Dining at the Governor's Mansion

Dining at the Governor's Mansion

BY CARL R. McQUEARY

TEXAS A&M UNIVERSITY PRESS   COLLEGE STATION

Library of Congress Cataloging-in-Publication Data

McQueary, Carl.
    Dining at the governor's mansion / by Carl R.
McQueary. — 1st ed.
        p. cm.
    Includes bibliographical references and index.
    ISBN 1-58544-254-2 (cloth : alk. paper)
        1. Cookery—Texas—Austin.   2. Texas Governor's
Mansion (Austin, Tex.)   I. Title
TX715.M4754   2003
641.59764—dc21   2002152757

To my parents,
Walter and Hollie Cleo Aaron McQueary,
to whom I owe everything, even my life,
with undying love and respect

Tell me what you eat,
and I will tell you what you are.

—ANTHELME BRILLAT-SAVARIN

Contents

Preface

The inspiration for this work comes from many places and many events in my life. My interest in the history of the Texas Governor's Mansion began when I was very small. The first time I remember seeing the mansion, my parents and I had just driven the eighty jillion miles from Amarillo and arrived in Austin to see the sites. Driving around the capital city in our big green Ford LTD, we saw Mount Bonnell and the Capitol (of course), and then as we rounded the corner off Eleventh onto Colorado Street, there it was—the Governor's Mansion. The gleaming white building, with its vast manicured lawn, was unlike anything this boy from the Panhandle had ever seen. I asked my mother what that place was, and she calmly stated that it was where the governor of Texas and his wife lived. My father joked that I had better straighten up because the governor was expecting us for supper. For a brief moment I believed him, until Mother laughed and said in her usual way, "Oh, Mac."

Thirty years later, while writing the history and cataloging the personal recipes of Gov. Miriam Ferguson (one of my favorite residents of the mansion), I discovered along the way little-known recipes of many of the other first ladies. Noted and documented, these mansion recipes and food references were stashed away in a large, black portable file case. I had no idea then what I would ever do with this information, but the recipes were interesting and as a collection they became increasingly significant. My research on Miriam Ferguson, a consuming passion for many years, was eventually completed. After it was published, Governor and Mrs. Bush asked me to be an after-dinner speaker and talk about the Fergusons' time in the mansion. Two dozen invited guests gathered for the meal, as guests have done for almost a century and a half, in the candle-lit State Dining Room. This time the governor really *was* expecting me for supper.

The evening was like something out of a dream. As I climbed the front steps leading to the mansion, the iron gate opened automatically, even before I reached it. A steward met me at the front door and offered me a drink. The governor looked at my new suit and said to Mrs. Bush, "See, Laura, his coat doesn't have a vent either." I thought this statement was some sort of code until the governor explained that his tailor had started cutting his suits without a vent slit in the back of the jacket. Mrs. Bush smiled at me and guided her guests into the dining room. She was a gracious hostess, and the governor was as congenial a host as the mansion could want. They made everyone feel absolutely at home.

The dinner was strictly Texas food, prepared and presented in a creative and artistic manner. I sat next to oil and business entrepreneur T. Boone Pickens, and our table was regaled with tales told in his inimitable style. When Mrs. Bush stood and introduced me, I arose and was a hair's breadth from being completely overwhelmed. The enormity of the events that have played out over the course of the last 150 years, in that very room, was almost palpable. I talked about Mrs. Ferguson and the State Dining Room and of the mansion's role in Texas history. In closing, I had everyone turn over his or her knife, forks, and spoons. Each implement is hand-engraved with the Great Seal of Texas, the name of the governor who lived there when it was added to the collection, and the year it was obtained. Since no one fell asleep, I guess I held the attention of those gathered.

After the dessert course had been removed and coffee served, I managed to slip away from the other guests and make my way to the back hall and into the kitchen. There, I offered my thanks to the staff for a wonderful meal. In talking with Sarah Bishop, executive chef at the mansion, I asked where the archives of the historic recipes of the first ladies were kept. She shook her head sadly, as only a chef who realizes the importance of food history could, and said that aside from her files from recent administrations, the mansion had no formal records documenting early food or food service. In a place where history is engraved everywhere, even on the silverware, I found this situation hard to believe. Ten years of research and an unforgettable journey are the results of the conversation in the mansion kitchen that night.

This book is intended to be more than a collection of recipes. Rather, it is a culinary history of the Governor's Mansion and its occupants. As such, it has as its central focus those elements of history relating to the state's first ladies: food, the preparation of food, entertaining at the mansion, and the challenges these women faced keeping the old structure together. In these pages there are neither discussions of the politics of the governors nor their political accomplishments. In fact, the governors themselves take a subordinate role in the text, allowing their spouses to shine as the true stars—a recognition they so richly deserve—in the history of the chief executive's house.

Like most historical texts, both the old and the new versions of the vast *Handbook of Texas* relegate the mention of all but a few of the first ladies to one sentence in the narrative of the husband's life. That one sentence is usually the one preceding a closing statement about the governor's death date and place of burial. However, two biographical sources relating to the first ladies do exist.

In 1915, Pearl Cashell Jackson wrote the earliest collection of biographies of the first ladies of Texas. Her wonderfully sentimental and poignant narrative, appropriately entitled *Texas Governors' Wives,* chronicles the lives of these remarkable women up to the second decade of the twentieth century. It details much of what is known about them. Many of the earliest first ladies were still living during Mrs. Jackson's lifetime, so the information she gathered generally came from first-hand reminiscences of either the former first ladies themselves or from those who knew them. The flowery, conversational style of her work offers us an intimate, personal glance at life in the mansion.

The second book, *First Ladies of Texas: The First One Hundred Years, 1836–1936,* by Mary D. Farrell and Elizabeth Silverthorne, published in 1976, chronicles the lives of the first ladies, including the wives of the presidents of the Republic of Texas. This comprehensive work is a thoughtfully researched testament to the lives of these enterprising women. Neither of these works focuses primarily on food and its place in the lives of the first ladies and their families, however. Rather than duplicate what has already been written, this book strives to complete a missing portion of a fuller picture of life in the mansion.

Because food and entertainment in the mansion are the focus of this book, the biographical sketches of the first ladies printed here do not dwell on the unpleasant aspects of their lives. Readers may assume, at first glance, that these women were somehow superhuman. They were not. In fact, the first ladies have little in common with the mythical Betty Crocker or the infamous Martha Stewart. The first ladies tenaciously endured their share of hardships, disappointments, and joys before, during, and after their time in the mansion. The daily routine of the mansion did not just happen. It required, and still does require, a great deal of work to make things run smoothly. The challenges these women faced and dealt with, more or less successfully, were very real. Without laboring the point, we can say that each of these unique women was a product of the era in which she lived. Their reactions to the problems and travails of daily life are rooted in the societal expectations of the time, as is the documentation of their shortcomings and foibles.

Because the biographical sketches in this book are intended to focus on the first ladies' period of residence and style of life in the mansion, they are relatively brief. However, they do highlight the indelible imprint that each of these women left on the Governor's Mansion and on the history of Texas. Books, like people, evolve over time. During a decade of research and years of writing, many changes have occurred in both the scope of the project and in my life.

Special individuals whom I had always hoped would be in my world forever have gone, while new relationships, completely unforeseen previously, have developed during the final stages of writing this book. The inspiration and creative force provided by these people, especially those who are no longer a part of my life, are gratefully and lovingly acknowledged.

There are, however, amazing friends who have remained a constant through my every success, crisis, and joy. Together, they have provided continuing love, support, and understanding regardless of the circumstances. Never have they lost faith in me or abandoned me just when I needed them. Rather, they have always been there, poised, at the ready.

This publication would never have been more than endless lunchtime banter were it not for my pal Jane Karotkin. As administrator of the Friends of the Governor's Mansion, she has endured the topic of Texas food during countless lunches at Las Manitas on Congress Avenue in Austin. Jane has been my unceasingly gracious mentor, through thick and thin (including the time she saved me from a seven-foot-tall wax Amazon). I thank you, Jane.

Many others have also helped: Wallace Saage, curator of the Harris County Historical Society in Houston; Judy Baldwin, of the Sam Houston Memorial Museum in Huntsville; Dorothy Copeland, library manager of the Texas Collection, Baylor University; Kristin Kraemer, at the Republic of Texas State Historical Park complex; Dr. William Seale; Madge Roberts, historian and descendant of Sam Houston; Kathleen B. O'Conner, education director at the Bayou Bend Collection and Gardens; and Dorothy Taylor, also of Bayou Bend.

In Austin my thanks go to Steve Williams and John Wheat of the Center for American History; Allen Fisher of the LBJ Library; the unflappable Donaly Brice and John Anderson, Bill Simmons, Sergio Velasco, and others at the Texas State Library and Archives; Dr. Ron Tyler, executive director of the Texas State Historical Association; Julie Morgan Hooper, executive director of the Austin Heritage Society, and to the Society itself; Wayne Bell of Austin (to whom I owe a gallon of Ima Hogg's Fish House Punch); Dorman Winfrey, retired director of the Texas State Library and Archives; Elton Prewitt of Prewitt and Associates, Inc., for his expertise on the mansion privy; Rebecca Rich-Wulfmeyer, archives and manuscript curator, Margaret Schlankey, photocurator, and the staff of the Austin History Center of the Austin Public Library; Jim Haley, a gracious friend and historian; Heather Brand, head of public relations for the Bob Bullock Texas State History Museum; Pat Sharpe, food editor, and intern Chamlee Williams at *Texas Monthly;* Sally Baulch, curator of the Texas Memorial Museum; and Anne DeBois, retired administrator of the Texas Governor's Mansion. Sarah Bishop, executive chef at the mansion, is incredible, and I was honored and touched to be given so many of her recipe "jewels." I also thank Janan Grissom, administrator of the Texas Governor's Mansion; Phyllis Munson, Assistant Administrator and tour director;

and Margit Johnson. I also wish to thank, from the Texas Historical Commission, my dear treasured friend, the late executive director Curtis Tunnell, as well as the current executive director, F. Lawerence Oaks, and Dan Utley, Charles Peveto, and Barbara Putrino.

Thanks also go out to the staff of the libraries at Abilene Christian University: Marsha Harper, director; Karen Hendrick, head of public services; Virginia Bailey, reference; and Jana Davis, cataloger. Across town at Hardin-Simmons University, Carol Hamner of the History Center and Kena Stringer, her student assistant, brought me a mother lode of vertical files.

The first ladies of Texas have been a joy. Nellie Connally is, to put it succinctly, a hoot. Linda Gale White offered favorite stories and recipes, and Rita Clements was a tremendous help. Mrs. Daniel's son, Houston, sent me a ream of anecdotal information and recipes from his mother. He gave me a Texas history lesson I will never forget. Thanks also to Laura Bush and to the lovely current first lady of Texas, Anita Perry, and to Wendy Bengal in the governor's press office.

Still others to be thanked include Ronald Chrisman of the University of North Texas Press; Elizabeth Silverthorne, the delightful Texas historian and expert on the first ladies of Texas; Dr. Rebecca Sharpless of the Institute for Oral History at Baylor University, who reined me in on numerous points, including my treatment of the "Lost Cause." Her attempts to make me politically and academically correct (a daunting task) are appreciated. Thanks also to Cissie Pierce and Susan Brock of the Dan Moody Museum of Taylor, Texas. Additional thanks for helpful suggestions go to my friends Elaine Davis, Martha Utterback, and Dora Guerra; to Runnels descendants Ann Burch Freeman and her mother, Ann Runnels Burch, and Jacqueline Espy; to members of the Sterling family, including Clay and Albert Sterling, and the irrepressible Francis Sterling Thurow; to Dr. Francis "Ab" Abernethy, *the* authority on Texas folklore, and Dr. Archie McDonald at Stephen F. Austin State University in Nacogdoches; Micheal Toon; Sharry Cox, president of the Wichita Falls Woman's Forum, and incoming president Doris Altman; and Becky Morrison, assistant administrator of the Wichita Falls Public Library. Special thanks also go to the staff of Texas A&M University Press, who made what could have been an onerous journey into a pleasant and fulfilling odyssey.

I am indebted as well to my brilliant son Kendall, who has helped me and laughed with me and reminded me constantly not to take anything too seriously, and to my amigos Audrey Tyler, Randi Carter, and Pat Doty. To my special friend and patron Moina C. Ellis, I thank you for your courage, wisdom, and support. Lastly, to my mysterious longtime friend Phineau Lineaux, wherever you are, thank you.

Dining at the Governor's Mansion

Introduction

An interesting and entertaining way to become familiar with a place
is to learn about the food served there. The Texas Governor's Mansion is a good example. One of the state's most venerable and historic structures, the mansion reveals itself in a whole new light when
viewed though the kitchen door. Since the mid-1800s, countless
cooks, usually mentioned in historical accounts only by a first name,
have prepared food for the governors and first ladies of Texas and
those guests fortunate enough to share their hospitality.

Social life at the mansion has always revolved around the governor's table, and in many ways the dining room has been the center of activity for generations. Every item in this room, from the
state china to the sterling silver flatware, has a story, yet the elegant
crystal, silver, and china pieces are only a small part of the narrative.

This study of food and its preparation within the specific setting of
the Governor's Mansion provides an intimate portrait of Texas life
from the mid-nineteenth century forward. The study also reveals that
the foods enjoyed by the governors and first ladies, especially in their
private meals, have been surprisingly similar to those consumed by

even the humblest of Texans. Until the 1950s, when entertaining at the mansion became much more formal, the governors, their families, and, to a degree, their guests, basically ate the same types of food, prepared in the same ways, as did residents of deep East Texas, where Southern food traditions were strongest. These Texas recipes reflect the most common social tastes and the most fundamental ingredients.

Most of the domestic chores done behind the closed door of the mansion kitchen are hidden from view and have not often been recorded in history. A cook's recipes, however, may describe the people being fed in an indirect way. Reflecting the times in which they were created and used, these historical "receipts" reveal more of Texas' economic, social, and cultural identity than one might expect from a simple listing of ingredients.

One reason that dining habits at the mansion were not well documented is that cooks traditionally passed food preparation instructions from one generation to another orally. This oral tradition, compounded by the fact that cooks of long standing often memorized their regularly used recipes, meant that many of the earliest recipes used in the mansion kitchen were never recorded in writing. Fortunately, a few cooks did scribble down some recipes, often on whatever scrap of paper was available at arm's reach.

The surviving flour-dusted, gravy-spattered documents are often the only record of a mansion cook, even though the cook, like many servants, worked either at the mansion or for the governors' families for decades. If the recipes were not passed on as generations of cooks hung up their aprons and retired, the recipes disappeared as well.

Those heritage recipes that survive are rare, vital, and treasured, but their wealth of information has never been fully documented and compiled until now. The first ladies' recipes that have been preserved generally are the result of the first ladies being asked to contribute their favorites to an endless array of charity cookbook projects, Sunday school fundraisers, and county fairs. A first lady would ask her mansion cook to write down a recipe for one of these causes, and thus it would be preserved for posterity. However, the cookbooks in which those recipes appeared were usually published in small numbers, in scattered locales, and for very specific audiences. These factors, coupled with the passage of time and changing fashions in food and food preparation, pushed the earliest of these books out of general circulation, where they were forgotten for decades.

The recipes in this book come from a wide variety of sources, many far removed from their point of origin at the mansion. Hundreds upon hundreds of Texas cookbooks have been read, newspaper accounts consulted, and interviews with former and current mansion staff and support staff conducted. Archival records and documents and interviews with former first ladies and their families have also yielded recipes and stories contained within this work. Many of the stories have been told so often as to gain an almost folkloric quality. A few of the tales presented on these pages are in written form for the first time.

Each of these historical recipes is, to use East Texas parlance, "the real deal." The governors of Texas and their families actually used the ones attributed to them. Their cooks prepared most of them in the mansion. With the exception of those governors who lived in the mansion briefly during the Civil War and Reconstruction, most of the first ladies are represented by at least one of their favorite recipes. The original recipe names have not been altered or modified. In fact, the only changes to the recipes are those involving formatting for consistency and occasional minor insertions relating to missing details or obscure instructions. For example, not many cooks of the twenty-first century know exactly how hot a "quick" oven is. Cooking times were also tested and included where none had existed previously. After some trial and error and many hours in my tiny condo test kitchen, I hope that I have made this work not only a fascinating historical account but also a collection of recipes that today's cooks will enjoy.

◆ A BRIEF MANSION HISTORY ◆

The Governor's Mansion of Texas is arguably the most historic house in the state. Situated in the center of a manicured expanse of lawn, bordered by carefully tended gardens, the mansion commands a spectacular view of the Texas Capitol. Construction began in 1855 and ended in 1856, making the mansion the oldest continuously occupied governor's residence west of the Mississippi. The building has been designated a National Historic Landmark as well as a Texas Historic Landmark.

The office of the chief executive in Texas is much older than the mansion, however. In fact, the position is older than the United States and predates the office of the presidency of the United States by almost a century. Depending on which Texas historian one consults, the political beginnings of Texas occurred in 1691, when the Spanish crown appointed Domingo Terán de los Ríos governor of the province of Texas. His name is first on a long list of *gobernadores,* presidents, and governors who have overseen the affairs of Texas. They all have left, in some way, a mark upon the state, and prior to 1856—with the exception of a few fortunate Spanish governors—they did not have a permanent, government-owned roof over their heads.

During the turmoil immediately after Texas gained independence from Mexico in 1836, the location of Texas' capital seemed to change with the political winds. In the new government of the young republic, providing a permanent home for the chief executive was not a top priority. In one of the earliest attempts to provide a state-owned executive residence, a large "President's House" was somewhat hurriedly constructed in Austin in 1842. Built of green lumber, the wooden structure literally pulled itself apart as the wood dried and cured. It quickly became uninhabitable and was torn down. The thrifty Texans salvaged a lot of the materials, however, since sawn lumber was still an expensive commodity. Many of the furnishings were also rescued from the house. Fittingly, some of them, though showing signs of age and wear, saw use again in the Governor's Mansion after its completion.

With ratification of statehood on February 19, 1846, the Republic of Texas joined the United States. Considering the other pressing matters with which the newly created state had to contend, providing a home for the chief executive was once again a low priority. There was no official residence for the first four governors of Texas, and from all indications, they did not seem to mind.

The first governor's wife, Frances Cox Henderson, did not even venture to Austin during the term of her husband, James Pinckney Henderson. Her absence was not without some justification. The

The Texas President's House. This rare drawing, circa 1840, of the home
built for the president of the Republic shows how the home was to have
looked. It stood a short time before falling into ruin.
Taken from a drawing by Edward Hale.
Courtesy Austin History Center, Austin Public Library, PICA 01083.

new capital in Austin was a wilderness outpost for all practical purposes, and the Hendersons continued to call San Augustine home.
San Augustine was not necessarily safer than Austin, but at least the
Hendersons' sturdy house there offered some protection from the
dangers of the frontier. Despite the privations of living in remote
East Texas, Mrs. Henderson was a consummate hostess. Her hospitality was well known in the social and political circles of the Republic
and, later, the state of Texas. While James was in Austin carrying out
his duties as governor, Frances supervised the operations of their
farm and cared for her five children. She was thus too busy tending
to the business of daily life to come to Austin even had there been
an official residence for her to occupy.

In many ways, Frances Henderson was the prototype for the subsequent first ladies of Texas. Her father had moved his family to Paris, France, when she was quite young so that she and her siblings could have the best education available at the time. That education included languages, and she was eventually fluent in eighteen.

In Paris, nineteen-year-old Frances met James Pinckney Henderson, who was then serving as chargé d'affaires to France from the Republic of Texas. A surviving portrait of Frances, done about the time she came to Texas (she was a Philadelphia native), shows a round-faced young lady with large, intelligent eyes. Following a brief courtship Frances and James were married in London in 1839. Arriving in Galveston, Texas, in 1840, they built their first home near San Augustine. Six years later, following a successful political assent, James became the first governor of the newly formed state of Texas.

The next three governors did not really require a designated home for the chief executive of the state any more than did the Hendersons. Gov. George T. Wood lived and ate at Bullock's Hotel in Austin during his term. Martha, his wife, made only one trip to Austin during his administration, and that was for his inauguration. She was far too occupied raising their five children and taking care of their home in Pointblank, Texas, on the Trinity River, to be concerned with the social goings-on of Austin. Governor Wood, who was often unkempt and seldom wore socks, rode his mule, Pantalette, back and forth from Austin to his plantation during the time he was in office.

Governor Wood's successor, Peter Hansborough Bell, also lived in an Austin boardinghouse and ate his meals at one of several establishments, of varying quality, that served food. A bachelor who sported shoulder-length hair and a flowing black beard, Bell did not need an official residence. He resigned in 1853 and was succeeded by his lieutenant governor, James Wilson Henderson. This Governor Henderson was in office only about a month, so he also did not have time to worry about the lack of an official residence.

Legislation for the construction of a governor's residence was proposed in 1853. However, since Austin was slated to be the capital of Texas only until 1870, the residence was perceived to be temporary and legislators were not willing to spend a great deal of money on its construction. The amount of $14,500 that the legislature finally approved in 1854 was somewhat of a compromise from the $20,000 originally proposed. Additionally, a mere $2,500 was allotted to furnish and outfit the new home.

Gov. Elisha Pease served on the committee charged with getting the mansion built. Ads were placed in Texas newspapers seeking a contractor to design and complete the structure. After a good deal of political wrangling, the contract went to Austin master builder Abner Hugh Cook. (That two of the three members of the mansion committee were living in homes designed and built by Cook could well have been a factor in the decision.) Cook's winning design was a skillful and ambitious adaptation of Greek Revival architecture. Popular on the East Coast, the style was still relatively new on the frontier of Texas.

Cook was a shrewd businessman, and his construction-related enterprises were diverse. He owned or had an interest in almost every aspect of the various trades required to construct the Governor's Mansion. His holdings included a large interest in the sawmill and lumbering operations at Bastrop that provided the lumber. Cook also owned the clay pit on the Colorado River where the buff-colored bricks for the Governor's Mansion were made.

Cook's Greek Revival design for the house called for a square structure with four main rooms on each of two floors. A semi-detached rear wing housed a dirt-floored kitchen and servants' quarters. The façade had six Ionic columns, twenty-nine feet tall, framing a veranda, with Cook's signature "X-and-Stick" balustrades forming the railings. Inside the house were high ceilings, tall windows, and wide hallways—all desirable features in such a warm climate. In the days before air-conditioning, large windows and cross-ventilation were the only means of cooling the mansion during the long, humid Austin summers.

The completion of the mansion was much anticipated by the citizens of Texas. To them the building symbolized a permanency of governance that reflected well on the reputation of the state. On August 18, 1855, the *Texas State Gazette* reported the latest news on the mansion's progress: "The new building is erected, and about being finished. In its large open rooms where sun and air of day can freely enter, we shall expect to see the people next winter welcome the successful candidate of Democracy. Its latch-string will always be open under the Democratic administration. The building is situated in full view of the Capitol, and is a neat and substantial structure, just what a republican Governor's house ought to be."

The governor's house was completed almost a year later. Construction delays and inclement weather pushed the finish date six months later than specified in the contract. (One of the terms of the contract required the builder to pay the governor's rent in a boardinghouse if the house was not finished on schedule.) On June 14, 1856, the building was finally turned over to the state. Texas' fifth governor, Elisha Marshall Pease, his wife Lucadia, and their daughters became the mansion's first residents. Shortly after settling in, the Pease family discovered living in the mansion required a special kind of determination. The house was hard to furnish, drafty, and prohibitively expensive to maintain, and the roof leaked. The Pease family and subsequent residents were expected accept these problems, plus a few other eccentric details that appeared over time, for the next 150 years.

The governor and his household were mostly self-sufficient, with the exception of staples such as coffee, salt, sugar, and flour. The first lady would have obtained flour from one of several local mills along the Colorado River. Milling was the first food-processing cottage industry in the state. While the mansion cook generally baked whatever bread and cakes were needed, a baking industry was developing throughout the state. Most bakers operated in conjunction with confectioneries. Buying "store-baked" bread was a novelty for most households, including the governor's. Goods baked in Austin, as a rule, were sold and used in Austin, since poor roads hampered the transportation of baked items.

One of the chief problems cooks at the mansion faced was spoilage. Cistern houses and cooling troughs in outbuildings were the only way to keep food moderately cool. The drying of fruit and vegetables was a popular way to keep food edible longer and to have something in the pantry during the long winter months. Drying food was not a new technique in Texas. Mary Austin Holley, a cousin of Stephen F. Austin, noted as early as 1836 that dried foods were an important pantry item, especially during lean times. Texan Gail Borden, of Elmer's Glue-All fame, introduced a dried meat biscuit that was used during the Civil War, but as with much of the dried food of the time, the biscuit was not very pretty to look at and required soaking in water before it could be eaten.

The governor could also partake of the fruit of the vine or beer produced in Texas prior to the Civil War. As early as the 1850s Texans were producing a considerable amount of whiskey, grape brandy, rum, and beer that was sold locally. The brewing trade was an important part of the Texas economy; by 1860 it ranked sixth in the industries of the state.

The occupants of the mansion not only withstood their home's problems, they often flourished despite the fact that war, love, death, civil unrest, marriages, births, and social change all visited this venerable historic home. Of course, most trying situations, from faulty plumbing to 'possums in the back bedroom, are made more tolerable when considered over a piece of pie. This revelation probably would not have been new to those people who have lived and served and labored at the mansion. The pages that follow offer a glimpse of the power of food in their lives.

A New Governor's Residence

WITH THE COMPLETION of the new governor's house, Texas' chief executive no longer had to sup with strangers at a boardinghouse. Instead, the governor and family members could dine together. Providing privacy and togetherness—and a venue for entertaining—were major home improvements for the young state government.

✦ LUCADIA CHRISTIANA NILES PEASE ✦
1853–1857, 1867–1869

Facing the vast expanse of freshly finished long-leaf yellow pine in the front hall of the Governor's Mansion for the very first time, Lucadia Pease might have reflected on the varied path that had brought her to that moment and that place. Lucadia, wife of Gov. Elisha Pease, would be the earliest of the many first ladies to step across the threshold of the mansion. The house was not unknown to her when she moved in, however. Lucadia and her husband were

*Lucadia Christiana Niles Pease was the first of many
first ladies to occupy the Texas Governor's Mansion.*
Courtesy Austin History Center, Austin Public Library, PICB 06781.

intimately familiar with the building project, having selected the
final site for the structure and overseen portions of its construction.
The couple also jointly faced the challenge of furnishing the home.
The mansion they so lovingly nurtured in its earliest days remains
much as it was during the first years after it was built. If Governor
Pease and his wife were to walk through the doors of the Governor's
Mansion today, they would no doubt quickly recognize it as the
house they once inhabited.

Lucadia married Elisha in 1850, and they came to Texas the same
year. They arrived in Brazoria, where Elisha was already established
as a lawyer, and set up housekeeping. A load of furniture, which

they had purchased in New York, arrived in the little Texas port city. As a result, the Pease family had one of the most smartly furnished homes in the region. Brazoria, however, was still very much a frontier town, with no paved streets. The Pease property had no fences, weeds grew hip high, and livestock would wander through the yard. Lucadia's patience with this state of affairs was probably taxed further when stray cows ate the new woven doormats off her front porch.

Lucadia was not without creature comforts in Brazoria, however. The future governor ordered her a fine carriage, possibly the first in Texas, so that she would not have to deal with the mud-filled streets of town.

Life changed for the Pease family in 1853, when Elisha was elected governor. This turn of events meant closing the compact Brazoria home and selling most of the furnishings. It would have been impractical to ship all their belongings by ox cart to Austin, so the Pease family arrived in the new capital with only a few trunks containing their clothing, personal effects, and the family silver.

Prior to the mansion's construction, the Pease family boarded in Austin with Col. William and Susan Ward. This arrangement worked well, for when the colonel was appointed consul to Panama and moved there, Lucadia was able to acquire some of the Wards' sturdy mahogany furniture. Many of these pieces remained with the Pease family for the rest of their lives.

The family had to stay with the Wards longer than expected, as completion of the mansion ran six months behind schedule. The building project had moved sluggishly from the start. The amount of money initially allotted by the legislature proved to be inadequate, so the plans for the governor's house were reduced in scale. As a result, the architect had to cancel plans for two grand wings adjoining either side of the main house. Still, despite the changes and setbacks, the house slowly took shape. In May, 1856, the *Texas State Gazette* reported, "The Governor's new mansion is progressing towards completion. The house is erected, and the inside finished and neatly painted. From appearances, the grounds will be laid off with much taste, and the whole, when finished will present an imposing spectacle."

The scant furniture the Peases owned would not fill the large public rooms, even with addition of the few random pieces that had been brought in from the rather sad dwelling occupied by the president of the Republic. The legislature had also appropriated twenty-five hundred dollars toward furnishing the home. Governor Pease sent trusted family friend S. M. Swenson, a successful Austin merchant, to New York on a buying trip. Furniture was expensive, and Mr. Swenson quickly ran out of money before he could acquire all of the necessary items. As a result, the downstairs was almost completely furnished, but three of the bedrooms were empty. But Swenson had excellent taste, and Lucadia approved of all of his selections. Several pieces of the Pease furniture, including two beds, a desk, and a sofa, still occupy places of honor in the mansion.

The kitchen, originally designed as a separate structure, was ultimately incorporated as a semi-attached wing with servants' quarters above. A kitchen being even partly attached to the main house was an interesting innovation. Most kitchens during this period were separate structures; it was widely held across the South that one did not cook in the same building as one lived. Also, because of the danger of fire, a detached kitchen had always been considered a safer arrangement.

With limited funds Lucadia managed to assemble a workable kitchen. Like even the finest homes of the time, the mansion's kitchen floor was dirt. On the other hand, the new mansion kitchen boasted one of the first wood-fired iron cook stoves in the region. Melvina "Viney" Fontaine, the family cook, had always cooked on an open hearth and at first had no idea how to use the stove, but she gradually became comfortable with the new device. Viney prepared meals for the Pease family at the mansion and later worked as a maid for Lucadia. In addition to working for the Pease family, Viney served several subsequent administrations at the mansion.

Immediately prior to the mansion's completion, Lucadia, her sister, and the children went to visit their family back East. The governor stayed behind and hosted a levee, which is a French word for reception. On August 20, 1856, the curious citizens of Austin arrived in droves for the party. An undated contemporary account, most likely from the *Texas State Gazette,* describes the event: "The elegant mansion reared by the liberality of the State, was illuminated and thrown open from cellar to garret. The cellar was emptied of wines, and the kitchen and pantry of viands, and the coops and stys of poultry and pigs. The parlour and study, the halls and galleries, the chambers, and the yard, were all full of people, and the dining-room and the back-yard were full of tables."

Five hundred people came, and three hundred stayed for supper. "Dutch" John, owner of a local restaurant, cooked the food, and several of Lucadia's friends helped the governor with other preparations. Six turkeys, two dozen chickens, two fat pigs, forty loaves of bread, five pounds of butter, ten pounds of almonds, ten pounds of candy, and all of Lucadia's home-canned preserves and brandied peaches were consumed by the crowds. Once the dust cleared, the governor was presented with a bill for $121.00, which included $35.00 for cakes and $8.30 for broken crockery. It was a huge success, though, and the governor was pleased. He wrote Lucadia detailed accounts of the celebration.

Upon her return Lucadia set about transforming the bare mansion grounds with flowers and other plantings, such as Irish potatoes and peas. Hogs were slaughtered, and she and the mansion servants rendered lard and cured hams. She also set a schedule for entertaining Austin society at the mansion.

If the dishes she wanted to serve her guests were too involved or beyond her skills or those of the mansion cook, she would hire local trades people to prepare the food. Austin confectioners, for example, were often set to work making dainty sweets for the governor's soirees. Lucadia would make cakes herself, and occasionally she prepared what was a novelty in Texas at that time—lobster salad. But her table was almost always laden with whatever local foods were in season. High cut-glass pedestals held jellies and custards, while large epergnes overflowed with various fruits. Such an extravagant table setting probably made a lasting impression on those citizens fortunate enough to view the spectacle, since many of Austin's twenty-five hundred residents likely still ate their daily meals from wooden bowls or on heavy stoneware plates. Lucadia's graciousness and hospitality at the mansion established a standard of excellence that endured.

Lucadia Christiana Niles Pease
◆ CORN PONES

The word *pone* originally meant "small oval loaf," but it now refers to a variety of cornmeal-based concoctions. Corn pones were a staple of the cuisine in the Republic of Texas. They could easily be made from ingredients that were often the only items available in most homes. Variations of these delicious little morsels have been made for hundreds of years.

Many of the first ladies served them proudly. This tradition continues, as they were among the fare offered at the mansion's annual picnic for 2001. This event is always held on the mansion grounds on the anniversary of Governor Pease's first levee. Serve these corn pones hot, with plenty of butter.

> 1 cup cornmeal
> ¾ cup flour
> 2 heaping teaspoons baking powder
> 1 egg
> A little salt
> 1 cup milk
> Water sufficient to make batter

Beat well. Drop into hot fat [a few drops of water will sizzle] and brown. ❧

Lucadia Christiana Niles Pease
◆ QUEEN OF PUDDINGS

This recipe yields a cross between bread pudding and custard. Lucadia did not specify what flavor of jelly to use. I had very good results using orange marmalade or lemon chutney.

Modern cooks know that egg mixtures should be cooked for safety. Try adding the meringue before the custard is fully baked.

> 1 pint nice bread crumbs
> 1 quart milk
> Yolk of four eggs

Grated rind and juice of 1 lemon
Piece of butter the size of an egg
1 cup sugar

Bake like custard. When baked spread over the top slices of jelly, and cover the whole with the whites of eggs beaten to a stiff froth with one cup of sugar and the juice of the lemon.

Lucadia Christiana Niles Pease
♦   SPONGE CAKE

Sponge cakes can be tricky, even under the most ideal conditions. Preparing this recipe in the oven of a wood-fired cook stove, as was done in Lucadia's day, would be a daunting task indeed.

2 cupfuls of powdered sugar
2 cupfuls of flour, sifted
2 teaspoons baking powder
4 eggs
¾ cup boiling water
Pinch of salt
Lemon to taste

[Preheat oven to 350 degrees.] Beat the whites and yolks of the eggs separately. [Combine sugar, flour, and baking powder, and then stir in egg yolks.] Gently fold the egg yolk–flour mixture into the egg whites about ¼ at time. Add boiling water after all of the ingredients have been mixed. Do not stir or cake will not be spongy. Gently turn batter into an ungreased tube pan. Bake in [350-degree] oven for about 40 to 50 minutes. Immediately turn pan upside down and let cool. Once cake is cool, remove it from the pan.

Lucadia Christiana Niles Pease
♦   WASHING PREPARATION

Not all of the products of Lucadia's recipes are edible; some were simply useful. Viney Fontaine and the other female servants of the

Pease family would have been very familiar with this mixture, as every Monday a large fire was built under an enormous iron kettle at the back of the mansion property. The governor's family's laundry was then subjected to the rigors of wash day and hung to dry, often on the pickets of the back fence. This recipe produces a form of lye, which is a caustic alkaline solvent and can cause severe burns if not properly handled—in other words, don't eat this.

> 2 pounds soda ash
> 1 pound unslacked lime (also called quicklime)
> 1 gallon water

Boil 20 minutes. Then add 2 gallons cold water and let it stand and settle. Then bottle. Use 1 teacup full to two pails water. Heat the water, then put the clothes in and boil them. Suds and rinse and they are nicely washed. ≈

◆ MARTHA CAROLINE ADAMS RUNNELS ◆
1857–1859

Immediately after his election, Gov. Hardin Richard Runnels realized he had a problem. He was a bachelor, and he knew that the social activities at the mansion would amount to more than he could handle alone. Seeking someone to assist him, he asked his mother, Patsy Runnels, to move to Austin, live in the mansion, and act as his hostess. Feisty Patsy apparently was not impressed by the invitation. Her sister had married the first governor of Georgia, and her brother-in-law was the governor of Mississippi, so another governor in the family probably did not inspire any feelings of awe in Patsy. Despite her son's plea, she flatly refused to be the hostess at the mansion, saying that one household was enough to tend to and she had no desire to move anywhere.

The governor then asked his twenty-one-year-old sister-in-law Martha if she would like to serve as his first lady at the mansion. She was honored and agreed to his offer. Her husband Howell, the governor's brother, was serving in the Texas Senate at the time so the arrangement was perfect. Engaging, smart, and attractive,

Martha Caroline Runnels, the beautiful sister-in-law of
Governor Hardin Runnels, during the time she served as
hostess of the Mansion.
Courtesy Ann Burch Freeman and Ann Runnels Burch.

Martha quickly assumed the duties of first lady and began arranging the various functions at the mansion, setting the governor's table
with the china and crystal she had received as wedding presents.

Her background had prepared her well for the job. Born in Georgia in 1836, she had moved with her family in a wagon train to
Marshall, Texas, a short time later. Her father eventually became one

of the largest landowners in the northeastern part of the state. Cultured and possessing a keen sense of both humor and tact, Martha could keep guests at the mansion amused as well as ably manage the governor's slaves. Outside the mansion though, political winds were shifting, and heated controversy over slavery and secession prompted the governor to wear two Colt pistols strapped to his belt. Troubles on the Texas-Mexico border, Indian problems, cattle rustling, and mob rule all caused turmoil during Governor Runnels's term.

Two years later, when he was not reelected, the Runnels family group left the mansion. Hardin Runnels returned to farming, and Martha and her husband, Howell, moved to a home near Texarkana and eventually had fourteen children.

Martha Caroline Adams Runnels
◆ NUT CREAM

This custard-like recipe has been passed down through the Runnels family for generations. It produces a light, layered dessert, perfect for a Christmas buffet. Ann Burch Freeman and her mother, Ann Runnels Burch, made this recipe available for inclusion.

> 2 cups sugar
> 1 quart whole milk
> 6 eggs, separated and beaten
> Enough corn starch to thicken
> 2 cups finely cut English walnuts
> Vanilla to taste

Cook sugar, milk, egg yolks, and corn starch on top of the stove. Stir constantly until thick, but not too thick. Do this until the mixture congeals. Then pour into baking dish.

Beat egg whites, spread on top, then put in oven and brown. Dish out into a serving dish. Place one layer of custard, then add nuts and sprinkle with vanilla. Add another custard layer and top with more nuts. Use *a lot* of vanilla. Serve with plain cake.

◆ MARGARET MOFFATT LEA HOUSTON ◆
1859–1861

Margaret Lea Houston arrived at the mansion in 1860 with her husband, seven children, twelve slaves, the family belongings, a team of mules, several horses, and numerous dogs. Of the slaves, five were generally house servants, presided over by Margaret's personal maid, Aunt Eliza, who was always by Margaret's side and worked long hours in the mansion.

When she arrived at the mansion, Margaret had been married to Sam Houston for twenty years. She had first been introduced to the general at a party in Alabama. Despite an age difference of twenty-six years and vastly different upbringings, after a year-long, long-distance courtship they were married on May 9, 1840. Soon after the wedding, members of her immediate and extended family moved to Texas with the couple. Sam's election to the governorship of Texas was just one of many events that marked their lives together. Wherever they went, Margaret always tried to make a comfortable home for her husband and family. She and Sam moved many times, so setting up housekeeping in new places had become almost routine.

Making the Governor's Mansion comfortable proved to be a challenge, even for Margaret and her cadre of slaves. The furnishings in the home were sparse when the family moved in, consisting largely of those left from the Pease administration and the ramshackle remnants salvaged from the old "President's Home" a few blocks away. In anticipation of the need for additional furniture, Sam ordered a large, canopied bed from a cabinetmaker in Seguin. It was a duplicate of one he had admired many years before in the home of a friend. Crafted in mahogany, and extra long to accommodate Houston's height, the bed, known now as the Sam Houston bed, remains in the mansion to this day.

Margaret's efforts to make the house livable were largely successful, and soon the mansion was visited by an increasing number of family, friends, and distant kin. One of the most notable guests at the mansion was army officer Robert E. Lee, who was stationed near San Antonio but visited Austin during his time in Texas.

Margaret Moffatt Lea Houston.
From the author's collection.

Aside from the visits of relations and a few other callers, Margaret, in failing health and pregnant with her eighth child, did not entertain a great deal while living in the mansion. Austin society had come to expect a certain level of social interaction at the mansion, and Margaret, weakened by asthma and occasionally bedridden with complications resulting from her pregnancy, simply could not meet their expectations. On August 12, 1860, with the female slaves by the bed stirring the air with large palmetto fans, Temple Lea Houston, Sam and Margaret's eighth and last child, was born. He was the first baby to come into the world at the mansion. Two weeks later Margaret was well enough to receive visitors.

The residence of Sam Houston during his time as president of the Republic of Texas in 1837–38. The building stands in sharp contrast to the home Texas built for its governor just twenty years later.
Courtesy Texas State Library and Archives Commission (1/103-506).

As political tensions mounted in Texas, Houston found himself faced with the increased desire among the populace to secede from the Union and join the newly formed Confederate States of America. On March 15, 1861, Margaret had the evening meal served as always, and as usual Sam read aloud a chapter from the Bible and led the assembled family and slaves in prayer.

At about eight o'clock that evening, a messenger knocked loudly at the front door of the mansion. He had been dispatched to inform the governor that all state officials must swear an oath of loyalty to the Confederacy. Houston spent the night pacing the large upstairs hall in his stocking feet, deciding whether or not to take the oath. Shortly after sunrise, Sam descended the winding staircase and said, "Margaret, I will never do it."

Later that day in the Capitol, as officials came forward to swear loyalty to the Confederacy, Houston's name was called three times. Houston remained in his office, whittling stoically, as the position of governor was finally declared vacant and Lt. Gov. Ed Clark was sworn in as Houston's successor. Two weeks later, the Houston family was packed and ready to leave the mansion, and fortunately, there had been no attempt to force them out sooner. In late March, Margaret walked down the steps of the mansion for the last time.

Margaret Lea Moffatt Houston
♦ REPUBLIC OF TEXAS COFFEE

In Lenoir Hunt's book *My Master,* Jeff Hamilton, the slave of Gen. Sam Houston, reveals that the general liked two cups of coffee a day. You can drink this coffee without cream and sugar, as Sam Houston often did (though he sometimes used sugar), but it is a pretty lethal brew for modern tastes. The eggshells help the grounds to settle out, and the egg whites smooth the consistency of the drink. The salt evens out the taste and reduces bitterness.

    1 egg and shell, crushed
    1 cup cold water, divided
    1 cup coffee, freshly roasted and ground
    1 pint rich cream
    1 egg white, beaten
    Sugar to taste
    6 cups boiling water
    Pinch salt

Scald the coffeepot. Beat egg slightly, add $\frac{1}{2}$ cup cold water, the crushed eggshell, and the coffee. Mix well and boil 3 minutes. Add rest of the cold water to settle the grounds and clear the coffee. Let stand over low heat for 10 minutes. To serve, add the cream to egg white, place this mixture with sugar in cups, and then add the coffee mixture to which the boiling water has been added.

Margaret Moffatt Lea Houston
◆ SAM HOUSTON WHITE CAKE

Modern cooks will treasure this elegant cake recipe belonging to Margaret Lea Houston. As each successive generation of Houston family members used this recipe, they updated it to reflect the innovations of the times. The recipe has also been printed many times. It made one of its first appearances in the *Blue Bird Circle Cook Book* in 1941. Imperial Sugar Company also features the cake in a number of its publications from the 1940s. It is a wonderful, thick cake.

    1 cup butter
    2 cups sugar
    3 cups sifted flour
    3 teaspoons baking powder
    $\frac{1}{2}$ teaspoon salt
    $\frac{1}{2}$ cup milk
    $\frac{1}{2}$ cup water
    1 teaspoon vanilla
    1 teaspoon almond flavoring
    6 egg whites

Cream butter until soft and bright. Gradually add sugar and continue creaming in order to incorporate as much air as possible. Combine flour, baking powder, and salt. Sift three times. Add flavorings to milk and water. Add flour and liquid mixtures alternately to creamed mixture, beating well after each addition. Beat egg whites until stiff but not dry and fold into batter. Blend well but do not beat. Pour into three greased and floured 9-inch layer cake pans and bake at 350 degrees for 25 minutes. Cool 5 minutes, then turn onto cake racks and remove pans. When cake layers are cool, frost. ❧

Margaret Moffatt Lea Houston
◆ SHINY CHOCOLATE FROSTING

The original recipe calls for egg yolks, but today's bakers may wish to omit them because the frosting is not fully cooked.

3 squares unsweetened chocolate
3 cups powdered sugar
$\frac{1}{8}$ teaspoon salt
$\frac{1}{4}$ cup hot water
3 egg yolks
$\frac{1}{4}$ cup butter, melted
1 teaspoon vanilla

Melt chocolate over hot water and stir in powdered sugar. Add salt and hot water. Beat in eggs yolks, one at a time. Add melted butter a little at a time, and vanilla. Mix well. Allow to cool if too warm and spread between cake layers and over completed cake. ❧

Margaret Moffatt Lea Houston
◆ LEMON CURD

Use this lemon curd as an alternative to the Shiny Chocolate Frosting between the layers of the Sam Houston White Cake. Both recipes are from the Houston kitchen, and both are delicious.

2 eggs
1 cup sugar
Juice of 4 lemons ($\frac{1}{2}$ cup)
$\frac{1}{2}$ cup butter
Zest of 1 lemon, grated

Whisk eggs until smooth in medium-heavy, 1-quart saucepan. Add sugar and lemon juice, whisking until well mixed. Cook slowly over medium-low heat, stirring constantly, until mixture thickens enough to coat back of wooden spoon (10 to 12 minutes). Remove pan from heat. Cut butter into tablespoon-size pieces and stir, one piece at a time, into warm mixture until melted and fully absorbed. Stir in lemon zest. ❧

Margaret Moffatt Lea Houston
♦ HOUSTON CORN PONES

This perennial mealtime staple helped sustain the Houston family and their slaves in even the leanest of times. Corn pones, with minor variations, have been served at the mansion from the mid-nineteenth century to the present day.

$\frac{1}{2}$ cup boiling water
1 cup white cornmeal
2 tablespoons shortening
1 teaspoon baking powder
$\frac{1}{2}$ teaspoon salt
$\frac{1}{4}$ cup cream

Pour boiling water over cornmeal and chill mixture for about an hour. After mixture is well chilled start your oven [at 400 degrees] (moderately hot). Put 1 tablespoon shortening in a heavy skillet (one you can put in the oven) and heat skillet until the fat melts.

Now pour remaining tablespoon of shortening (melted) into cornmeal along with baking powder, salt, and cream. Mix well and drop by tablespoonfuls into the hot skillet. Flatten with the back of a spoon and bake 20 to 30 minutes or until nicely browned. Makes 8 to 10 pones. ❧

Margaret Moffatt Lea Houston
♦ CHICKEN SCRAPPLE

This recipe originally called for a plump, freshly butchered stewing hen. It has been updated slightly, saving you the trouble of wringing a chicken's neck. This recipe now cooks in minutes rather than hours, as it did in Margaret Lea Houston's day.

14 ounces boned, cooked chicken
3 cups plus 1 cup water, divided use
2 chicken bouillon cubes
2 teaspoons salt

1 teaspoon onion salt
¼ teaspoon pepper
¼ teaspoon thyme
1 cup corn meal
2 eggs
¼ cup fat [may be shortening, salad oil, or butter]

In a large saucepan, toss chicken, 3 cups water, bouillon cubes, salt, onion salt, pepper, and thyme. Cook to the boiling point, then reduce heat and cook mixture slowly for about 5 minutes. During the cooking, break the chicken up in little pieces with a fork.

Now mix cornmeal with 1 cup water until smooth. Stir into the chicken mixture and cook until thick, stirring constantly. Lower heat and continue cooking 10 minutes longer. Transfer the mixture to a large rectangular kitchen tray and level surface. Chill and cut into 2-inch squares. Dip each square into slightly beaten egg and fry in hot melted fat until crisp and brown on both sides. This takes just a few minutes. Serves 6 to 8. ❧

Margaret Moffatt Lea Houston
◆ DEVILED TOMATOES

Margaret Lea Houston raised most of her own vegetables. In a letter dated December 26, 1853, she mentions raising beets, lettuce, artichokes, squash, long green cucumbers, eggplants, long scarlet radishes, and three early varieties of cabbages. The Houston family was also fond of tomatoes. This is a delicious summertime side dish.

3 hard-cooked egg yolks
3 tablespoons butter
3 tablespoons vinegar
1 tablespoon sugar
1 teaspoon prepared mustard
Dash salt
½ to 1 teaspoon cayenne pepper
3 eggs
5 tomatoes

Mash the hard-cooked egg yolks with a fork. Melt butter in the top of a double boiler. Remove from heat and stir in mashed yolks, vinegar, sugar, mustard, salt, and cayenne.

Beat the whole eggs until frothy, stir into seasoned mixture, and cook over hot water until water in the bottom of the double boiler comes to a boil. Now turn off the heat and let the mixture stand in the double boiler for about 10 minutes. Give it an occasional stir.

Meanwhile, start your oven [at 350 degrees] and cut tomatoes in half horizontally. Bake about 7 to 10 minutes or until the tomatoes are tender but still keep their shape. Arrange on a warm serving platter and pour the hot deviled egg sauce over the tops. Serves 4 to 6. ◅

Margaret Moffatt Lea Houston
◆ FRIED GREEN TOMATOES

Madge Thornall Roberts, great-great-granddaughter of Sam and Margaret Lea Houston, often speaks of the general's penchant for fried green tomatoes. A venerable Southern favorite, they are still as easy to prepare and as satisfying today as they were during the Houstons' stay in the mansion.

> 3 tablespoons of bacon fat drippings
> 3 or 4 firm green tomatoes
> ¼ cup flour
> 1 cup dry, fine bread crumbs
> Salt & pepper
> 2 eggs, beaten

Heat frying pan and add the bacon fat. Slice your tomatoes into ½-inch thick slices. Combine flour, bread crumbs, and salt and pepper. Taking each slice individually, dip it into the egg, covering each side, then place in flour and bread crumb mixture, covering entire slice. Repeat with each slice until all are coated. Then, place them into the frying pan, with the bacon fat, and fry slowly. Slices should become golden brown. Add salt and pepper to taste. ◅

Margaret Moffatt Lea Houston
◆ TEXAS APPLE DUMPLINGS

The origins of the names for many of Margaret Houston's recipes
are not known. In the earliest sources they are merely printed with
the names they carry to this day. Some of the earliest mentions of
these recipes are in articles published in *Southern Living* in the 1940s.
As to whether Mrs. Houston or a creative copywriter for the magazine bestowed these titles on the recipes is unknown.

> 3 apples
> 6 tablespoons sugar
> $\frac{1}{4}$ teaspoon cinnamon
> $\frac{1}{4}$ teaspoon nutmeg
> 2 cups pastry dough
> 3 tablespoons butter

Peel, remove cores, and cut apples in half crosswise. Mix sugar,
cinnamon, and nutmeg together. Now roll the pastry on a
floured board into a rectangle about 8 inches by 12 inches and cut
into equal squares. Put pastry squares in a large shallow baking
pan and put a half apple on each square. Fill apple cavities with
sugar mixture and dot with butter. Wet the edges of squares with
a little cold water and lift all four corners up to a point. Press the
points with your fingers until they seal securely.

Cook 1 cup of sugar, $\frac{1}{2}$ teaspoon cinnamon, 1 tablespoon
butter, and 2 cups of water together to the boiling point and boil
for 3 minutes. Pour syrup around dumplings and bake 35 minutes
or longer. Serve warm with sauce over the top. ~

Margaret Moffatt Lea Houston
◆ BUTTERMILK BISCUITS

Have plenty of fresh butter on hand to enjoy with these dense but
delicious biscuits.

1 cup sifted all-purpose flour
1 teaspoon baking powder
¼ teaspoon salt
½ teaspoon sugar
¼ cup shortening
⅓ cup buttermilk

Start your oven [at 375 degrees]. Sift flour, baking powder, salt, and sugar together in a mixing bowl. Add shortening and cut in with two knives or a pastry blender until mixture looks mealy. Stir in the buttermilk with a fork until dough holds together in a soft ball.

Dump on a floured board and knead lightly. Roll about ⅓ inch thick and cut with biscuit cutter. Bake on an ungreased cookie sheet 15 to 20 minutes or until golden brown. Serve immediately. Makes about 12 medium-sized biscuits. ≈

Margaret Moffatt Lea Houston
◆ DUMPLINGS

These substantial, wonderful dumplings are every bit as delicious now as when they were served at the mansion during Houston's term. They are usually cooked in the rich stock made from a stewing chicken, although beef or veal stock can be used.

2½ cups sifted all-purpose flour
1 teaspoon baking powder
½ teaspoon salt
Dash pepper
½ cup shortening
5 to 7 tablespoons milk

Sift flour, baking powder, salt, and pepper together several times. Cut in the shortening with two knives or pastry blender until the mixture looks mealy. Add milk, a tablespoon at a time using spoon and pastry blender, until you have a soft ball of dough.

Roll dough on a floured board about an ⅛ of an inch thick and cut into inch-wide strips. Drop into boiling stock (you'll need at least 2 quarts). Cook slowly for 15 to 20 minutes. Serves 6. ≈

Margaret Moffatt Lea Houston
◆ CABBAGE RELISH

Once "put up," this delicately flavored relish will be a welcome addition to winter foods such as pinto beans or hearty soups. It is also an interesting addition to harvest-time buffets, spread on very dry toasted baguette rounds.

> 1 medium head cabbage
> 10 carrots
> 4 large onions
> 3 green peppers
> 2 tablespoons salt
> 2 teaspoons mustard seed
> 2 teaspoons celery seed
> 1 cup sugar
> 1 cup wine vinegar
> 1 cup water

Work cabbage and carrots through your food grinder. (The results should yield 4 cups of each). Grind onions and peppers. Put the ground vegetables and all remaining ingredients in a large kettle. Cover the kettle and cook over medium heat for about 1 hour. Give relish an occasional stir. Spoon into sterilized pint jars and seal securely. ⤖

Margaret Moffatt Lea Houston
◆ AUNT 'LIZA'S APPLE CRISP

Aunt Eliza was the Houstons' cook at the mansion. This apple dessert is wonderful when heaped atop a large bowl of vanilla ice cream.

> 6 sliced apples
> $\frac{1}{2}$ cup water
> $\frac{1}{2}$ cup sugar
> $\frac{3}{4}$ cup sifted flour
> $\frac{1}{2}$ cup butter

Pinch of salt
Pinch of cinnamon

Slice apples and place in greased pan and add water. Mix remaining ingredients and spread over apples. Bake [at 400 degrees] for 40 minutes.

Margaret Moffatt Lea Houston
♦ BREAD PUDDING

The addition of a well-baked meringue to the top of this pudding provides an elegant finish to the dessert. The finished product literally melts in your mouth.

3 eggs, separated
1 quart milk
Sugar to taste
1 pint broken bread pieces
Rind of lemon, grated
3 teaspoons butter
½ cup raisins

Beat yolks of eggs. Combine with milk and add sugar to taste. Pour over bread pieces. Add grated rind of lemon, butter, and raisins to taste. Sit pan in hot water and bake [at 350 degrees] until set. Prepare meringue with remaining egg whites. Spread on pudding and bake until brown.

Margaret Moffatt Lea Houston
♦ MOLASSES PIE

Sorghum syrup was produced by hundreds of home farms through the nineteenth and early twentieth centuries. Making syrup is a labor-intensive process of cooking the juices of the sorghum stalk, which produces the sugars and gives the finished syrup its unique "bite." If you can find home-produced sorghum syrup, the result is well worth the effort it takes to locate. The interesting taste of the syrup infuses this century-old recipe with what one guest at a recent dinner party described as "the taste of the past."

2 eggs
1 cup sugar
1 cup sorghum syrup or molasses
1 tablespoon flour
1 tablespoon butter
1 teaspoon vanilla
Dash of nutmeg

Beat eggs and add sugar. Stir well and add molasses and then add remaining ingredients. Pour into a prepared pie crust and bake [at 350 degrees] until pie is set and crust is brown. ~

Troubled Times

DURING THE YEARS of the Civil War (1861–65) and the Reconstruction period in Texas (1865–73), the state had little money, and only the most necessary appropriations for the mansion were made. The Union army had advanced south within a month after the surrender of Galveston in 1865, and the *Austin State Gazette* reported that a portion of the New York cavalry had arrived in Austin. Gen. Wesley Merritt and his staff established their headquarters at the Governor's Mansion. For the first time in several years, the U.S. flag flew on the Capitol building.

Vandalism of the mansion during the decade after the Civil War was not uncommon. A variety of tenants—some beloved, many not—lived in the old house during the next eight years, some of them leaving the mansion in a sorry state upon their departure.

Supplies were expensive and scarce. Union blockades of the major shipping ports caused dire shortages on Texas tables. Items that could not be grown or produced at home were in short supply. Thrifty and enterprising Southerners made do with what they had. "Confederate coffee," a wicked blend of whatever was on hand—

Martha Melissa Evans Clark.
Courtesy Friends of the Governor's Mansion.

sweet potatoes, roasted cornmeal or peanuts, even blanched corn—
stood in for the real commodity.

♦ MARTHA MELISSA EVANS CLARK ♦
MARCH 16−NOVEMBER 7, 1861

Melissa Clark had a very short period of residence in the Governor's
Mansion. Originally from Marshall, Texas, she and her husband
Edward had moved to Austin several years prior to his governor-

ship. They lived in a house at Twelfth and Nueces Streets, from which Edward could make a quick commute to the Capitol and the various positions he held there before being elected lieutenant governor in 1859.

In the spring of 1861, when Sam Houston refused to take the oath of allegiance to the Confederacy, Edward Clark was elevated to the position of governor. The Clark family left their Twelfth Street home in Austin and moved into the Governor's Mansion. Melissa shared the role of first lady somewhat begrudgingly with her proud and domineering mother-in-law. The elder Mrs. Clark's father and later her husband both served as governors of Georgia, and when her son was promoted to the governorship of Texas, Mrs. Clark felt somewhat entitled to preside over the affairs of the mansion. When the Clarks left the mansion less than a year later, they returned to their home on Twelfth Street. At the close of the Civil War, Governor Clark briefly sought sanctuary in Mexico, as many former Confederates did. Upon his return, he, Melissa, and the family returned to Marshall.

<div style="text-align:center">~~~</div>

Martha Melissa Evans Clark
♦ OYSTER LOAF

In the mid-nineteenth century, before the process of canning oysters was perfected, obtaining them in Austin was a daunting, if not impossible, task. Small canning operations were in place on the Texas coast shortly before the Civil War, so the transport of oysters to the far inland reaches of the state was made easier. Bette Anne Clark, a great-granddaughter of Melissa and Edward Clark, submitted this ancient Clark family recipe.

To prepare bread:
Cut top from unsliced loaf of bread.
Scoop out middle, leaving $\frac{3}{4}$-inch sides and bottom.
Lightly brush inside with egg white.
Spread outside with butter.
Bake [at 350 degrees].

Filling:
Drain and save liquid from 2 pints oysters.

Make white sauce using:
4 tablespoons butter
4 tablespoons flour
2 cups oyster liquid (add milk to make enough if there is not enough)

Melt butter in saucepan over medium heat, whisk in flour, and gradually add oyster liquid, stirring until thick. Add oysters and heat thoroughly but do not boil. Season with lemon juice, sherry, or Worcestershire sauce. Pour filling into bread shell and serve immediately. Use scooped-out bread chunks or other bite-size items to dip into filling.

◆ ADELE BARON LUBBOCK ◆
1861–1863

Adele Baron of New Orleans, a bride of sixteen, married twenty-year-old Francis Lubbock in 1835. Adele's French father had passed along to his daughter a keen wit and a love of entertaining. Her training as a fine hostess and homemaker would serve her well as she followed her husband in his political career.

The couple tried several business ventures ranging from breeding fancy poultry to raising camels, but Francis's heart and mind were in politics. He held several offices before being elected to the governorship of Texas in 1861, by only 124 votes. He staunchly supported the Confederacy. At the end of the Civil War, Lubbock was imprisoned and kept in solitary confinement for eight months before being paroled.

Contemporary accounts record the couple as being very content together. Some of the couple's devotion for one another can be gleaned from passages in Lubbock's memoirs. His life story is, for the most part, woven around a loving tribute to his life partner of fifty years. He wrote the following of their time in the mansion: "We made the Governor's Mansion a cheerful, bright home and we

Adele Baron Lubbock.
Courtesy Friends of the Governor's Mansion.

loved to have our friends enjoy it with us; our house was always open to visitors. At an early date we had a levee for the Legislature and all citizens were invited. We never dined alone, invariably having from two to a dozen members of the Legislature with us, so that during the session every senator and representative has been at our table."

The couple brought four slaves with them to the mansion. Two were young girls who were trained in housework and two were men who cared for the horses and did other jobs around the house. The first lady supervised every detail of running the mansion household. Although the Civil War was already raging, provisions for the first family were still usually available during the war's first year. Turkeys could be purchased for fifty cents.

One year later, however, due more to a severe drought than the hardships of war, provisions were increasingly hard to buy in Austin. When supplies in Austin were exhausted, Adele went into the countryside, some twenty miles away, and bought game and vegetables for the mansion table. As hostess of the home of the chief executive during a very uncertain time in Texas, she still managed to make the Governor's Mansion one of the social and political centers of the South.

Adele Baron Lubbock

◆ BIRDS, SQUABS, SQUIRREL, RABBIT, OR CHICKEN EN CASSEROLE

As the title indicates, this recipe may be used for preparing a variety of meats. Historian T. Lindsay Baker uses a preparation similar to this one when he prepares opossum. The test kitchen decided to stick with chicken.

Split the backs of 2 young fryers, dredge with flour seasoned with salt and pepper, and fry in hot fat. Place in oiled casserole with backs up. Add strips of broiled bacon, 2 tablespoons butter broken into bits over bacon, and 1 minced onion. Surround with small carrots (and tiny onions if desired). Cover with hot water and cook in oven half an hour. Sprinkle over them 1 teaspoon each of sugar and paprika. Add a glass of sherry wine and continue cooking birds in oven until browned. Strain gravy over them to serve. Birds, squabs, squirrels, and rabbits may be cooked the same way.

Adele Baron Lubbock

♦ FRESH CORN AND OKRA

Two of the great-granddaughters of Adele and Francis Lubbock, Augusta Breed Fenley and Laura Breed Haden, preserved this recipe by contributing it to the Harris County Heritage Society's cookbook. Augusta and Laura were the granddaughters of Theodore Uglow Lubbock, who was orphaned as a baby and adopted by Governor and Mrs. Lubbock. This corn and okra dish is very Southern and very delicious.

   1½ cups of okra, cut thin
   1 small onion, cut into small pieces
   ¼ cup bacon grease
   6 ears of fresh corn, with kernels cut from the cob
   ¼ cup water
   Salt
   1 small portion of pepper
   Dash of paprika

Fry okra and onion in bacon grease until light brown. Add corn with ¼ cup of water. Cook slowly until well done. Season with salt, pepper, and paprika. ✄

Adele Baron Lubbock

♦ ORANGE MARMALADE

This recipe was also passed down in the Lubbock family. The simple flavors of the fruit make this recipe very appealing. Yes, it really does gel if you cook it slowly and carefully.

   3 oranges
   1 lemon
   1 pint water
   6 cups sugar

Place fruit in a saucepan and fill with enough water to cover pieces. Boil until a silver fork can go through the orange and the lemon. Allow to set overnight. Run boiled fruit through meat grinder. Add the 1 pint of water and the sugar. Cook over low flame until it gels. Put in sterilized jars and seal. ≈

♦ SUE ELLEN TAYLOR MURRAH ♦
1863–1865

Though no documented recipes of Sue Ellen Murrah survive, the story of her time at the mansion must be told. It is possibly the saddest tale of all of the first ladies. The daughter of a wealthy planter, she married Pendleton Murrah, a dashing young lawyer, in 1858. He was elected governor in 1863, during one of the most tumultuous periods in Texas history. Murrah's inauguration supper gives an indication of the impact the Civil War had on life at the mansion. The guests ate what was probably the simplest inauguration meal ever—they dined only on corn cakes—and there was no inaugural ball.

The Pendletons' marriage was loveless, and Sue Ellen was a wife in name only. The rift apparently came on the Murrahs' wedding night, when joyous friends and relatives "shivareed" the couple, as was the tradition. Unbeknownst to Pendleton, they took Sue Ellen captive as a prank. He grimly waited in the bridal chamber all night for a bride who never arrived. His pride wounded, he stubbornly withheld his affection for his wife from that point forward. Never fully understanding why her husband was distant, she endeavored to be personable to those around her. The story of her unhappy condition would possibly never have been told, had it not been for one fateful event at the mansion.

On a cold and drizzly night, Sue Ellen was sick in bed when downstairs, a huge, flaming log rolled out of the fireplace in the library and set the room on fire. Governor Murrah came to her bedroom, wrapped Sue Ellen in a blanket, and carried her downstairs and out the back door. Across the street, safe in bed at a neighbor's house, ill and with fever, she related how her husband, as he carried her down the stairs, had called her "my dear." This phrase was the first term of endearment he had spoken to her during their entire wedded life. Between her sobs, the tale of her sad married state then came spilling out to the stunned ladies gathered near her bed.

At the close of the Civil War, even after Gen. Robert E. Lee's surrender, Murrah urged Texans to resist the Union forces. When it was obvious that the Union troops could not be stopped, Murrah, fearing imprisonment, vacated his office and fled from Texas to Mexico, as did so many former Confederate loyalists. Sue Ellen, broken-hearted and abandoned, was left in the mansion with two slaves to look after her. She then returned to her former home in Marshall. Sue Ellen never saw her husband again. The long trip was too much for Pendleton. Weakened by what was probably tuberculosis, he was bedridden upon reaching Monterrey, Mexico, and died there on August 4, 1865.

◆ MARY JANE BOWEN HAMILTON ◆
1865–1866

Mary Jane Bowen was born in Georgia in 1828 and later moved to Alabama with her parents, Judge and Mrs. John D. Bowen. A young lawyer named Andrew Hamilton was soon brought in as a partner in Judge Bowen's Alabama law firm, and he was frequently a guest at supper. As the months passed, Mary Jane discovered that she enjoyed Andrew's company very much. A courtship began and progressed, and the couple married in 1843. The Hamiltons, like so many of their generation, had heard of the vast lands and opportunities offered to those relocating to Texas. They moved to Texas in 1847. In 1849 the couple moved to Austin, and Mary Jane settled into their dusty little log cabin. Once in the city, Andrew, who was loyal to the North and Union causes, quickly became involved in state politics.

The outbreak of the Civil War brought great suffering as food and supplies became increasingly scarce. Shortly after the war had begun, Andrew Hamilton met with President Abraham Lincoln and received a commission as a brigadier general in the Union army. His actions may not have been well received back in Austin. The Hamiltons' home burned in 1864 under mysterious circumstances, and the family lost everything. Undeterred, Hamilton used his commission to gain political visibility, and because of his efforts during the war, President Andrew Johnson appointed him

*The earliest known photograph of the Governor's Mansion, taken by Austin
photographer H. B. Hillyer in the mid-1860s. This picture dates from
the time Sue Ellen Murrah was first lady or slightly
after, when the house was abandoned.*
Courtesy Friends of the Governor's Mansion.

to be provisional governor of Texas in the summer of 1865. At the close of the war, with the South beaten and former Confederates returning home to be ruled by their former enemies, emotions ran high.

Hamilton's position as governor, which he held for a year, did little to endear him and his family to Texans still loyal to the Southern cause. Many considered him a traitor. His time as the chief executive in Texas during Reconstruction was difficult and frustrating. Whatever measure of success the governor enjoyed was due in part to the capable assistance of his wife. Her gentle spirit and quick wit soothed tensions at the mansion on more than one occasion.

Mary Jane, tall and striking in appearance, did all she could to maintain a peaceful and structured home life for her children. The Hamilton family's life in the Governor's Mansion was a bright spot amid the turmoil. In addition, with the help of five servants, she gave some of the first levees after the war. In their own way, these

Mary Jane Bowen Hamilton.
Courtesy Friends of the Governor's Mansion.

events did a great deal to lessen the tension between the old Southerners and the new Northerners in the capital.

Among the Northern guests at the mansion were General and Mrs. George Custer, who were stationed at the Blind Institute. The Hamilton family would dance the Virginia reel with the invited citizens of Texas, and their levees were remembered with great fondness by those who did not let political alliances keep them from attending. Throwing a party during the years immediately following the Civil War was not an easy task. Supplies were often restricted and astronomically expensive, but for the year Mary Jane was first lady, she always managed.

Mary Jane Bowen Hamilton

◆ CONFECTION CAKE

The intense, old-fashioned nature of the filling of this cake makes it a wonderful addition to a holiday get-together. The difficulty in obtaining many of the ingredients, especially immediately after the Civil War, must have made this dessert a true delicacy at the mansion.

    2 cups granulated sugar
    $\frac{2}{3}$ cup butter
    1 cup sweet milk
    $2\frac{1}{2}$ cups flour
    2 teaspoons baking powder
    6 egg whites

Cream sugar and butter; add milk, then flour, then baking powder and whites last, beaten very stiff. Bake in three large layers and fill with the filling.

Filling:
Beat 2 eggs until stiff. Boil 2 cupfuls sugar in a cupful of water until it drops like thick honey; then add a pinch of cream of tartar and pour onto beaten eggs, beating constantly while pouring. Beat until thick, then add 3 cups of stoned and chopped raisins, 1 heaping teaspoonful each of chopped figs, dates, citron, candied cherries, almonds, and hickory nuts, add 1 teaspoonful vanilla, and spread [between layers]. Put plain boiled icing over top and sides. ⌐

◆ ANNIE RATTAN THROCKMORTON ◆
1866–1867

First Lady Annie Throckmorton never lived at the mansion. When her husband James became governor in 1866, Annie basically wanted nothing to do with the troubled state's capital. She felt more

Ann Rattan Throckmorton.
Courtesy Friends of the Governor's Mansion.

secure at home with her ten children in Collin County, and James, determined to be both governor and a good father, divided his time between Austin and their home.

A no-nonsense woman who maintained absolute order in her household, Annie was conservative in both manner and dress—the only jewelry she ever wore was a single brooch and her wedding ring. She was also well read and something of a folk physician in her own right. When James, who was a physician by training, was away on house calls and later when he was in Austin pursuing his political career, she was desperate for books to read. Pulling down his medical books, she studied them and soon became adept at minor treatments.

One of the seven legislators who had dared to vote against secession, James Throckmorton had nevertheless served as a Confederate brigadier. Elected to succeed Andrew Hamilton as governor, he was removed from office by decree of Gen. Philip Sheridan, who replaced him with the more placid former governor, Elisha Pease, who eventually resigned in disgust.

When Throckmorton was removed from the governor's office by federal officials, he returned to the family home in Collin County. Annie was no doubt glad for him to be home and away from the intrigue and dangers of political life in Austin. After Reconstruction ended, James once again left his home and family and served four terms in Congress. While he was gone, it was once again up to Annie to take care of the children and the farm.

The years immediately after the war were an uncertain time for Texans. In 1867, the U.S. Army sent Gen. Joseph Jones Reynolds to oversee the federal government's military control of Texas, and he took up residence in the mansion. The *Texas State Gazette* of October 19, 1867, optimistically stated upon his arrival, "Maj. General Reynolds has established his headquarters for the present in this city. We are told the new Commander will occupy the Governor's Mansion, and we hope his administration in Texas may be distinguished by judgment and mercy."

To many Texans, General Reynolds's brief tenure probably seemed anything but just and merciful. His actions disenfranchised many former Confederates, and other Northerners placed in positions of authority seemed to follow his lead. The arrival of Reconstruction forces in Texas compounded the tension in the state for the next three years. In the hands of strangers, the fate and future of the mansion remained uncertain. Increasingly tired of years of unrest, military occupation, and reflecting the general anxiousness of the population of Texas, the *Tri-Weekly State Gazette* questioned on April 30, 1869, "When shall it [the mansion] be filled again with a real old fashioned Governor? We trust as soon as possible. Hurry up reconstruction. You will never find the people more anxious or better disposed than at present. Let us have a live, whole-souled, patriotic Governor of some sort, and let him give a rousing Re-union in the mansion, signifying that the war is over and peace restored."

The condition of the mansion worsened. Untended and ignored, the yard and gardens grew up in weeds. Many of the windows were broken, and the majority of the shutters hung at odd angles. To local residents, the state of the home was a reminder of occupation by a conquering army. On August 4, 1869, the *Tri-Weekly Gazette* once again brought the status of the mansion and the governance of Texas to issue: "The Governor's Mansion we understand, is now left in charge of some slaves, who are having a good time of it. If we ever get a ligitimate [*sic*] Governor, a good deal of repairs and cleaning up will be necessary."

Texas got an elected governor late in 1869. The voters had two candidates from which to choose, and both were men with Northern loyalties. The federal military occupation forces controlled the election. Even though the man who was elected was not ideal in the minds of the Texas populace, he was still better than being under the control of the military.

◆ ANNE ELIZABETH BRITTON DAVIS ◆
1870–1874

Anne Elizabeth Britton, known as Lizzie, was the daughter of Forbes Britton, a loyal Confederate, state senator, and friend of Sam Houston. She was a Southerner through and through. E. J. Davis, the man she loved, was described during his lifetime as being tall, gaunt, cold-eyed, and commanding. He was also a man with significant Union loyalties. The two overcame their families' concerns, ideological differences, and disparate backgrounds and married on April 6, 1858, in Corpus Christi, Texas. She supported her husband fully and was ready to do what she could to help him.

Because her husband joined the Union forces, Lizzie fled Texas during the Civil War and sought refuge in Mexico. After she had been there for four months, E. J. joined her in hiding. One evening a gang of angry Southerners, seeking revenge, captured E. J. and

Anne Elizabeth Britton Davis.
Courtesy Friends of the Governor's Mansion.

other Union loyalists. Lizzie, grief-stricken, threw herself on the mercy of the marauders and identified herself as a loyal daughter of the South. The mob was unmoved and took their captives away. Shortly thereafter, one of the men they had captured was found hanging from a tree.

Lizzie did not know for days whether E. J. was dead or alive. Not eating, scarcely able to walk, she was near collapse when E. J. finally returned to her, severely beaten but alive. He explained that the only reason he was spared was through the efforts of the United States consul and the Mexican authorities. After his harrowing narrow escape, E. J. Davis's loyalties to the Union and its ideals were guaranteed. In 1869, during the trying days of Reconstruction in Texas, Davis ran for governor against former governor Andrew Hamilton, and in an election fraught with fraud on both sides Davis won by only eight hundred votes.

Having fought for the Union in the Civil War, the newly elected Governor Davis arrived in Austin as a much-derided "carpetbagger." As such, his time in office was controversial, and his governorship was added to the list of woes surrounding the challenges of Reconstruction in Texas. The bitterness of a Northern victory was ingrained in almost every white inhabitant throughout the South, and the citizens of Austin were no exception. Life was not easy for him or his two sons, or for that matter his wife.

Despite the animosity of the locals on a personal level, Lizzie oversaw many improvements to the mansion. The years of neglect and vandalism during Reconstruction had taken their toll on the old house, but she began to clean and put the mansion in order. One of her most lasting changes was the "graining" of the interior doors of the mansion. In fashion immediately after the war, the painted graining effect imitates fine hardwood such as oak or walnut.

The grounds of the mansion also received her special touch. Lizzie hired the mansion's first official gardener, William Davenport, in 1870. Together they undertook an extensive landscaping project. A variety of seeds and plants were ordered from Pennsylvania, Maryland, and New York. Lizzie selected hyacinths, narcissus, tea roses, petunias, and hollyhocks. William brought in thousands of yards of topsoil to level the gardens and grounds. A new fence surrounded a vegetable and herb garden, and William planted more flower gardens. The front lawn was replanted with grass and decorated with wooden benches. Large cast-iron pedestals were placed at key positions along winding gravel paths. The crowning touch to the outdoor improvements was a summerhouse or gazebo that was built on the south lawn.

Despite the signs of progress around the mansion, sugar, flour, coffee, and other basic commodities were still difficult to obtain, even for the governor and his family. The extreme shortages experienced immediately after the Confederate surrender were lessening somewhat, although prices remained high. This situation did not keep Lizzie from opening the house to Austin citizens for a few special receptions. The mansion was not as crowded for these parties as it had been before the war. In addition to supervising the public events, she oversaw arrangements for the first wedding at the mansion. E. J.'s pretty young niece married George T. Sampson at a small private ceremony in January of 1872.

Lizzie remained relatively calm during her time as first lady. Even when the locals had shown open animosity toward her husband and refused to come to her parties, her face never revealed her anguish. The last few days at the mansion, however, were a different matter. The political situation in Texas, unstable at best during the final days of Reconstruction, worsened. E. J.'s administration was faltering, and he refused to give up control, even after he was technically voted out of office. Desperate to remain in power, he sent an urgent plea to his one-time fellow Union army officer, President Ulysses S. Grant, asking for military support in his plight. Grant flatly refused and, in effect, turned his back on Davis.

The president's rebuff was the last straw. Always serene, always reserved in the past, Lizzie's composure shattered in an instant. When she learned that help for her husband would not be coming, she marched down the winding stairs of the mansion, yanked Grant's portrait from its place of honor, and stamped her heel through the picture, glass and all. Her actions, though atypical for her, mirrored the sentiments of most of the citizens of Austin toward the president.

Ultimately, U.S. troops were not deployed, and her husband finally yielded control of the government of Texas and quietly left office. When Lizzie moved from the mansion, she remained in Austin, where her husband practiced law. She would continue to deny the story of her tantrum with the picture of Grant for the rest of her life. But those who heard her refuting the event could not help notice the twinkle in her eye and the satisfied smile on her face, even while she innocently recounted her own story of how the portrait came to be ruined.

◆ MARY EVANS HORNE COKE ◆
1874–1876

Two large portraits of Governor and Mrs. Richard Coke hang in the small parlor of the mansion, as they have for decades. The images look down into the elegant room and beyond. The small grin on the face of the first lady gives insight into the gentle spirit Mary Coke possessed, even during the complicated days during which she resided in the mansion.

Mary Evans Horne was born in Georgia in 1836 and at the age of thirteen moved with her family to Waco, Texas. Waco was scarcely more than a collection of rude log cabins and other ill-constructed "huts" and as such was not a very pleasant place in which to live. The Horne family was not alone, however. Dozens of other early pioneer families lived in the region. Mary's father was a physician and rapidly grew acquainted with the people of the area. At the age of fifteen she met Richard Coke, a young Waco lawyer. Mary's dainty "Cinderella" feet had first attracted Richard's eye. (As unusual as it may sound, he admired them so much he always insisted on selecting her footwear.) Soon after they met, she married him. Dr. Rufus Burleson, the man who baptized Sam Houston, solemnized the wedding vows.

When the Civil War began, Coke enlisted as a private in the Confederate army. He served for the entire war, eventually reaching the rank of captain. With the war and Reconstruction behind him, Coke ran for governor and won, entering office in 1874. The family left Waco and moved to Austin. Mary, a slender woman of medium build, was never strong. The trials of the move to Austin and the stress of life as first lady during a hectic time in the city's history practically rendered her an invalid. Governor Coke was, in contrast, an enormous man with a massive brow and a bushy black beard.

Social life in Austin was slowly emerging in full force for the first time since the conclusion of the war. Despite her frail constitution, Mary assisted the mansion kitchen staff in preparing food for an increasing number of spring and summer receptions. Mary and her cook prepared the cake and food for the second wedding to take place in the mansion when Richard's widowed cousin married an army officer. The fancy foodstuffs (especially those that had to be

Mary Evans Horn Cooke
Courtesy Friends of the Governor's Mansion.

imported from back East) and produce needed for these events were slowly becoming available again on Texas tables. Newly installed gaslights further dissipated the lingering specter of war from the mansion.

At the end of her husband's term, Mary left the demands of entertaining at the mansion behind and with her family returned to Waco, her home for almost fifty years. There, the Cokes built an imposing house where she spent the rest of her days caring for her husband and children.

Janie Roberts Hubbard.
Courtesy Friends of the Governor's Mansion.

✦ JANIE ROBERTS HUBBARD ✦
1876–1879

Janie Roberts was born in Georgia in 1849, and at the age of twenty she married Richard Hubbard in Tyler, Texas. When her husband, then serving as lieutenant governor, became governor after Richard Coke resigned the office, Janie entered the mansion and began to hold the usual receptions and events. Repeatedly described as a clever hostess at the mansion, Janie was a sturdy woman of medium stature, with elegant manners and a stately bearing. She was quickly accepted by Austin society and became a popular hostess.

The war years had deprived citizens of many of the standard social events, so the new schedule Janie set was eagerly embraced. She hosted the third wedding at the mansion in March of 1877 when Nettie Houston, daughter of Sam Houston, married Maj. W. L. Bringhurst, a teacher at the Military Institute in Austin.

The skill with which Janie prepared food at the mansion might be inferred by the size of her husband. Richard dwarfed her. Governor Hubbard was so large, in fact, that political wags of the time said he looked as though he had swallowed his predecessor, the also sizable Gov. Richard Coke. Hubbard, Texas' largest governor to date, weighed in at nearly four hundred pounds. His closest friends called him Jumbo.

In his later life, when President Grover Cleveland named Hubbard an envoy to Japan, Janie traveled with him. She took over the official residence in Japan as she had the mansion. Her first project was teaching her cook Yin, who was from China, how to prepare food "Texas style." The experience she received as first lady of Texas helped to prepare her for her new role at her husband's side. She later recalled that even though she had bowed before an empress and met the full court of the imperial palace in Japan, she had never had a better time than when she was first lady of Texas.

Gracious Years

In the 1870s Mark Twain and Charles Dudley Warner wrote a novel called *The Gilded Age,* a phrase now synonymous with the late nineteenth century in America. It was an era of big steel, railroad magnates, labor disputes, and ostentatious displays of wealth by industrial magnates of the Northeast.

Although the Gilded Age did not have such a blinding glare in Texas, life at the Governor's Mansion during this period began to emerge from hard times and adopt contemporary styles. It was good practice for the next century, when oil was discovered and a more sophisticated style of entertaining became affordable.

◆ FRANCES WICKLIFFE EDWARDS ROBERTS ◆
1879–1883

Frances Edwards was born in 1819 and raised in her home state of South Carolina. When her family moved to Ashville, Alabama, she entered school, something still rather rare for a woman. When she met Oran Roberts he was studying law, but he allowed himself enough time away from his studies to pursue her. Courtship and marriage apparently did not interfere with his studies, for Oran was admitted to the bar in 1837. Shortly after their wedding, the lure of opportunity brought Oran and Frances to the newly formed Republic of Texas. The young pair lived first in the rough-edged frontier town of San Augustine but eventually settled in Tyler. There, the Robertses' seven children were born.

During the Civil War, Frances established a hospital for the 11th Texas Infantry in a tiny structure adjacent to the family plantation. She and the family's slaves took care of a steady stream of the sick and wounded. She also wove cloth to outfit four soldiers, even though the dust and fibers aggravated her asthma. Frances's health, never good, was further weakened by the demands of life during the war.

One simple act of sharing by Frances became one of the few satisfying moments during that unsettling time. During Union blockades, coffee was virtually impossible to get. Texans, as well as most other Southerners, resorted to an endless array of substitutes. Peanuts, barley, rye, and even oats were roasted, ground, and brewed in an attempt to find a replacement. Frances never developed a taste for "Confederate coffee" as it was called, but Oran lucked into a small bag of rich coffee beans in Houston and brought it to his wife. She had intended to make it last through the war, but once she saw the longing eyes of the wounded when they smelled the wonderful aroma of brewing coffee, she shared her precious cache with them.

When at last the war was over, Frances and Oran were deeply in debt. The expense of caring for the wounded soldiers and managing the farm had emptied their reserves. Frances insisted that they sell their home and land to pay their creditors. Once the accounts had been settled, the Robertses moved. Oran practiced law and eventually served on the Texas Supreme Court for a number of years. The family was settling in at their new farm near Tyler when a telegram arrived. Oran read the notice informing him that the Democratic convention of 1878 had met and he had been selected as the Democratic candidate for governor. He talked with Frances and agreed to accept the nomination. When he was elected to the governorship, Frances, now fifty-nine and ailing, oversaw the running of the mansion as she had her own home.

Frances Wickliffe Edwards Roberts.
Courtesy Friends of the Governor's Mansion.

Oran, best known for smoking a corncob pipe (which was rescued from the old Capitol building during the fire of 1881), accomplished a great deal during his two gubernatorial terms. State expenditures were reduced, and the burdensome debt left from Reconstruction was slowly erased. The contract for the present Capitol in Austin was finalized during his time in office, and the cornerstone for the University of Texas was laid in 1882. One year later, shortly before his term as governor ended, the University of Texas opened in Austin.

Running water was installed at the mansion during the Robertses' time in the house. This innovation did not come about as a result of the state's concern for the governor's comfort, but rather as a precaution against fire. When the old Capitol burned in 1881, Frances oversaw the dismal job of removing the burned and scorched paintings for safekeeping to the mansion. Because of her sense of history, she preserved much of what would have otherwise been dumped with the other rubble from the burned-out building. After that disaster, legislators voted for an ounce of prevention and appropriated funds for running water in other state properties.

Frances was very proud of her husband and wanted to ensure that those visiting the mansion were both well received and well fed. Her first levee was for members of the Texas legislature. The cook made gallons of coffee, an expensive commodity, for the party. Under Frances's careful, practical eye, dozens of other large receptions were held for elected officials and the citizens of Austin alike. The Governor's Mansion became a popular spot again and was often the first stop for prominent visitors to the capital city. While she was first lady, Frances converted the back parlor into a bedroom to accommodate the throng of visitors who came to stay with them.

Elizabet Ney, the famous sculptor, was a guest at the mansion on her first visit to Austin. The bohemian, freethinking artist and the conservative, plainspoken first lady seemed to have gotten along quite well. Never one to stand on ceremony, Frances once startled supper party guests when they found her out in the back garden of the mansion gathering turnip greens for their evening meal. Despite her frailty, she always helped her husband during his time as governor through her tireless efforts to make the mansion a welcome retreat. When their residency at the mansion ended, she and her family remained in Austin.

Frances Wickliffe Edwards Roberts
♦ MOLASSES PIE

Mrs. A. C. Graham, daughter of Gov. Oran M. Roberts, provided this variation of a traditional Southern favorite. The cinnamon and nutmeg finish the mixture nicely.

1 cup ribbon cane syrup
1 cup sugar
3 whole eggs
1 tablespoon butter
1 teaspoon each of cinnamon and nutmeg

Line a pie plate with rich pie crust. Mix the above ingredients in order given. Pour into pie pan and bake in slow oven until firm. ↩

◆ ANNE MARIA PENN IRELAND ◆
1883–1887

Anne Maria Penn was born in Henry County, Virginia, on July 7, 1833, to Columbus and Frances Rives Penn. After several years in Virginia, the Penns moved to Mississippi and later relocated to Reutersville, Texas. John Ireland, a young lawyer and recent widower, lived in nearby Seguin. Through mutual friends, he and Anne were introduced. Following a year-long courtship, they were married and eventually had four daughters. When war broke out in 1861, John joined the Confederate army and quickly organized a company of soldiers, which he led to the Texas coast.

Ever supportive of her husband, Anne closed their serene home at Seguin and moved with her husband and the troops. Living near the camp, she immediately became cook, nurse, and mentor to the soldiers living there. The war years took their toll on Anne and fostered in her a desire to provide a quiet life for herself, her husband, and her children. She did not care for the constant demands of her husband's political life and expressed little or no interest in politics.

When her husband was elected governor in 1882, she accepted the role of first lady with quiet humility. She did not attend the inaugural, however, as she did not believe in dancing and expressed her beliefs openly. Nor did she especially relish the thought of moving to Austin. Judging from the condition of the mansion shortly before the Irelands moved in, her reluctance was well founded. The *Austin Daily Statesman* gave this assessment of the governor's house: "The legislature is contemplating an appropriation for the improve-

Anne Maria Penn Ireland.
Courtesy Friends of the Governor's Mansion.

ment of the executive mansion. . . . As it is, it is not fit for a residence. The dampness of the walls, the exhalations from vapory
and various cellars, the leaky roof, and other notable faults, making it unfit for human beings to dwell in. . . . The *Statesman's*
advice to him [Governor Ireland], in fact, . . . would be not to
take his family into the mansion unless it be thoroughly renovated
as we suggest."

Despite the deplorable state of the mansion, the Ireland family
moved their personal furniture and belongings into the drafty old
house. Anne bore the shortcomings of the mansion and the duties

of official hostess that were expected of her. She performed her role as first lady mainly out of a sense of loyalty to her husband, as was expected. To ease the pressure of hosting these large parties, her stepdaughter Tillie assisted. Her precocious adopted son Pat, typical of young boys living at the mansion, pulled a few memorable stunts. He outdid many of his predecessors by riding a pet donkey up the front steps and practically into the front hall.

Being the wife of the governor did not change Anne. She continued to work as she had before, cooking and cleaning alongside her servants. When a waiter left in the middle of a dinner honoring Confederate veterans, she carried his tray and served the guests herself. She also controlled the behavior of the governor's household. When Tillie was caught playing raucous popular tunes on the piano for some friends, Anne walked up to the instrument, closed the lid, locked it, and pocketed the key.

As mistress of the Governor's Mansion, Anne hosted the mansion's fourth wedding when their daughter Rosalie married E. S. Hurt. These and countless other events became routine for Anne, but she primarily used her position to perform charitable works. She could be seen on many occasions in her carriage taking food and other provisions to the needy of Austin. She is also remembered for darning socks for countless boys attending the University of Texas during the time her grandson was a student. After her husband's time as governor, she and her family returned to Seguin, away from Austin and away from the limelight.

♦ ELIZABETH DOROTHY TINSLEY ROSS ♦
1887–1891

Elizabeth "Lizzie" Ross stepped off the train in Austin and faced a huge throng of people anxious for their first glimpse of the new governor and his family. It was cold and late, after 1:00 A.M., when the Ross family finally made their way down the platform and climbed aboard a carriage. The trip to the Driskill Hotel was slow as hundreds of people ran alongside the carriage and frequently crowded the streets to the point that the driver had to stop altogether. Lizzie, her husband Sul, and their six children tried to rest

Elizabeth Dorothy Tinsley Ross.
Courtesy Friends of the Governor's Mansion.

that night amid the clamor in the hotel. The inaugural reception was held the next day, and she spent the early part of the afternoon greeting callers who came to their suite in a nearly endless stream. The final inaugural supper that evening was an elaborate meal featuring the best the Driskill could provide. She was exhausted by the end of the night. The last well-wisher and reveler did not leave until the wee hours of the morning.

The mansion was a welcome retreat for the first few days after the inaugural of Lawrence Sullivan Ross. Lizzie oversaw the unpacking of the last of the family's belongings and saw that the children had worked out the division of the bedrooms without too much bloodshed. The Ross servants were given their assignments and made familiar with the kitchen. The male servants were shown the outbuildings and instructed on the other details of the vegetable gardens and the stables. Lizzie was familiar with the old house, having often visited her friends the Cokes when they lived in the mansion.

Florine Ross, the oldest daughter, quickly made friends in Austin, and Lizzie encouraged her to bring them to the mansion. Lawrence, the eldest son, also developed a large circle of friends who, along with the other Ross children, kept the mansion alive with activity. It was a prosperous time in Texas during Lizzie's time in the house, with one of the most important events she would oversee just on the horizon. The new Capitol was nearing completion, and Lizzie was asked to be the official hostess for the dedication ceremonies.

Her focus was not on the Capitol, however; it was on getting the mansion ready for the hundreds of visitors who would no doubt flock to Austin for the event. With all the dignitaries and officials and potentates and socially prominent people in town for a once-in-a-lifetime celebration, she knew the house would have to shine. Her main concern was where the overnight visitors to the mansion would sleep. As it was, the children filled every available bed in the house, and short of having them sleep in the servants' quarters or over the stable, she did not know what she would do. The Mexican delegation would be in Austin with all the ambassadors and their wives, and they were bringing the Mexican National Band.

Lizzie had to oversee myriad details. Would all of the guests fit in the double parlors for the private receptions? How would the seating arrangements be made? Where would the extra chairs needed to accommodate everyone be obtained? What would they serve the Mexican National Band? The house received a thorough cleaning. The attic and cellar were emptied and straightened (even though chances are they would not be seen). All of the outbuildings were freshened, and anything that was not useful or presentable was either hauled away or stored out of sight. The grounds were raked and the bushes and shrubs trimmed. Those plants not meeting her critical approval were chopped down and replaced. Throngs of visitors began to stop by the mansion on their way to admire the enormous new Capitol.

As the day of the grand opening dedication for the Capitol dawned, Lizzie rose early. Preparations at the mansion were drawing to a close. The servants had their instructions for the day. The children, pressed, pinned, and tucked into their best clothes, stood ready to follow their parents to the new Capitol's front steps. The day was magnificent, and Lizzie was proud of her husband. The time they shared in the mansion was considered a highlight of their marriage and marked a period of calm and prosperity for Texas.

Elizabeth Dorothy Tinsley Ross
◆ ORIOLE'S NEST

Tastes have changed a great deal during the time the mansion has been in existence. This dessert was created during an era of intense creativity in culinary circles throughout Texas. Novelties and theme desserts were the rage, and Elizabeth Ross, like many first ladies both before and after her, strived to serve those items that were sure to amaze and delight her guests. Frankly, the results we obtained with this recipe, after protracted and involved experimentation, could be termed neither amazing nor delightful. In reality, this is merely a variation of a Jell-O® mold. I believe the jelly to which Elizabeth refers is actually gelatin. The finished product is supposed to resemble a bird's nest containing tiny white eggs. I have tried it both with gelatin and with good plum jelly. Both resulting variations were pretty silly, but the flavored gelatin variation was the most successful. Perhaps your results will yield something more appetizing.

Blanc Mange (for the egg shapes):
3 tablespoons sugar
2 eggs, beaten
1 teaspoon vanilla extract
3 tablespoons cornstarch, diluted with a little cold water
2 cups milk, scalded

Mix sugar, eggs, vanilla extract, and cornstarch together. Beat well. Pour in the milk gradually. Place mixture on fire [burner] and allow to boil for 2 minutes, stirring constantly. Mold blanc mange in half eggshells, having emptied and washed as many of them as will make a pretty nest. Remove the blanc mange from the eggshells when set.

Having made a stiff jelly, partly fill a bowl with it and place the blanc mange egg shapes upon it, in such a way as to look well when turned out. All around and over the eggs place long strips of preserved orange rind to resemble straw. Melt a cupful of the jelly reserved for the purpose and pour over the whole. After it is thoroughly congealed, turn out upon a glass dish. ⮬

◆ SARAH ANN STINSON HOGG ◆
1891–1895

Sarah "Sallie" Stinson married James Stephen Hogg on April 22, 1874, on a rainy day at the Stinson family home near Quitman, Texas. The newly married couple settled into their first house, a tiny four-room frame structure. In January of 1875, their first child, William Clifford, was born. A daughter, Ima, was born on July 10, 1882. Named for the heroine of a Civil War poem written by her uncle, Thomas Elisha, she was in later years known affectionately as Miss Ima. Michael was born in 1885, and Thomas Elisha Hogg was born in 1887. Sallie worked tirelessly to make the small cottage a home for the growing Hogg family.

Jim had political aspirations beyond being merely the justice of the peace of Wood County. He ran for a variety of offices and in 1886 was elected attorney general of the state of Texas. This event necessitated a move to Austin, and the family arrived in December of 1886. Austin was a town of more than fourteen thousand people, and the Hogg family found it to be a vast change from small-town life.

The new Capitol was being built not too far from the boarding-house where the family lived for a time. Eventually, Jim bought his family a two-story house on Fourteenth Street. These moves had tired Sallie. She was expecting her fourth child, Tom, and after his birth she never fully regained her vitality. A wet nurse fed him along

Sarah Ann Stinson Hogg.
Courtesy Friends of the Governor's Mansion.

with her own infant. Caring for the four Hogg children was challenge enough, but Sallie's workload was about to increase. In early
1889, Jim announced his plans to run for governor. In 1891, he was
the first native-born Texan to be elected governor. The Hogg family moved to the mansion in January and began to settle into a daily
routine. Sallie, suffering from chronic headaches and in increasingly
poor health, did her best to manage the daily duties of the house.
Her daughter Ima later wrote that her mother had very fair skin but
not much color during this time.

Sallie set about, undeterred, trying to put the mansion in order. The house was somewhat dilapidated, and her first task was hiring a cadre of painters and carpenters. The men worked for several weeks to complete the job. Sallie had the mansion walls papered for the first time. In 1891 the mansion's single bathroom contained little more than an enormous tin tub installed almost thirty years earlier for Sam Houston. The other "necessary facilities" (that is, the privy) were still a distance from the main house. Heating the water on the kitchen stove took a very long time, so as a rule the Hogg men would bathe in the cistern house, which was a chilly experience. Along with substantial work to modernize the bathroom, new furniture was ordered for the front parlors and library, and the antiquated kitchen received much-needed updates.

Sallie divided the plot of ground behind the house into smaller plots that included a vegetable garden, a croquet lawn, a pool, flower beds, and a small fruit orchard containing fig, peach, quince, and plum trees. The vegetable garden provided most of the family's needs, and the fruit trees offered a large enough harvest to keep the mansion cook busy canning and preserving.

Frail and weak, and never weighing more than one hundred pounds, Sallie nevertheless attended every function given at the mansion, even though she often had to remain seated or lean on a stool in order to do so. The Hoggs started a weekly "at home" day when they would open the mansion to receive guests. Sallie was a meticulous housekeeper who oversaw every detail of these endless receptions and events with the help of her maid, cook, and a gardener.

In addition to holding frequent receptions in which the carpets were rolled back and the Virginia reel would be danced until the wee hours of the morning, the Hoggs would often hold euchre parties, which were as popular in the 1890s as bridge became in the next century. For these events, refreshments, including the occasional champagne, were served at around 4:00 or 5:00 P.M. Party suppers were served much later than they are today, usually beginning at about 10:00 P.M. Often, the ailing first lady would give servants instructions for these receptions from her bed.

The four children, ranging in age from three to fifteen, stayed busy with their collection of dogs, cats, squirrels, raccoons, and a Shetland pony. Among the menagerie living at the mansion was

The governor's mansion during the time the Hogg family lived in the house, circa 1890s. The old privy stands in the south side yard.
Courtesy Friends of the Governor's Mansion.

Jane, a large green parrot that would cry "Papa! Papa!" and fly out to meet the governor as he arrived home. Most days, if not outside tending to the animals or playing croquet, the Hogg children could be found indoors careening down the banister of the grand staircase. When the youngest, Tom, fell off and cut his chin, an exasperated Governor Hogg hammered tacks down the banister and ended the fun. The tacks were removed long ago, but the holes they left are still visible.

The governor also lost patience because the picket fence around the mansion had to be repaired so often. The younger children kept removing boards in order to make it easier for their friends to crawl through. On one occasion, according to an oft-told family story, Tom tried to solve the problem by almost burning the fence down.

The governor loved his wife and family, and on one occasion when they were away visiting the Stinson grandparents in East Texas, he wrote from the mansion, "Around the house here from morning 'till night there's not a sound of a rat, cat or cricket. The cow, parrots, the dogs, are all gone. I am like a ghost in a two-story barn deserted."

Sarah Ann Stinson Hogg
+ HOGG FAMILY BREAKFAST

The following is a typical breakfast served to the Hogg family in the 1890s. The morning meal was always served promptly at 7:00 A.M. and consisted of a bowl of oatmeal with thick cream or a small bowl of fresh clabber. The Hoggs' Hereford cows provided the dairy products at the mansion. Home-cured ham, sliced and fried, along with grits and redeye gravy, eggs fried on one side, and butter biscuits or cornmeal batter-cakes with ribbon cane syrup rounded out the meal. If any were biscuits left over till the next day, they were split, toasted in the oven, and spread with molasses. ⤙

Sarah Ann Stinson Hogg
+ BOILED WILD DUCK

Miss Ima, the daughter of Jim and Sallie Hogg, preserved this recipe. Duck is a tricky, greasy dish to prepare, but the results are crispy and delicious. Make sure your duck is a young and fresh one.

Take a wild duck, after cleaning, and scrub well with soda water and rinse thoroughly. Then cover it well with cold water, after placing $\frac{1}{2}$ apple or onion inside the duck to absorb the odor, and boil a few minutes. Then throw this water away. Now place duck in boiling water which has the following seasoning: slices of lemon, thyme, bay leaf, garlic, onion, peppercorns, red pepper, allspice, and cloves and boil until tender. While duck is still hot, place in a deep dish and marinate with a rich French dressing, which should include garlic and tarragon vinegar. The duck should be turned over frequently and basted with the dressing. It should be served cold and is better if it stands in the dressing 24 hours. This is a delicious Sunday night supper dish served with preserved orange slices or preserved kumquat. ⤙

Sarah Ann Stinson Hogg
◆ FRENCH DRESSING AND MARINADE

This modern version of a wonderful marinade from the Hogg kitchen works equally well with most meats and is really delicious when used on chicken.

> 1 cup water
> 1 cup red wine vinegar
> 1 teaspoon sugar
> Juice of one lemon
> 2 teaspoons fresh tarragon, chopped
> 1 tablespoon salt
> 1 tablespoon ground black pepper
> 1 tablespoon Worcestershire sauce
> 1 tablespoon dry English mustard
> 1 clove garlic, minced
> 3 cups extra virgin olive oil
> 1 cup walnut or grapeseed oil

Blend together all ingredients except the oils. Using a whisk or food processor, combine the oils and add them in a very fine stream, continuing to whisk until the mixture is well combined. Chill and shake thoroughly before serving.

Fresh dill or rosemary can be added. This dressing is an excellent base for ranch, Caesar, or Thousand Island dressings. It is a marvelous marinade not only for duck but also for vegetables, fish, or other meats that are to be broiled or grilled. ❧

Sarah Ann Stinson Hogg
◆ SPICE COOKIES

Miss Ima Hogg loved her mother's cookies. These were a perennial favorite at the mansion in the 1890s.

> ½ pound butter
> 2 cups sugar
> 3 whole eggs

½ package figs
1 cup chopped almonds
½ teaspoon soda
1 tablespoon boiling water
4 cups flour
1 teaspoon cinnamon
1 teaspoon allspice
1 teaspoon ginger
Almonds, split

Cream the butter and sugar well together. Add the eggs, one at a time, beaten well. Add the figs after grinding. Add the chopped almonds and soda, dissolved in the boiling water. Then sift the flour with the spices, working into the dough. Then put in the icebox and let chill. Roll out very thin and cut with fancy cutters. Place a split almond on the top of each cookie and bake slowly in a moderate oven.

Sarah Ann Stinson Hogg
♦ FISH HOUSE PUNCH

There's a little place just out of town,
Where, if you go to lunch,
They'll make you forget your mother-in-law
With a drink called Fish-House Punch.
                    —*from* The Cook (*1885*)

This concoction is older than the United States. Fish House Punch was first served in 1732 at the State in Schuylkill Fishing Club in Philadelphia, Pennsylvania, where it was much enjoyed by one of the club's most famous members—George Washington. His diary has several blank sections that have long been attributed to this potent drink.

Despite its rather unappealing name, this was a favorite recipe of Miss Ima Hogg. She served it at many functions held at her home, Bayou Bend, in Houston, and those held at her beloved retreat at Winedale. Miss Ima cautioned to "be careful, but not too careful when making it." One should also be careful when drinking it. It packs a Texas-sized wallop.

Make a syrup of 3 quarts of water, 1 pound of brown sugar. Pour while hot over the rinds and juice of a dozen or a dozen and a half lemons and simmer. Cool.

> Add:
> 2 quarts Jamaica Rum
> 1 quart Brandy
> Dash well with Peach Brandy to make it mellow
>   and extra fine.

This is the base for the punch, which can be kept in the icebox. The lemon rinds should be removed before juice is bottled. Dilute the base of the punch with fruit juice (grapefruit and pineapple juice mixed, and ginger ale can be used instead of water). The punch should be served immediately in a punch bowl containing ice made of fruit juices. The base is diluted according to one's taste and judgment. ∽

◆ SALLIE HARRISON CULBERSON ◆
1895–1899

Sallie Culberson is remembered time and again in mansion histories as the first lady who first served cranberry sauce at the mansion in individual molds. Transported to Texas by train, fresh cranberries, a fairly expensive commodity, were shipped in wooden barrels. Each barrel weighed one hundred pounds. The reason Sallie's innovation was so noteworthy at the time has been largely lost to history. Her novel method of serving the red berries must have been quite an impressive feat to gain so much notoriety.

Mansion luncheons and dinners were her special talent, and she planned the menus down to the minutest detail. She made the house comfortable and stylish by moving in her own beautiful rugs and furnishings. The Culbersons also installed one of the first heating stoves in the mansion, thus ending the reign of the fireplaces as the only source of heat in an often cold and drafty house. The decor of the mansion interiors during her time as first lady is remembered as being among the most elegant of the nineteenth century.

Sallie Harrison Culberson.
Courtesy Friends of the Governor's Mansion.

Like his wife Sallie, Charles Culberson was a handsome and perfectly dressed individual. Together they hosted many open houses and receptions. One of the most reported events during the time the Culbersons lived in the mansion was their New Year's Day reception in 1898. The mansion drawing rooms had been decorated with palms, flowers, and bamboo. William Jennings Bryan and his wife attended, as did the former governor of Missouri. The dining room table was piled high with what the *Austin Statesman* described as "most tempting viands."

Despite the brave façade she presented to the public, Sallie was weak and in poor health during her time in the mansion. She often traveled to the sanitariums in Battle Creek, Michigan, in order to build her strength. Her condition grew so alarming that the legislature appropriated forty dollars a month to pay a housekeeper to help with the mansion chores. Sallie's widowed sister also came to live with the family at the mansion, in part to keep Sallie company, but also to help with the social obligations. The invitations and constant demands on the first lady tired Sallie. She had little use for the social set and only accepted those invitations that she truly wanted to attend. She kept her sister and the mansion servants hopping, however, often issuing orders while resting on a chaise longue.

Sallie was keenly aware of the importance of the mansion and was one of the first first ladies to be actively involved in preserving mansion history. She placed a plaque on the Sam Houston bed to identify its significance to future generations. She considered her years at the mansion to be among the happiest of her life, and despite her frequent bouts with ill health, she lived for almost thirty years after leaving the old house.

◆ TURN OF THE CENTURY ◆
1899–1918

Life in Texas was good at the beginning of the new century. The mansion received much-needed updating, the roof was repaired, and electric lights illuminated opulent dinner parties enjoyed by invited guests. The style of the time called for meals featuring multiple courses—sometimes as many as eighteen—which could take three hours to complete. The first lady orchestrated the details and made sure that the guests—most still arrived at the mansion via horse and buggy—were comfortable and well fed. The mansion's full-time cook and housemaids worked seventeen-hour days to keep the household running smoothly.

Behind the scenes, the mansion's wood stove—constantly stoked—kept the kitchen blisteringly hot. Food had to be gathered shortly before it was prepared because the icebox was the one of the only ways to keep perishables cool. The mansion had a weekly standing order with the iceman (usually from the Lone Star Ice Company) that was augmented for parties and special events. The produce for the governor's table was still generally grown in the mansion's backyard. Butter was churned on site, and the milk was obtained from his cow, which shared a lean-to with the laying hens. Fancy foods and staples such as coffee, sugar, flour, and salt, along with some meat, were generally the only foods that had to be purchased during the first decade of the twentieth century. The canning industry developed in parts of the state where produce was grown in quantity, especially the lower Rio Grande valley, but for the most part food was still grown by individuals for their own consumption. The governors' and first ladies' agrarian roots were reflected in the way the mansion was almost self-sustaining.

The first ladies living in the mansion during first decade of the new century would be among the first to try the new sweet onions grown in Texas. The Bermuda onion was introduced into South Texas in 1898 when a packet of onion seed was planted near Cotulla. By 1904, approximately five hundred acres of Bermuda onions were planted in South Texas. In spring, 1907, 1,011 carloads of onions were shipped from South and southwestern Texas. By 1909, twelve coastal counties shipped 2,920 train carloads throughout the United States. Mansion cooks would incorporate the new onion into their recipes in a variety of ways.

One of the most lasting innovations impacting food and food preparation was implemented during the early twentieth century: the enforcement in Texas of a pure-food statute. It had been originally passed in 1883, but money for enforcing it was not regularly appropriated until 1907, when the legislature finally created a monitoring agency. Called the Dairy and Food Commission, its role was the administration of newly passed food and drug laws. The second major innovation affecting food was the standardization of the units of measure for cooking in the United States. Prior to this time recipes called for vague units of measure such as a pinch of salt or an amount of lard "the size of a goose egg." Standardized measuring cups and spoons brought an end to much of the mystery and made cooking in the mansion more of a science and less like conjuring.

Immigration was at an all-time high during the first two decades of the new century, bringing new tastes and textures to the state.

Chop suey, spaghetti and meatballs, and chow mein found their place on menus in homes around Texas. In addition, brands of processed foods that remain a part of the food culture to this day were introduced in the first ten years of the decade. Texans began to eat Oreo® cookies, Hellmann's® mayonnaise, Aunt Jemima® syrups, Crisco®, and Quaker Puffed Wheat®.

Before the production of alcoholic beverages was halted on June 25, 1918, and the era of Prohibition began, mustang grape wine, favored by more than a few of the governors, was produced in several regions of the state. A clever Texan patented a beer cooler in 1885 for use in saloons and hotels, although most of the beer (except that produced locally in small volume) in Texas was imported. Anheuser-Busch had opened a brewery in Houston, Texas, by 1890, and two other major breweries were established soon after in San Antonio. Some breweries survived Prohibition and went back to full production with the repeal of the eighteenth amendment in 1933.

◆ ORLINE WALTON SAYERS ◆
1899–1903

Orline Sayers, or "Lena" as she was usually known, is often considered to have been one of the most popular of the early first ladies. She loved living in the mansion, and in fact her connection with the house had begun in 1879, when Governor and Mrs. Oran Roberts held a wedding reception for Lena and Joseph Sayers in the front parlors. When Joe was governor, he indulged her creative tastes and encouraged her love for the old house. During her time in the mansion, the legislature granted more than eight thousand dollars for improvements. Lena used this money to simplify the mansion garden areas. The fountains installed by First Lady Lizzie Davis were removed, and on the south lawn Lena added extensive rose beds. A carriage house with two floors was built, with the upstairs rooms housing the maids.

One of the improvements to the mansion—possibly Lena's favorite—was the installation of electric lights. The formal parlors and the State Dining Room no longer depended on the malodorous and uneven glow of gaslight. Electricity was considered so prestigious

First Lady Lena Sayers in her best bonnet, circa 1903.
Courtesy Center for American History, University of Texas at Austin,
Prints and Photographs Collection, CN 00307.

that early lightbulbs were usually left unadorned in order to show them off to best advantage. In Austin, electric power was shut off just before ten o'clock in the evening, sometimes earlier if the city's water-driven power plant was experiencing difficulties—which it frequently did.

In 1901, Lena completed the redecoration of the mansion in late Victorian fashion. Mirrored over-mantels were added to the fireplaces, and large molded plaster cornices were placed around the parlor ceilings. Gilt parlor furniture, in the French style, was purchased. Two large crystal chandeliers were acquired for the visit of President William McKinley. These fixtures, exactly like those that hung in the White House in Washington, remained in the downstairs parlors for the next seventy years. Lena even touched up the historic portraits herself.

In preparation for the president's visit, the house was cleaned from attic to cellar, and dozens of potted palms were brought into the lower parlors. Animosity over the Civil War lingered in Texas, even forty years afterward, but Gov. Joe Sayers, a Confederate veteran, and President McKinley, a former Union officer, helped ease those tensions, dining together in the State Dining Room. The president even joked that Lena was the "governor of the Governor."

Lena carried out her duties with the skill of a diplomat, something she had learned to do while attending balls and receptions in Washington when her husband was a member of Congress. She made the mansion in Austin a welcome stop for the likes of Jay

The entry hallway decorated in Victorian Splendor, circa 1902.
A cast iron heating stove is proudly displayed. Note the
stove-pipe running out the back of the hall.
From the author's collection.

The State Dining Room decorated for the visit of
President William McKinley, circa 1901.
Courtesy Center for American History, University of Texas at Austin,
Prints and Photographs Collection, CN 00340.

Gould and governors from Mexico. The ease with which she entertained delighted her next presidential visitor.

When President Theodore Roosevelt was honored at the
mansion, the grand reception was perhaps the highlight of her
time as first lady. Throngs of curious admirers gathered on the
front lawn hoping to catch a glimpse of the popular president.
When she was not entertaining dignitaries, Lena would open the
mansion to visitors and greet guests herself every Tuesday afternoon. Joe and Lena Sayers were very good friends with Elizabet
Ney, by now an Austin resident, and the artist was a frequent
guest. Joe got her the important commission of sculpting the
statues of Stephen F. Austin and Sam Houston for the Hall of
Heroes in the Capitol in Washington.

Joe and Lena Sayers led a very comfortable life during their four years in the house. When they had to depart for the last time, Joe and Lena were not the only ones sad to move. The family Saint Bernard had become so fond of the home that he refused to leave. He was adopted by the next governor, S. W. T. Lanham. The Sayers cat apparently felt no remorse and lived out her days with Lena and Joe in Bastrop.

Orline Walton Sayers
◆ LENA SAYERS'S SUNSHINE CAKE

The egg whites make this cake especially light and fluffy. The recipe was given to President McKinley after his visit to the mansion and was prepared at the White House for many years.

> 1 teaspoonful of cream of tartar
> 1 cup of unsifted flour
> Whites of 11 eggs
> Yolks of 3 eggs
> 1½ cups of sugar
> 1 teaspoonful of vanilla

Put cream of tartar into the flour and sift it. Beat whites to a very stiff froth; beat the yolks well and add them to the whites. Add sugar carefully, then the flavoring, and last the flour. Mix thoroughly, but lightly and quickly; turn into a 9-by-9 ungreased pan and bake in a moderate oven 45 minutes. ≈

Orline Walton Sayers
◆ FRUIT CAKE

Lena was famous for her fruitcake, and for decades the old guard of Austin would not use any other recipe. This cake was first introduced into the mansion by Lena's dear friend Mrs. J. W. Parker, of Taylor, and it was served at all the receptions given there in the winter. Use a good brand of whiskey in the preparation of this cake.

4 pounds raisins
1½ cups whiskey
1 pound butter
1 pound sugar
1 cup molasses
10 eggs
1 pound flour
Spices to taste
1½ pounds citron, slivered
½ pound figs, cut
½ pound dates, cut
½ pound orange and lemon peel
1 pound almonds, blanched
2 cups pecans, cut

Soak the raisins in the whiskey overnight. Cream butter, sugar, molasses, and eggs. Combine flour and spices and add to mixture. Do not dredge the fruit in flour, but add all the fruit and nuts to the raisins and whiskey, mixing well before adding to the cake. Bake 4 hours in a moderate [300 degrees] oven in a round spring-form pan well-lined with greased paper. ❧

Orline Walton Sayers
◆ PRUNE MERINGUE

Prunes (or "dried plums," as they are now officially known) are a wonderful, nutritious snack on their own. When prepared as they are in this recipe, they become caramelized and delicious. Traditional pudding baking dishes can still be found at many cooking specialty shops.

Take as many prunes as will fill your pudding dish and stew with just enough sugar and water to cover them. This must be done the evening before you wish to use them. Place the prunes in a dish without the syrup, and make one and a half pounds of sugar into icing and pour it over the prunes until they are well covered, then set the dish in a warm oven to brown. ❧

Orline Walton Sayers
◆ SWEET MILK COOKIES

Rolling these traditional cookies very thin is the key to obtaining an almost cracker-like crunch. They are the perfect garnishes to many other desserts, or they can be eaten on their own.

1 cup white sugar
½ cup of butter
1 egg
2 tablespoons sweet milk
2 teaspoons baking powder

Add sufficient flour to roll thin. Bake in hot oven [400 degrees] until golden brown. ✐

Orline Walton Sayers
◆ BUTTERMILK CAKE

There is no need to ice this wonderful, delicate cake. Just serve it sliced very thin with ice cream or sherbet.

1 cup of butter
2 cups of sugar
6 eggs, separated
1 teaspoon soda
2 teaspoons cream of tartar
1 cup of buttermilk
3 cups of flour
1 clove nutmeg, ground
1 teaspoon vanilla

Cream butter, sugar, and add well-beaten egg yolks. Then dissolve the soda and cream of tartar in the buttermilk. Mix nutmeg with the flour and add it and buttermilk, alternately, to the creamed mixture, mixing well. Beat egg whites to stiff but not dry. Do not overbeat the egg whites as they will lose air and fluffiness and become dried out. Eggs (and other ingredients) should be at room temperature. This will make a larger, lighter cake. Add, folding in by hand, stiffly beaten egg whites. Add vanilla, pour into greased, floured, tube pan. Bake slowly at 300 degrees for an hour or an hour and a half. It is done when the top springs back lightly when it is touched. When done it is a golden brown and is pulling away from the sides of the pan.

Orline Walton Sayers
♦ COCOANUT CAKE NUMBER ONE

The late-nineteenth-century spelling of coconut was used in all of Lena's recipes calling for that ingredient. In the late 1890s and early 1900s coconuts, though readily available, were still considered somewhat unusual on Texas tables and were considered an exotic fruit.

Cake:
2 cups sugar
$\frac{1}{2}$ cup butter
1 cup milk
3 cups of flour
3 eggs
2 teaspoons of yeast powder

Mix ingredients together and bake in jelly cake tins at 325 degrees for 35 to 45 minutes until golden.

Filling:
The meat of one grated cocoanut (6 to 8 ounces)
3 eggs, whites only
$1\frac{1}{4}$ cup powdered sugar

Take three-quarters of the cocoanut meat; add egg whites, beaten to a stiff froth with 1 cup of powdered sugar. Frost sides of cake and spread between layers. Mix with the remainder of cocoanut and $\frac{1}{4}$ cup of powdered sugar and spread quickly over top of cake.

Orline Walton Sayers
+ SWEET PICKLES

These are delicious pickles. You can use any variety of available pickling spices.

> 1 pound of sugar
> 3½ quarts water
> 1 pint vinegar
> Spices (commercially available pickling spices)
> Cloves
> Cinnamon
> Mace to taste

Put in as much fruit as syrup will cover well. Boil from 15 to 30 minutes. Put up in jars. ⤚

Orline Walton Sayers
+ COLE SLAW

This recipe produces an interesting variation of traditional slaw. Lena also utilized cabbage from the garden to prepare sauerkraut for the governor in the fall and winter months.

> 1 head cabbage
> 1 pint vinegar
> Salt, pepper, sugar to taste
> 1 tablespoon butter
> 2 or 3 eggs
> 2 tablespoons cream
> 2 or 3 hardboiled eggs, for garnish

Have your cabbage finely shredded and place in a salad dish. Put in a saucepan vinegar, salt, pepper, and sugar to taste, with butter, and set over the fire. Break 2 or 3 eggs and stir constantly until it thickens, then add cream. Pour while hot over the cabbage, then cut 2 or 3 hardboiled eggs over the top. ⤚

Orline Walton Sayers
◆ JELLY CUSTARD

3 eggs
1 cup sugar
1 cup of jelly
1 tablespoon butter
Lemon and spice to taste

This must be baked with only an undercrust. Bake until golden brown.

Orline Walton Sayers
◆ CREAM CUSTARD

Orange-flower water may be purchased at most specialty shops, especially Indian groceries.

2 eggs
1 cup cream
1 cup sugar
1 tablespoon butter
2 tablespoons flour
Nutmeg
Orange-flower water
Citron

Combine all ingredients except citron, which should be very thinly sliced and laid on top. Bake in a crust. ⤚

◆ SARAH BEONA MENG LANHAM ◆
1903–1907

Sarah Beona Meng, the daughter of Garland Meng, a planter, and Suzannah Thomas Meng, was born on October 8, 1845. The family lived about four or five miles from Pacolet, South Carolina, and Sarah attended school and was courted by S. W. T. Lanham. After

Sarah Beona Meng Lanham.
Courtesy Friends of the Governor's Mansion.

he returned from fighting in the Civil War, he and Sarah married on September 4, 1866. Almost immediately the young couple said good-bye to their families and started out for Texas in a covered wagon. They settled first in East Texas and taught school for a year at Old Boston. In 1868 the Lanhams moved to Weatherford and opened a school there. The school they established was in a primitive log cabin with an attached lean-to shed room. Here they lived as well as taught their students.

Eight of the Lanhams' nine children were born in Weatherford. When the children were all grown and on their own, Sarah took a

Congress Avenue looking north between 3rd and 4th Streets.
John Orr provided groceries to the Governor's Mansion.
Note the trolley tracks in the middle of the street.
Courtesy Texas Department of Transportation.

home-based course of study for four years. Widely read, she mastered the German language after she was forty years old. Despite her iron will, Sarah was never very healthy, but she still maintained a comfortable home for her family. She supported her husband's career in politics even though his frequent trips away on the campaign trail left her to care for the home and family alone.

Sarah was fifty-eight years old when her husband was elected governor. The *Dallas Morning News* of January 20, 1903, described the inauguration and associated balls and receptions as being a "splendid success." Texas newspapers, following the patriotic mindset of the time, frequently compared her to Martha Washington. Religious to her toes, Sarah did not allow alcohol to be served in the mansion or at state functions. As a result, her husband's inaugural was a little less jovial than those of many of the other governors. This limitation, unpopular though it was among legislators and guests of the governor, was overlooked due to her genuine manner and gracious hospitality.

Austin, although greatly changed since the days of the Republic, had only begun to add modern conveniences for its citizens. The city had only one paved street, no permanent city sewer system, and irregular electric power service. The mansion, like most other houses in town, still relied on its own garden for vegetables, and the governor's chickens still provided for the needs of the kitchen. Despite being the wife of the governor, Sarah herself worked to see that meals were on the table when they were supposed to be and that her guests were provided for in the best manner possible. Even though she had several servants and a cook, she was not above doing whatever it took to keep the daily routine of the mansion under control.

Sarah Beona Meng Lanham
♦ CHOCOLATE PUDDING

A daughter-in-law of Gov. S. W. T. Lanham provided this recipe for baked pudding.

> 1 tablespoon butter
> 1 tablespoon flour
> 1 cup milk
> $\frac{1}{4}$ pound sweet chocolate
> 4 eggs, beaten separately
> $\frac{1}{2}$ cup sugar
> 1 teaspoon Adams Best vanilla

Make a thick sauce of the butter, flour, and milk, and allow to cool. Melt the chocolate, beat the egg yolks, and add both to the sugar, mixing well. Then add the sauce to the chocolate mixture. Beat egg whites, adding them and vanilla to mixture. Put in a buttered casserole and bake slowly for 1 hour. Serve hot with whipped cream. ✎

Sarah Beona Meng Lanham

◆ LANHAM MAHOGANY CAKE

This cake, like many others in this book, is a true period piece of culinary history. Rich and chocolaty, with a texture from another time, it is a delectable treat when served with coffee ice cream.

Cake:
2 ounces bitter chocolate
6 tablespoons boiling water
½ cup butter
1½ cups sugar
4 eggs, beaten separately
½ cup milk
1¾ cups flour
2 rounded teaspoons baking powder

Dissolve the chocolate in the boiling water and allow to cool. Cream the butter and sugar together and add the egg yolks that have been beaten light. Pour in the cool chocolate. Add the milk, flour, and baking powder. Lastly, add the beaten egg whites. Bake in a 350-degree oven for 20 to 25 minutes.

Filling:
3 cups powdered sugar
½ cup butter
1 egg yolk
2 teaspoons chipped chocolate
1 ounce cocoa
5 tablespoons strong hot coffee
2 teaspoons Adams Best vanilla
1 tablespoon cream
1 cup pecans or walnuts (optional)

Cream the sugar, butter, and egg yolk. Mix the chipped chocolate and cocoa with the hot coffee. Stir well into the powdered sugar mixture. Add the vanilla and cream last. Beat smooth. Put nuts in the filling or dough or both. ◀

Mansion Improvements

The Governor's Mansion underwent many cosmetic changes during the early part of the twentieth century. It was also during this period that the only substantial addition to the house was constructed. The various improvements greatly enhanced the quality of life for the governor and first families.

✦ FANNIE IRENE BRUNER CAMPBELL ✦
1907–1911

When Fannie Campbell arrived at the mansion, she found the grounds to be overgrown and neglected and the remaining fencing (that which had not already fallen down) to be beyond repair. House proud, she believed the small state appropriation for refurbishing the house should be used for improvements on the outside of the mansion. The governor, she reasoned, owed it to his visitors, and those passing by, to keep the place as presentable as possible. As a result, improved curbing, new front steps, and the removal of

Fannie Irene Bruner Campbell.
Courtesy Friends of the Governor's Mansion.

the old fence changed the appearance of the grounds considerably. Fannie's love of flowers prompted the construction of greenhouses on the nearby Capitol grounds.

Her artistic flair made entertaining at the mansion almost second nature. The well-being of the guests of the governor was her first priority. As a result, company was made comfortable and fed the best she could provide. However, everyone who lived at the mansion, from the governor on down, soon learned that their comfort was secondary to that of visitors. More than once the cook was

{ 94 }

awakened from a deep sleep to make coffee for guests who had an early train to catch. Fannie's daughters, who slept in the Sam Houston bedroom, often had to give up their room on very short notice for some overnight caller. Fortunately, the space under the huge bed was an ideal place to quickly hide any clutter that might have been an embarrassment to their mother.

Fannie was always immaculately "turned-out," and for her bigger receptions she pulled out all the stops. Contemporary newspapers give her clothing almost as much coverage as the pressing matters of the state. The traditional New Year's Day reception for 1909 was probably her most spectacular party. The reception rooms were festooned with pink and white garlands. The dining room was done in Christmas colors, with cedar bows, gray moss, and red-berried holly decorating the mantels. Every light in the house was turned on, and the "electrical effects" were impressive. Students from the Institute for the Blind furnished the music.

The happy, house-proud Campbell family shown in front of the Governor's Mansion, circa 1908.
Courtesy Austin History Center, Austin Public Library, CO 2730.

Despite the elaborate decorations, it was Fannie who stole the show. Wearing a princess gown of white satin–striped crepe trimmed with delicate rose point, she descended the mansion staircase to greet the guests. The music stopped and all eyes turned to the gaze upon the woman who in many ways typified the elegance of the Edwardian era in Texas.

Fannie Irene Bruner Campbell
◆ SWEET MAYONNAISE DRESSING

This is a nice version of a very old and traditional type of mayonnaise dressing. For a true early-nineteenth-century experience, serve it on a quartered wedge of lettuce.

> 1 tablespoon butter
> 1 tablespoon sugar
> 1 tablespoon flour
> $\frac{1}{2}$ cup hot vinegar
> 2 egg yolks
> Little French mustard
> Cream

Mix ingredients. Add cream last. Chill and serve. ⌇

Fannie Irene Brunner Campbell
◆ TOMATO SOUP–CREAM CHEESE SALAD

An easy and delicious luncheon addition, this salad really shines when the optional ingredients, such as the wonderful preserved green olives, are included.

> 2 cans tomato soup, undiluted
> 1 large pkg. cream cheese
> 3 envelopes gelatin (plus 1 cup cold water)
> $1\frac{1}{2}$ cups mayonnaise
> 1 tablespoon onion juice (or $\frac{1}{2}$ grated onion)

Lemon juice ($\frac{1}{2}$ lemon)
Dash Worcestershire sauce (optional)
Salt to taste
Pepper
Pinch of sugar
Sliced stuffed olives, or 1 cup chopped celery and 1 cup
    chopped bell pepper (all optional)

Melt tomato soup and cream cheese together in saucepan. Beat with egg beater [or Mixmaster] until smooth. At same time be softening gelatin in 1 cup cold water. After soup and cheese mixture has cooled slightly, beat in gelatin. Then beat in mayonnaise. Add seasonings. Pour in mold and congeal in icebox slightly. Add the olives or celery, etc. Small shrimp, salmon, etc., may also be used. Serves 10 to 12 generously.

Fannie Irene Bruner Campbell
   ✦ COFFEE PUDDING OR SPRING FORM

Fannie Campbell passed this recipe down to her daughter Fannie Campbell Womack. It has been used in the Campbell family for many years.

48 marshmallows
$\frac{3}{4}$ cup cold coffee
1 pint whipping cream
$2\frac{1}{2}$ dozen lady fingers

Melt marshmallows in coffee in double boiler. Cool. When cold add whipped cream. Line mold with lady fingers. Pour in mixture and let stand from 3 to 24 hours.

Fannie Irene Bruner Campbell
   ✦ MARSHMALLOW MOUSSE

Old-fashioned and sumptuous, this pudding is the perfect close to a special evening meal. It was a favored dessert at the mansion.

1 cup sugar
$\frac{1}{4}$ cup water
$\frac{1}{2}$ pound marshmallows
3 egg whites
1 tablespoon vanilla
$1\frac{1}{2}$ cups heavy cream

Put sugar and water in saucepan, bring to boiling point, and let boil until syrup will spin a thread. Add marshmallows, cut in halves, and when partially melted beat, using an eggbeater, until mixture is smooth. Beat egg whites until stiff, and gradually pour the marshmallow mixture into the egg whites, beating until cold. Then add vanilla and cream. Beat until stiff. Freeze, as you would mousse. Do not stir while freezing. ⤙

Fannie Irene Bruner Campbell
♦ SKILLET CAKE

Garnish this dessert with fresh whipped cream and crushed pineapple.

Batter:
4 eggs, separated
1 cup sugar
1 cup flour
3 teaspoons baking powder
1 teaspoon vanilla

Base:
$\frac{1}{4}$ pound butter
1 cup pineapple
1 cup nuts
1 cup sugar

Beat eggs separately. Add cup of sugar to yellows. Add flour and baking powder to yellows, and then add vanilla. Last add whites. Put butter in cold skillet. Put pineapple in next, and then add the nuts. Over this add a cup of sugar. Then put in batter. Cook in slow oven 40 to 45 minutes. ⤙

ALICE FULLER MURRELL COLQUITT
1911–1914

The invoices of the daily expenses at the mansion during the Colquitt administration are among the earliest and most complete. Previously, these papers had not usually been considered important enough to retain after a governor left office. The surviving Colquitt records, now in the State Archives, provide a fascinating record of the actual costs involved in the operation of the mansion. Bills for electric power, coal, wood, and routine services fill several small file folders. They document a period of immense change and improvement in the Governor's Mansion.

When Alice Colquitt, sturdy and statuesque, moved into the mansion in 1914, the home was in desperate need of repair. Patching and painting over the problems was no longer adequate. There was not enough room to accommodate overnight visitors, and the old kitchen was, by this time, a relic. Governor Colquitt prevailed upon the legislature, and funds for the needed changes were appropriated. After months of planning by an unknown architect (possibly the contractor), the ancient kitchen was removed and a large new kitchen wing built in basically the same configuration. Nalle and Company provided the cement; Calcasieu Lumber Company provided the lumber for the project. Numerous rooms were replastered at this time.

A new family dining room was included on the main floor, and additional living space was added upstairs over the new addition. The antiquated bathroom was replaced with two additional modern tiled versions reflecting the improvements of the time. To warm the new addition, an ancient heater was replaced with gas radiators throughout. The exterior of the mansion, which had always been unpainted, was given its first coat of white paint. These changes represent the only major structural additions to the mansion in 150 years. C. H. Page was paid $8,459.00 for constructing the new portions of the building and for repairs on the existing structure.

Alice hired a decorator, and the parlors, front hall, and library were redecorated. The parlors were papered in silvery gray colors with matching carpets; halls were repapered in dark green with coordinating carpeting. The dining room was done in brown and

*The path from the Capitol to the Governor's Mansion during
the Colquitt administration.*
Courtesy Center for American History, University of Texas at Austin,
Prints and Photographs Collection, CN 08806.

greenish blue. A new bronze chandelier was suspended from the
ceiling of the dining room, and new lighting fixtures were placed in
many of other rooms. A Baldwin grand piano was purchased so that
there could be live music for the many receptions. At other times,
popular dance music from Victrola records sold by the J. R. Reed
Music Company could be heard echoing through the mansion parlors. Governor Colquitt was the first mansion resident to own an
automobile (more than likely a Buick), and it was housed in the
converted carriage house at the back of the property.

Alice ordered numerous items to use when entertaining guests at
the mansion. She selected new upholstered chairs for the State Dining Room and had a new banquet top made for the dining table.
She added to the dishes and silver used at the mansion as well. Elegant Haviland china was selected, and Vredenburgh Jewelers sold
Alice twenty-three sterling silver orange spoons and twenty-three
salad forks, for a total of forty dollars.

The mansion staff in 1911 consisted in part of Hanna Johnson, cook; Ester Free, housemaid; and Emmet Plummer, porter. They each received twenty-five dollars a month for their services. Another cook, Clara Danz, joined the staff in 1913.

The staff of the kitchen got accustomed to using the items acquired on Alice's frequent shopping trips. During the time she was first lady, a new McCray refrigerator, three oscillating electric fans, a carpet sweeper, and a laundry list of other kitchen gadgets such as a pecan cracker, chop dishes, a waffle iron, and a plumber's friend (toilet plunger) were delivered to the mansion. A fish globe (fish bowl) and new sheets and pillowcases came from the E. M. Scarbrough Company. Groceries were delivered to the kitchen by W. A. Achilles.

Once the mansion updates were complete, Alice opened the house to the people of Texas, never dreaming that the work she oversaw would be the only major renovation to the mansion for the next forty years.

❧

Alice Fuller Murrell Colquitt
◆ COOKIES

These cookies were prepared in the new mansion kitchen by Alice Colquitt's staff.

> 3 eggs
> 1 cup brown sugar
> 1 cup white sugar
> 1½ cups hot butter
> 2 teaspoons cinnamon
> ¼ cup nuts
> 5½ cups sifted flour
> ½ teaspoon salt

Mix the ingredients in the order given, then divide and roll in three or four pieces of wax paper. Allow to stand overnight and use as needed, cutting in thin slices before baking in hot oven. ❧

◆ MIRIAM AMANDA WALLACE FERGUSON ◆
1915–1917, 1925–1927, 1933–1935

In the first decade of the twentieth century, the Fergusons were a typical upper-middle-class family enjoying peace and prosperity in Temple, Texas. Miriam Ferguson had a handsome, loving husband (Jim), two active daughters (Ouida and Dorrace), an elegant home in one of Temple's best neighborhoods, a large flower-filled yard, and servants to help with the household tasks. She was content and secure. However, Jim Ferguson dropped a piece of news in 1913 that would forever disrupt her tranquil idyll.

Miriam was trying on hats at Roddy Brothers in downtown Temple, as she did every Friday, when Jim rushed into that feminine retreat and stated that he was going to place his name on the ballot for the governorship of Texas. Without turning from the mirror, Miriam told him calmly that the whole idea was ridiculous and not to be late for supper. Six months later, Miriam Amanda Wallace Ferguson, who had been perfectly happy with things just as they were, was the first lady of Texas.

The Ferguson family arrived in Austin in a private car on the Santa Fe Railway. Their personal effects and furnishings were placed in storage in Austin, and the Temple home was rented out. The family stayed at the Driskill Hotel because Governor Colquitt had asked to be allowed to stay in the mansion until after the inauguration. Aunt Laura, the Fergusons' longtime maid, traveled with the family to help Miriam at the mansion, and her son Bud became the butler and yardman.

When the Fergusons moved from the Driskill to the Governor's mansion, they found a hot meal ready for them in the mansion dining room, prepared under the direction of Mrs. Colquitt. It was traditional for the outgoing governor to perform this courtesy for the new governor's family. The meal consisted of fried chicken, vegetable casserole, and Mrs. Colquitt's special cookies. Later, former first lady Lena Sayers hosted a reception to introduce Miriam to Austin society. Lena also assisted during Miriam's first mansion entertainments.

The Governor's Mansion was in fairly good condition when the Fergusons moved in due in part to the Colquitt improvements and

Miriam Amanda Wallace Ferguson.
From the author's collection.

renovations. Gov. Jim Ferguson added a comfortable screened-in sleeping porch along the front balcony, and Miriam added a retaining wall along the Eleventh Street side of the property. However, the roof still leaked and fireplaces still provided the majority of the heat during the winter. The first winter the old place got very cold; Miriam caught the influenza.

Following her illness, Miriam realized that the duties of the first lady were simply too much for her to handle on her own. She was exhausted by the demands of her role as first lady. She took the initiative and decided to hire a secretary to help her with the entertaining. This move set tongues to wagging. Austin's gossips thought it was pretty high-falutin' to hire a personal secretary. They remembered that Lena Sayers had managed just fine without one, so why did Mrs. Ferguson think she needed one? Times at the mansion had changed, though. The demands placed on the first lady were much greater now. The first secretary was soon replaced with Miriam's niece, Fairy Ferguson. Miriam and Fairy oversaw the big receptions and parties that had become tradition at the mansion. Some days, Miriam received almost as much mail as Jim did. Answering all the social correspondence was a huge job.

During this time, an important piece of furniture arrived as a gift to the mansion. The writing desk of Stephen F. Austin was shipped from Perry's Landing to the mansion and unpacked. The Perry family was related to Stephen F. Austin and had wanted the desk to be in the mansion during the Ferguson administration. It was a tangible piece of Texas history and provided a perfect backdrop for the numerous parties and receptions at the mansion.

On March 2, Texas Independence Day, Miriam held a large event that was catered by the Driskill Hotel. Mr. Stark, the hotel manager, set up his kitchen on the lawn of the mansion. Chicken salad, coffee, sandwiches, olives, bonbons, and little cakes were served in the State Dining Room. The tables and mantels were festooned with cut flowers, and the banister was draped in southern smilax and garlands of East Texas moss. The mansion's Swedish maid, Ruth, and Ethel the cook served while Essex, the butler, helped clear each completed course and poured the coffee.

Miriam's entertaining schedule was full. On Easter Monday, Miriam gave the children of Austin an egg rolling, much like the one at the White House in Washington, D.C. It was held on the sloping hillside in the southwest quarter of the Capitol grounds. The orchestra from the Institute for the Blind played, and ice cream was served. On August 31, Miriam gave Jim a "men only" birthday party. The table was decorated in a political motif with teddy bears dressed as public figures. The dinner began with shrimp cocktail and closed with toasts, informal speeches, coffee, and cigars with "Jim Ferguson" labels, which Miriam procured from their home town of Temple.

The family's first Christmas at the mansion was a memorable one. One hundred forty-eight friends and supporters collaborated and gave the Fergusons a five-hundred-piece silver service. Each piece was engraved with a large "F" and the year, 1915. A large mahogany silver chest with beveled glass doors was also presented to house the silver. The following year, after a popular stage production, *The Garden of Allah,* was performed at the Hancock Theater, Miriam served dinner in the dining room, which had been decorated in a Middle Eastern style. Dolls were dressed in harem veils and placed beside a small pyramid and a sphinx. Potted palms surrounded the table. Miriam used their new sterling silver flatware at each of the place settings.

Entertaining at the mansion called for decorating the dining table and the rest of the house with a large number of fresh flowers. Only one or two major florists operated in Austin and they were both very expensive, so Miriam asked Jim to approach the legislature for a small appropriation to build a greenhouse on the mansion grounds. The legislature granted the request and Miriam got a place to grow flowers. She instructed the man who was pouring the foundation of the greenhouse to carve her name and the year, 1915, in the threshold. Miriam also hired a gardener. He was an old German fellow named Hans who had been a noted horticulturist in Germany before he fled in fear of the Kaiser. Hans's wife Frieda had come with him from the old country, and together they helped Miriam tend her flowers. That spring her flowers were more beautiful than ever before.

Miriam went to the trouble of growing fresh flowers and doing the entertaining partly because she had to and partly because she enjoyed it. Kind-hearted Jim had been reluctant to tell her a governor was expected to personally pay for all refreshments and related expenses at the mansion. A governor's salary was only four thousand dollars a year, and the catering bills were mounting. The Driskill Hotel presented Miriam a bill for, among other things, chicken salad. That bill was inadvertently forwarded to the state treasurer, who paid it. These household bills were the beginning of a very troubling time for Gov. Jim Ferguson and his family.

The painful events that unfolded during the long, hot summer of 1917 stemmed in part from Jim's decision to veto the state

Dorrace Watt, youngest daughter of Miriam and Governor Jim Ferguson, holds family cat, Teddybear, circa 1926. Sambo the white Spitz relaxes on the steps. The player piano in the back corner hid a huge hole in the rug.
Courtesy Austin History Center, Austin Public Library, CO 2569.

appropriation for the University of Texas for a number of reasons. Angered, the powerful political alumni of the University of Texas rallied against the governor and in retaliation for his veto, they investigated every facet of the Ferguson administration. These proceedings escalated, and by September Jim was removed from office. Miriam received the unhappy news and, in her usual matter-of-fact way, had the servants begin packing at once. Having packed their belongings for shipment to Temple, the family climbed into Miriam's Twin Six Packard and pulled away from the porte cochere of the mansion. As they drove down the mansion's driveway, Miriam vowed that the Fergusons would one day return. She did not know how or when, but she was determined to see her husband's good name restored.

*Miriam Ferguson peels peaches on the back porch of her home
in Temple, Texas, on the day in 1924 that her nomination as
the democratic candidate for Governor was announced.*
Courtesy Underwood and Underwood.

It would take nearly eight years and an unimagined series of
events, but Miriam did indeed return to live in the mansion—twice.
Miriam, basically a shy housewife, had never made a public speech
before announcing that she was running for governor herself.
Riding on Jim's popularity, she was elected governor in her own
right, first in 1925 and then again during the dark days of the Great
Depression in 1933.

After leaving the mansion for the final time in 1935, her days in
Austin were mostly quiet. Often the only sound in her home on
Windsor Road came from the small gold clock on the mantel. The
clock had been a gift from friends to Miriam and Jim when they

Governor Miriam Ferguson and Will Rogers stand on the steps with Miriam's grandson George Nalle at her side. Miriam's daughter Dorrace is directly behind her. Governor Jim Ferguson stands to the right of Will Rogers.
Courtesy Austin History Center, Austin Public Library, CO 2883.

moved into the Governor's Mansion in 1915. Its reassuring chime was a regular reminder of her six years at the mansion and of a life well lived.

❧

Miriam Amanda Wallace Ferguson
♦ WILL ROGERS CHILI

There are several versions of this chili recipe in the Ferguson family archives. This one differs slightly from the others. Will Rogers was a frequent visitor to the mansion during Miriam's terms as governor. He and Jim Ferguson were good friends who had many attributes in common. Will was extremely fond of Mexican food,

{ 108 }

and Miriam's cook happened to specialize in Mexican cuisine. A Mexican supper was always planned when Will was expected to arrive. The menu for Will usually started with chili con queso and was followed by guacamole salad, but the part he loved best was the chili and tamales, and he was never too bashful to take a second helping. The dessert was either pineapple or sherbet along with pecan pralines. One night, as the dessert being served, Will looked up at the servant and said, "No thank you, I don't want any of that. If I had more room I would take another bowl of that great chili."

> 4 pounds coarsely ground beef
> 1 large onion, chopped
> 2 cloves of garlic, minced
> 1 teaspoon comino seed
> 6 teaspoons of chili powder
> 2 cans of tomatoes—do not drain
> Salt to taste
> 2 cups of hot water

Combine meat, onions, and garlic in a large heavy skillet. Sear until light colored. Add comino, chili powder, tomatoes, salt, and hot water. Bring to a boil, lower heat, and simmer about one hour. Skim off fat as it cooks out to avoid greasy taste.

Miriam Amanda Wallace Ferguson
◆ MUFFIN CAKES

All her life Miriam found these little cakes to be the most delicious treat. She made them for her own children and, in later years, for visitors who dropped in to see her.

> 1 cup sugar
> $\frac{1}{2}$ cup butter
> 2 eggs
> $\frac{1}{2}$ cup sweet milk
> Pinch salt
> 2 cups flour
> 2 teaspoons baking powder
> 1 teaspoon Adams Best vanilla

Cream the sugar and butter together and add the eggs, milk, and other ingredients. Spoon into muffin tins. Bake at 350 degrees for 15 to 20 minutes until golden.

Miriam Amanda Wallace Ferguson
♦ GINGERBREAD

Miriam had marked this recipe in her favorite cookbook with emphatic lines, a sure sign that it was one of her favorites. Judging from the smudges and smears that cover the pages in the book, it was used many times. Mentions of this gingerbread appear in several articles written about Miriam.

½ cup lard
½ cup sugar
2 eggs, beaten
2½ cups flour
1½ teaspoons baking powder
½ teaspoon soda
½ teaspoon salt
1 teaspoon ginger
1 teaspoon cinnamon
¼ teaspoon cloves
1 cup molasses
1 cup boiling water

Cream the lard and add the sugar gradually while creaming. Add the beaten eggs, then sift together dry ingredients and add alternately with the molasses and water. Beat enough to mix thoroughly and then pour into a well-greased 12¼-by-8-by-2-inch pan and bake at 350 degrees for 40 to 45 minutes.

Miriam Amanda Wallace Ferguson
♦ KATY KORNETTES

In 1932, Miriam joined the race for governor with what the writer James DeShields called a "splendid fury," traveling the entire state on the Missouri, Kansas, and Texas Railroad. From the rear gondola of the train she made hundreds of campaign speeches in small towns. After eating dozens of meals in the dining car of the MKT Railroad, Miriam became very fond of its famous Katy Kornettes. So fond was she of these little cornbread nuggets that she wrote to the president of the line for this recipe. She wrote it by hand in the back of her copy of the Austin Woman's Club cookbook, *Treasure Pots*.

> 2 cups boiling hot milk
> 2 cups meal
> ¼ cup butter
> 1 scant teaspoon salt

Drop on greased pan; bake 20 minutes at 350 degrees.

Miriam Amanda Wallace Ferguson

♦ CHERRY PIE FILLING

This was a favorite recipe of Miriam's. Make a regular pie crust using your standard pie crust dough recipe and fill with this delicious mixture.

> 4 cups cherries, pitted
> 1½ cups sugar
> 3 tablespoons flour
> 3 tablespoons cornstarch

After the seeds have been removed from the cherries, add the sugar, flour, and cornstarch. Put into a 9½-inch pie dish lined with pastry and cover with the top crust in which openings have been cut. Moisten the edges of the crust, press together, flute, and trim. Bake at 425 degrees for 40 to 45 minutes.

If canned cherries are used, decrease the sugar to 1 cup, the flour to 2 tablespoons, and the cornstarch to 2 tablespoons.

Miriam Amanda Wallace Ferguson
♦ SPICED PEARS IN WHITE WINE SAUCE

Miriam did not approve of alcohol, but occasionally she would
bend the rules. These pears turn out really delicious and will impress
your guests.

½ cup sugar
1 cup water
1 cup California Hock, Sauterne, Chablis, Riesling, or any
    white table wine
6 fresh pears, peeled and halved
1 cinnamon stick, about 2 inches
12 whole cloves
½ lemon, sliced thin

Combine sugar, water, and wine. Add the pears and simmer
slowly about 15 minutes. Add spices and lemon slices and continue cooking until pears are tender. Chill and serve as accompaniment to meat course. ⤚

Miriam Amanda Wallace Ferguson
♦ RUSSIAN ROCKS

These simple treats were among Miriam's favorites and remained so
throughout her life. When asked later to contribute her favorite
recipes to various charity publications, Russian Rocks always filled
the bill.

1½ cups brown sugar
2¾ cups flour
1 cup butter
1 teaspoon soda dissolved in a little boiling water
A pinch of salt
3 eggs, beaten separately
1 teaspoon cinnamon
½ pound nuts, pecans, or walnuts
1 pound raisins

Combine ingredients in a bowl. Fill teaspoon and drop in buttered tins. Bake in moderate oven [325 degrees] for 12 minutes or until they look done. ~

Miriam Amanda Wallace Ferguson
◆ LITTLE RIVER CORN PONE

This is yet another version of corn pone. It seems that almost every first lady has her favorite version. With the addition of eggs, Miriam's pones are almost like cornbread.

    1 cup cornmeal
    ¾ cup flour
    2 heaping teaspoons baking powder
    1 large egg
    Pinch of salt
    1 cup milk
    Water sufficient to make batter

Combine ingredients and beat well. Drop into hot fat and brown. Drain and serve. ~

Miriam Amanda Wallace Ferguson
◆ SCHNITZEL A LA HOLSTEIN

Miriam obtained this European recipe from Madame Ernestine-Schumann Heink, a grand opera celebrity who was a favorite guest at the mansion. Though well past her singing days, the opera diva provided color to the sitting rooms of the mansion, where she would regale other guests with tales of her days performing before crowned heads of Europe.

    2¼ pounds veal from leg
    Salt
    1 pinch paprika
    2 eggs
    ⅛ pound butter
    ½ tablespoon flour

$\frac{3}{4}$ cup of water
$\frac{1}{2}$ tablespoon meat extract [probably bouillon]
4 eggs, hard-boiled
6 sardines
2 tablespoons chopped pickled beets
1 tablespoon chopped onion
1 small pickle, chopped
6 slices lemon
1 tablespoon capers

The meat is cut into six $\frac{1}{2}$-inch-thick slices, sprinkled with salt and paprika, and dipped in well-beaten egg. The butter is heated and the meat fried brown on both sides, then put on a hot platter. The $\frac{1}{2}$ tablespoon of flour is stirred into the butter, and $\frac{3}{4}$ cup of water is added with teaspoon of meat extract and salt, if necessary, then boiled and poured over the meat.

The hard-boiled eggs are chopped fine, the whites separated from the yolks. The sardines are drained and cut in half lengthwise, then rolled up. Now arrange your dish neatly, with little heaps of beets, onion, pickle, whites and yolks of egg, and lemon slices on each cutlet. Place each rolled sardine in the middle of a lemon slice, heap the rest around each slice, and place the capers singly in between. Should be prepared quickly but appetizingly. ❧

Miriam Amanda Wallace Ferguson
♦ MINESTRONE, MILAN FASHION

Here is another favorite recipe from frequent Ferguson guest Madame Ernestine-Schumann Heink, grand dame of the opera. According to legend, Jim Ferguson said she ate more than two field hands put together.

Chop 6 or 8 oz. of bacon, put into a stew pan with a piece of raw ham, a shredded cabbage, 2 or 3 handfuls of fresh string beans, either white or green, and pour over all these vegetables 3 quarts broth and place on hot fire. After 10 minutes of boiling, add 4 tablespoons tender celery roots, diced, some green peas and asparagus heads diced, a chopped tomato, 12 ounces of rice, as well as two or three Milan sausages. Continue boiling until rice is thoroughly cooked. At the last moment, add to the soup a handful of grated Parmesan cheese; then take out ham and sausages, cut up fine, and return to soup and serve. ∼

Miriam Amanda Wallace Ferguson
◆ CRABMEAT CANOES

These little morsels are a perfect addition for brunch or luncheon parties.

6 medium potatoes
2 tablespoon butter
4 tablespoons milk
1 tablespoon grated onion
½ teaspoon salt
1 cup crabmeat
½ cup grated American cheese

Bake potatoes; cut lengthwise and scoop out carefully. Mash potatoes; add next four ingredients and beat until smooth. Add crabmeat and refill shells, mounding slightly. Sprinkle with cheese. Bake in a slow oven [325 degrees] 20 minutes. Serves 6. ∼

Miriam Amanda Wallace Ferguson
◆ SUGAR CAKES

There is no estimating how many thousands of these delicious cookies were made and served at the many big receptions at the Governor's Mansion in Austin when Miriam Ferguson was in office as governor. Family members consider this to be her signature recipe.

1 pound butter
4 cups sugar
6 eggs
1 teaspoon salt
1 teaspoon nutmeg

$\frac{1}{4}$ cup brandy
8 cups sifted flour
1 teaspoon salt
1 teaspoon baking powder

Cream butter and sugar. Add well-beaten eggs, salt, nutmeg, and brandy. Beat mixture well. Sift flour, salt, and baking powder together. Add gradually to butter mixture to form a stiff dough. Put dough in covered bowl and refrigerate for 2 hours. Remove from icebox and shape into small rolls. Cut and bake in oven at 400 degrees until slightly brown, about 6 to 8 minutes. ↞

Miriam Amanda Wallace Ferguson
✦ TOMATO ASPIC SALAD

Miriam marked this recipe in her well-worn copy of *Treasure Pots* with a check mark and the notation for Alberta, her cook, to "use this one." The recipe came from Nellie May Miller, the wife of Tom Miller, Austin's popular longtime mayor. He was first elected during Miriam's second term as governor.

1 tablespoon plain gelatin
$1\frac{1}{2}$ cups tomato juice
1 cup stuffed olives
1 cup diced celery
2 tablespoons salad dressing (Miracle Whip®)
Salt to taste

Dissolve the gelatin in 1 cup of warm tomato juice and cool. Then add the rest of the tomato juice, the olives, celery, and salt to taste and congeal. Garnish with Miracle Whip®. Makes 6 servings. ↞

✦ WILLIE CHAPMAN COOPER HOBBY ✦
1917–1921

Willie Chapman Cooper was born in 1887 in Woodville, Texas, and spent much of her girlhood in Washington, D.C., while her father, Samuel Bronson Cooper, was a member of the House of Representatives. Living in the nation's capital in a political and social context provided many important lessons for Willie. Later, when she was living in New York, she became greatly interested in women's suffrage. Her belief in this cause would continue the rest of her life. She married William Hobby, her childhood sweetheart, in 1915 at

First Lady Willie Chapman Cooper Hobby shown seated
in the gown she wore to her husband's Inaugural, 1919.
The chair in which she is seated was added to the
Mansion during the time Lena Sayers was first lady.
Courtesy Austin History Center, Austin Public Library, Stocker Collection.

the Saint Charles Hotel in New Orleans. The social climate in which she was raised allowed her to assume a daunting schedule, first as the wife of a lieutenant governor and then as first lady when her husband became governor in 1918.

She did not entertain a great deal at the mansion during World War I, feeling it was inappropriate except when required. War shortages and conservation meant that many foods were not readily available. She followed government guidelines for the conservation of light foodstuffs and produce. One of the few major events she coordinated was a reception for Margaret Wilson, daughter of President Woodrow Wilson, during her tour of the nation raising funds for the war effort.

As first lady of Texas, Willie Hobby's tact and outgoing personality brought great praise from those who visited the mansion. The

*Governor and Mrs. Hobby on the front walk of the Governor's Mansion
with the Capitol in the background, circa 1918. The zinnias
appear to be in full bloom.*
Courtesy Austin History Center, Austin Public Library, Stocker Collection.

*The State Dining Room with the Mansion porters at the ready,
circa 1919. The chandelier hung in the room for decades.*
Courtesy Austin History Center, Austin Public Library, Stocker Collection.

Houston Press reported that she "made the Mansion at Austin a
Mecca for thousands. She reigned there with a democracy that
thrilled the most humble and brought equal praise from the most
aristocratic." Willie accorded her maid, Savannah Pearl, a mansion
wedding when she married General Jackson, a porter in the Texas
senate, in 1921.

The mansion, despite being the home of the chief executive of
one of the largest states in the Union, was still far from an ideal
place to live. Already nearly sixty years old, it was drafty and almost
unbearably cold during the winter months, despite large fireplaces
in almost every room. Willie prevailed upon the legislature for improvements in the mansion and was granted a small amount of
money that allowed for steam heating to be installed. She also
added a private bath to the north front bedroom.

The first lady admitted that even though she frequently made her own clothes, she could not cook and hated dishwashing. Fortunately, there was a large staff to handle those details at the mansion. Although Willie did not bother with domestic details, she did devote her energies to a number of causes related to the Great War. She could frequently be found in Red Cross workrooms making mittens, socks, and other items needed for the war effort. She also served during the war as a member of the Austin chapter of the State Council of Defense and the War Camp Community Service League. After Governor Hobby's term, the couple moved to Houston, where she became active in civic affairs, especially those related to women's issues.

The Conservatory of the Governor's Mansion. The room was added during the Colquitt administration in 1914. The Hobbys' maid, more than likely Savannah Pearl, is shown, circa 1919.
Courtesy Austin History Center, Austin Public Library, Stocker Collection.

Bedroom used by Governor and Mrs. Hobby, circa 1919.
Courtesy Austin History Center, Austin Public Library, Stocker Collection.

Willie Chapman Cooper Hobby
◆ CRAB GUMBO

The use of real, fresh crabmeat gives this delicious hearty gumbo an unforgettable flavor. Have plenty of good sourdough bread on hand to accompany a brimming bowl.

    1 large onion
    Thyme
    Bay leaf
    Parsley
    Salt, pepper, and a drop of Tabasco® sauce
    1 tablespoon lard
    Meat from 1 dozen crabs
    1 pound boiled shrimp
    Ham bone, bacon, or veal stew bone
    1 quart water

Chop up the onion and brown with seasonings in frying pan with the tablespoon of lard. When golden brown, add crabmeat, shrimp, and ham bone. Let brown. Then add a quart of water. Season and boil moderately for half an hour. ❧

◆ MODERN TIMES ◆
1917–1929

Prohibition of alcohol consumption went into effect in January, 1920, and it seemed to have little effect on the governors and first ladies of the 1920s because the public had simply never known them to drink a great deal. One governor, a "hard-shelled Baptist," did not drink at all. Although the mansion's parties were a little more somber as a result of Prohibition, they made up for it in the food and entertainment they featured. Texas prisons, meanwhile, soon filled with minor liquor violators and rum-runners.

Food trends in the state changed a great deal during the energetic 1920s. Roadside diners and cafeterias blossomed along the newly improved Texas highway system. Faster and more dependable automobiles made traveling easier than it had been previously, and the motorists who drove across the state ate at a wide of variety of these roadside establishments. More and more visitors stopped at the mansion to see the historic old home, and occasionally they were invited inside for a piece of pie.

In the mansion kitchen, the built-in icebox was finally removed and a small home-sized electric refrigerator, purchased by the governor rather than the state, was installed. Sales of the new refrigeration units escalated from 10,000 in 1920 to 800,000 in 1929 as electricity became available to a greater number of rural homes. A modern gas range augmented the mansion's wood stove. Labor-saving devices such as an electric coffeepot and a pop-up toaster were new to the home.

The cook's workload decreased. Store-bought food was slowly reducing the residents' dependence on the mansion garden. Although fresh vegetables were still important to the table, frozen foods were available at the end of the decade. Instant mixes and one-step foods were also coming into fashion. Canned goods made even out-of-season vegetables available year round and expanded the list of ingredients available. Jell-O® had been on the market since the late 1890s, but as the new refrigerators made chilling food so much easier, it quickly became a kitchen staple. Pre-sliced bread, introduced late in the 1920s, was heralded as one of the greatest food innovations of the century.

◆ MYRTLE MAINER NEFF ◆
1921–1925

Myrtle Neff was a shy and retiring woman who shrank from the spotlight placed upon her as first lady. She had never intended to be in the spotlight, but when her husband Pat, whom she married in 1899, was elected to the governorship in 1921, she went to the mansion willingly. She had had a taste of political life during the time Pat was Speaker of the House in the Texas legislature; in fact, she was the first of many Speaker's wives to set up housekeeping in the Speaker's apartments of the Capitol. There she entertained whenever she was required to do so. The Neffs, staunch Baptists, did not believe in drinking or dancing, so her events were slightly subdued.

When Pat left his position as Speaker, Myrtle was glad to get back to their home in Waco. At home she was completely at ease and liked nothing more than visiting with a few select friends and taking care of her two children, Pat, Jr., and Hallie Maud. She gardened and was active in the Baptist church.

Things were not to remain quiet for long, however, since Pat had decided to place his name on the ballot for governor. He traveled thousands of miles campaigning around the state. Myrtle occasionally would travel with him, but only for the shorter trips. She endured the time away from her home and gardens only because she knew that winning the governorship was important to Pat.

Pat won the election and Myrtle became the first lady of Texas, a position she was not really certain how to fill. For her husband's inaugural she planned a large banquet, which was held at the local country club. The Neffs did not endorse the traditional inaugural ball, as they did not believe in dancing.

The Neff family in the Mansion Gardens, circa 1921.
Courtesy Austin History Center, Austin Public Library, CO 8033.

Once ensconced in the mansion, Myrtle upheld tradition. She gave numerous receptions and opened the home every Tuesday afternoon to the public, as her predecessors had. Her best times were still when she was at home with her family, and she worried about Pat when he worked long hours and was frequently away from home on business. When he announced he was going to run for a second term, Myrtle conceded to his desires. He was elected by a handy majority, which meant two more years as first lady for Myrtle.

Despite the usual allotment of servants at the mansion, Myrtle did a large portion of the work herself. She planned numerous meals and luncheons for the visiting dignitaries and enjoyed working in the mansion greenhouse. One of her favorite duties was dressing the pulpit at her church with flowers she had grown. She added two large cedar closets to the upstairs bedrooms and had a small screened sleeping porch enclosed at the back of the house, away from public view. The State Dining Room was freshened, and the Sam Houston bed got new draperies and a matching coverlet.

When her days as first lady were drawing to a close, she wanted nothing more than to get back to Waco and continue her peaceful family life. Her dreams of a quiet rest went unfulfilled because President Calvin Coolidge appointed Pat to the National Railway Mediation Board. Myrtle packed up the family belongings and moved with Pat to Washington. In 1932, they returned at last to Waco, where Pat was asked to serve as president of Baylor University. Although she was required to entertain frequently in her role as wife of the president, at least she was back in Waco, among her friends and family.

Myrtle Mainer Neff
◆ STUFFED SQUASH

6 small white squash
1 cup milk
5 tablespoons flour
½ stick butter
½ teaspoon salt
¼ teaspoon black pepper
1 hard-boiled egg, chopped
½ cup blanched, chopped almonds
Bread crumbs

Cook squash until tender, scoop out centers (save), and drain well. Make cream sauce of milk, butter, flour, salt and pepper. Add chopped egg, almonds, and squash centers. Stuff with mixture, sprinkle with bread crumbs and melted butter. Brown in medium oven. ↼

Myrtle Mainer Neff
◆ CHEESE AND FRUIT SALAD

(For forty people)
3 envelopes gelatin
1 large can pineapple, drained (reserve juice)

1 large can white cherries, pitted and drained (reserve juice)
2 lemons, juiced
Red pepper and salt
⅓ cup sugar
1 quart cream, whipped
1 cup chopped pecans
2 pounds American cheese, grated

Soak gelatin in ½ cup cold water, dissolve in ½ cup boiling water. Add to fruit juices (from pineapple and cherries), lemon juice, salt, red pepper, and sugar. Set aside to cool. When thoroughly cool (not congealed) slowly add whipped cream, then fruit and nuts; last fold in grated cheese. Pour in molds to congeal. ≈

Myrtle Mainer Neff
♦ CRANBERRY SALAD RING

Cook 2 cups cranberries in 1½ cups water. When soft, add 1 cup sugar and cook 5 minutes longer. Pour boiling mixture over 1 package cherry gelatin. Stir until dissolved. Chill. When partially set, add ¾ cup diced celery, ½ cup chopped nuts, ¼ teaspoon salt. Pour into ring mold. Chill. Unmold on crisp lettuce. Serves 6. May be garnished with cooked, pitted prunes stuffed with mixture of 1 cup chopped coconut, ½ cup crushed pineapple, 2 tablespoons grated carrots, and salad dressing to moisten. ≈

Myrtle Mainer Neff
♦ CREAMED ONIONS AU GRATIN

Drop prepared, sliced onions into a quantity of boiling water and cook until tender. Drain at once. Save water for cream sauce. Make cream sauce and add onion. Place in greased baking dish and sprinkle with grated cheese. Dot with butter and top with bread crumbs. Place under broiler (moderate temperature) until browned. ≈

Myrtle Mainer Neff
◆ LEMON CAKE PUDDING

2 tablespoons butter
1 cup sugar
$\frac{1}{4}$ teaspoon salt
Juice and grated rind of 2 lemons
3 tablespoons flour, sifted
3 eggs, yolks and white separated
1 cup milk

Cream butter with sugar and salt. Add grated lemon rind and juice and sifted flour. Beat yolks of eggs, add milk. Combine two mixtures, beat well, and fold in stiffly beaten egg whites. Pour into pan, place in oven in pan of hot water, and bake slowly 45 minutes in a 325-degree oven. ❧

Return to Elegance

Despite the substantial addition to the mansion during the Colquitt administration, by 1925 the home of the governors was threadbare and worn again. First Lady Mildred Moody undertook a major re-decoration project, and her efforts made the mansion once again a source of pride for the citizens of the state. But, like all improvements to the mansion, the task was daunting, underfunded, and slow.

◆ MILDRED PAXTON MOODY ◆
1927–1931

Mildred Paxton Moody got her first glimpse of the interior of the Governor's Mansion while she was still a student at the University of Texas. During World War I in 1918, the daughter of President Woodrow Wilson came to Austin as part of a nationwide tour to sell bonds benefiting the troops. There was a reception for Margaret Wilson at the mansion, and Mildred Paxton happened to be in the

The mansion during a snow in the 1920s.
From the author's collection.

editorial chair of the *Daily Texan* at the University of Texas that day. She was determined to get an interview with the president's daughter. Mildred basically crashed the reception and gained entrance to the front parlor where Miss Wilson was being honored. Nine years later, Mildred was the first lady of Texas, and she was not only attending but also in charge of the receptions at the governor's house.

Mildred, however, had never been in charge of a household before moving into the mansion, having been married to Dan Moody only seven months prior to becoming first lady. Before her marriage on April 20, 1926, she had either lived with her parents or been in college. After graduating in 1917 from Simmons College (now Hardin-Simmons University) in Abilene, Texas, Mildred attended graduate school at the University of Texas. She returned to Simmons to teach but interrupted her teaching career to complete a journalism degree at Columbia University in New York. After returning again to Abilene, she taught journalism at Simmons and remained a staunch supporter of her alma mater for the rest of her life.

*First Lady Mildred Paxton Moody, during her time as a
student at Hardin Simmons in Abilene, circa 1917.*
Courtesy Abilene Photograph Collection at Hardin Simmons University.

Mildred did have some experience in the kitchen, however. For
a time she worked as the women's editor of her hometown newspaper, the *Abilene Reporter.* In this capacity she occasionally ran a
column of recipes from the "famous cooks of the community." A
few of these recipes she would try out in her mother's well-run
kitchen. Her efforts generally elicited the wrath of the Paxtons' effi-
cient cook, who would usually just shake her head and cross her
large arms while watching Mildred.

Every time Dan would come home for a weekend visit to West Texas during his time as the state's attorney general, Mildred would proudly make a pie for him. She considered making pies her only culinary talent. Week in and week out, Dan would dutifully eat the results of her efforts. One of the first shocks of Mildred's young married life was Dan's early proclamation that if there was one thing he did not like, it was pie.

During the weeks immediately after being elected governor but prior to moving into the mansion, the Moodys lived at the Stephen F. Austin Hotel in downtown Austin. Once in the mansion, Dan Moody, tall, lean, and red-headed, and young Mildred, with her smart "bobbed" hairstyle, quickly gained their bearings in the new surroundings. The other mansion residents—a canary, a Persian cat, and a white collie named "Tex"—did the same. Mildred rolled up her sleeves and began to supervise the endless array of special functions at the mansion, including the wedding of her sister, Helen Paxton, to Edward Weaver Moore in 1928.

When Mildred entered the front hall for the first time as first lady, she was shocked. The mansion was no longer the glittering showplace it had been for the reception of Margaret Wilson. In fact, it was, for all practical purposes, now merely a big, tired, drafty house. The wall coverings were in tatters; carpets were threadbare. An ancient player piano occupied a portion of the back hall and was allowed to remain there primarily because it was less unattractive than the large hole in the carpeting it concealed. The ancient plumbing would stubbornly allow only one person at a time to run a bath, and the heating system mysteriously failed, often on the coldest days of the year. State funds for upkeep were not forthcoming, and making ends meet was always a challenge. For almost one hundred years, first ladies had to contend with such problems.

Mildred began offering the receptions that local society expected. Keeping her recipes in a small wooden card file for easy access, she consulted them frequently as she and her kitchen staff prepared dishes for a large number of events. Many of the parties during the Moody administration were more casual "at homes."

The State Dining Room had, perhaps more than any other room in the house, been the heart of the mansion. Here, for generations, governors, their families, and fortunate guests had dined,

*Birthday party for little Dan Moody, Jr. The Moodys' family
dog can be seen in the background.*
Courtesy Austin History Center, Austin Public Library, CO 2865.

celebrated, and mourned. Unfortunately, by the time the Moody
family had moved into the mansion, the room was also one of the
least presentable in the house. Mildred finally persuaded the miserly
State Board of Control to appropriate funds to repaper the State
Dining Room.

She chose wallpaper produced by the venerable Zuber Company.
The paper, entitled "Scenic America," depicted American scenes
from the 1700s. T. S. Hill of Austin oversaw the repairs and redecorating. The "scenic" wallpaper was expensive, and the entire state
allotment was used to purchase it. The governor was so angry that
he refused to sign the disbursement form until he cooled off. The
lack of funds left the other rooms of the mansion no better off than
they had been when Mildred arrived, so Mildred called her banker
father and received from him the money needed to finish the other
rooms. John L. Martin installed the latest bathroom ensemble in the
mansion. The "Woodmere" bath and shower suite, along with the
necessary plumbing improvements, cost $359.00.

Among Mildred's other early improvements were the updating of the kitchen and pantry. Both rooms received much-needed paint and Armstrong straight-line "A" linoleum. A large piece of zinc was placed under the gas and wood range. The old built-in icebox on the back porch was removed once and for all, and the antiquated wiring was replaced in portions of the house. The ancient front porch steps of wood were replaced with a handsome concrete version that had an elaborate iron railing. The porch steps had not been high on Mildred's list of projects until they collapsed under the weight of a large crowd. Summer reception guests were sent sprawling across the lawn as the steps fell in on themselves. Mildred was determined that her successors should not have to face such deplorable conditions. She had to take action.

Because of the difficulty in securing funds for the mansion's upkeep, Mildred was determined that a committee should be appointed

The Sam Houston bedroom as it looked during Mildred Moody's time in the home. Note the crocodile skin on the floor and the electric cord stretched down from the ceiling fixture.
From the author's collection.

to manage the preservation and decoration of the house. This idea came to the public's attention in 1931 when the *Dallas News* published an article by Mildred about her experiences as first lady. In the article she recommended that a board be established to plan for furnishing the governor's home, preferably in a style that reflected its historic character.

Spurred on by the article and out of respect for Mildred, the forty-second legislature authorized a Board of Mansion Supervisors to oversee planning and improvements. The new governor, Ross Sterling, appointed Mildred Moody to chair the new three-person board. The committee had a great impact on the historic home, authorizing new furniture, floor coverings, roofing, and landscaping. Mrs. Moody continued to serve on the board until 1941. In many respects, her efforts as first lady and chair of the Board of Mansion Supervisors led the way in preserving the mansion, providing a benchmark of care for other first ladies to follow.

By the second decade of the twentieth century, the first ladies of Texas had achieved celebrity status across the state. As a result, their "unofficial" duties multiplied. As with other first ladies of this period, Mildred Moody was frequently asked to support county and regional charity efforts. These invitations came in the form of requests that she provide a favorite recipe, contribute a handkerchief for a silent auction, or fill a tiny apron pocket with the same number of pennies as her waist size.

Mildred Paxton Moody
♦ "EXPENSIVE" CHESS PIE

Making chess pies for all the legislators and visitors who dined at the Governor's Mansion table was an expensive proposition for the governor and his young wife. The governor's salary was four thousand dollars a year, and that did not go very far when one considers that the governor had to pay for all of the groceries used by the mansion's residents and guests.

2 cups of sugar
¾ cup of butter
5 eggs
2 tablespoons cream
1 teaspoon vanilla extract
2 tablespoons flour

Cream sugar and butter. Add eggs one at a time and mix well.
Add cream, vanilla, and flour to this mixture and blend well.
Pour mixture into 9-inch pie shell and bake at 350 degrees for 45
minutes or until set and brown on top.

Mildred Paxton Moody
◆ CARAMEL NUT PIE

The recipes for chess pie and caramel nut pie were Mildred's favorites. They came from a Mrs. Kincaid, who ran a hotel kitchen at
Buffalo Gap, just south of Abilene. That establishment was the only
thing approaching a "night spot" for the young people there.
Mildred Moody used her Grandmother Paxton's "infallible" hot
water piecrust—made with lard.

2 cups sugar, divided use
2 cups milk
4 eggs
2 heaping tablespoons flour
1 tablespoon butter
½ cup pecans, chopped

Brown 1½ cups of sugar—this means careful "browning" in a
heavy iron skillet. Put other sugar and remaining ingredients
[except nuts] in double boiler to heat, and then add to browned
sugar. Cook to a thick custard and fill pastry shell, already
cooked. Pecans are added to the custard. Delicious!

Mildred Paxton Moody

◆ GRANDMOTHER PAXTON'S "INFALLIBLE" HOT WATER PIE CRUST

$\frac{3}{4}$ cup lard (or shortening)
$\frac{1}{2}$ teaspoon salt
1 teaspoon milk
$\frac{1}{4}$ cup boiling water
2 cups all-purpose flour

In a large bowl, combine shortening, salt, milk, and boiling water. Whip with fork until smooth and creamy. Add 2 cups flour and stir with large round-the-bowl strokes until all flour is well mixed in. Makes enough crust for one double-crust pie. ～

Mildred Paxton Moody

◆ FAMOUS DEVILED OYSTERS

This special dish of Mildred Moody's is one of the few recipes by a first lady to appear in print during her tenure in the mansion. It was first published in *Farm and Ranch* in October, 1928. Mildred explained in the article that it was too expensive for her to serve except on special occasions.

1 small onion
$\frac{1}{8}$ pound butter or bacon grease
2 cans oysters for six people or 60 fresh oysters
6 crackers rolled fine
1 raw egg
2 hard-boiled eggs, crumbled
3 or 4 stalks parsley, minced
Juice of $\frac{1}{4}$ lemon
$\frac{1}{4}$ bottle of Worcestershire sauce
1 pimento
Salt and pepper to taste
Dash of Tabasco® sauce

Fry onions in butter until tender. Cut fine the drained oysters with a knife or scissors. Mix all ingredients and let cook until thickened. If necessary, add cracker crumbs. Take off stove and let stand until cool. Place in washed shells or ramekins. Top with cracker crumbs. Dot with butter and bake 20 minutes. ꩜

Mildred Paxton Moody
✦ DAN MOODY'S FAVORITE DESSERT

This recipe also appeared in the October 13, 1928, issue of *Farm and Ranch*. The dessert, which has a custard base, contains ingredients that would have been on hand in almost any kitchen of the era.

    1 quart milk
    6 eggs, separated
    1 cup sugar
    Vanilla to taste
    12 ladyfingers
    12 macaroons
    Nuts
    Whipped cream

Put milk in double boiler and let it get hot. Beat yolks and add sugar. Stir into milk until thick. Do not cook too long as milk will curdle. Flavor with vanilla.

Around a large platter place two layers, one of ladyfingers and one of macaroons, leaving the center of the platter open. While the custard is hot, pour slowly over the cakes and allow them to absorb it. Scatter a few drops of vanilla over the whole dish, then over the custard spread the stiffly beaten egg whites. Sprinkle with nuts, almonds or pecans. Place in oven just long enough to brown. Remove and, when cool, fill the center with whipped cream. Slice and serve at table. ꩜

Mildred Paxton Moody
◆ SALMON LOAF

3 cups salmon
2¼ tablespoons sugar
¾ tablespoon salt
¾ tablespoon flour
3 egg yolks
2¼ tablespoons melted butter
¼ teaspoon cayenne pepper
1¼ cups milk
⅓ cup vinegar
2 tablespoons gelatin
3 tablespoons cold water

Cook salmon. Place in colander and rinse well with hot water. Pick out bones and skin and let drain.

In top of double boiler, blend the sugar, salt, and flour. Add the egg yolks, melted butter, cayenne pepper, milk, and vinegar and cook, stirring constantly, until thickened. Soften gelatin in cold water, then blend gelatin into thickened cream sauce.

Add cooked salmon chunks and refrigerate, either in individual molds or in one large mold, such as one that is shaped like a fish, and let congeal. When ready, turn out of molds and garnish. Pour cucumber dressing over the top to serve. ⤚

Mildred Paxton Moody
◆ CUCUMBER DRESSING

The recipe for Mildred Moody's cucumber dressing was not complete in the source where it was found. I have added dill, which is standard for this type of dressing. The addition of a clove of garlic, finely chopped, gives the mixture a bit more zing. Yogurt may be substituted for the heavy cream if you prefer. This dressing is good pureed smooth in a food processor or blender, (either of which would have been a welcome addition to the mansion kitchen in the 1930s), although several to whom it was served said that they liked the larger pieces of cucumber.

1½ cups cucumber, shredded fine
¾ cup heavy cream
3 tablespoons vinegar
1 teaspoon fresh or dried dill
¾ teaspoon salt

Peel, seed, and shred cucumber. Add cream, vinegar, dill, and salt.
Add pepper to taste. Chill for 30 minutes. ⬿

Mildred Paxton Moody
♦ PATIENCE CANDY

To prepare this candy perfectly does indeed take some patience, but
it is really good.

3 cups granulated sugar, divided use
1 cup milk
2 tablespoons white syrup
1 cup pecans, chopped

Put 2 cups sugar, milk, and syrup in a very large kettle to boil. At
the time you put above mixture to boil, put in an iron skillet the
1 extra cup sugar, cooking until brown, then add it to the first
mixture, stirring all the time. Cook until it forms a hard ball in
cold water, and then add 1 cup chopped pecans. Make into a roll
and slice. ⬿

Mildred Paxton Moody
♦ ROLLED SANDWICHES

These would be perfect additions to afternoon bridge parties or
informal luncheons.

3 eggs
2 cups sweet milk
⅓ cup butter, melted
Flour
½ teaspoon red pepper

1 pound cheese, grated
Bread

Beat eggs together with milk and melted butter; add enough flour to make mixture as thick as mayonnaise dressing. Add a scant half teaspoon of red pepper to 1 pound of grated cheese. Cut bread very thin and spread the mixture of cheese and other ingredients over bread. Roll sandwich like jelly roll and use toothpick to hold together. Put in stove when ready to serve and toast lightly brown. Serve while hot with tea and mints. ➤

Mildred Paxton Moody

◆ ALMOND OR PECAN SLICES (ICEBOX COOKIES)

The advent of the electric refrigerator changed the way Texans cooked. Versions of these cookies occur in most every Texas cookbook of the 1920s.

5½ cups sifted cake flour
1 teaspoon soda
3 eggs, slightly beaten
1 cup sifted brown sugar
1 cup granulated sugar
1 cup hot melted shortening (part butter preferred)
1 cup chopped almonds or other nut meats

Sift flour once, measure, add soda, and sift three times. Mix other ingredients in order given, adding the flour last. Pack tightly into 8-by-8-inch pan lined with waxed paper and chill overnight. Remove loaf from pan and cut in half. Slice crosswise in thin slices. Bake in a hot oven [425 degrees] for 5 minutes. Makes about 6 dozen. ➤

◆ THE DEPRESSION ◆
1930–1937

The Great Depression hit Texas hard, but the Governor's Mansion was still the scene of many entertainments and receptions for special visitors. Despite hard times, governors still had to maintain the status of their office with these receptions and pay for them out of their own pockets. In the 1930s, these receptions were generally more casual and less spectacular than those of the preceding decade, but social tradition called for the mansion to be open. Afternoon teas and small luncheons were popular—and less expensive—than large and lavish parties.

The leaner times gave the first ladies a chance to be creative, both with the food budget and the decorations. The frugal mansion cooks made every penny count. Macaroni, soup, and the perennial Jell-O® were popular staples on the mansion table. During the darkest days of the depression, Gov. Miriam Ferguson had the mansion cooks bake bread to distribute to the needy in Austin.

New electric kitchen gadgets were popular additions to a home of the 1930s, with beautifully designed chrome wonders like waffle irons, toasters, and chafing dishes arriving in the mansion kitchen. Appearing more like sculpture than work-a-day machines, these streamlined marvels were also labor-saving devices. The mansion also boasted a new commercial refrigeration unit. Weighing almost as much as a small Buick, the huge machine was a star attraction. More than once, a female guest at one of the parties would whisper to the first lady and the two would walk back into the kitchen, where they could be found discussing the features of the gleaming new refrigerator.

✦ MAUD ABBIE GAGE STERLING ✦
1931–1933

Maud Sterling was a woman with a commanding sense of humor. One of the stories frequently told about her involved what she was going to wear to her husband's inaugural ball. Her family implored her to buy a new dress. Maud prolonged their anguish by telling them the old brown lace dress she already owned was good enough. What she did not tell them was that she had already purchased a new dress—in an uncharacteristic splurge—from Neiman Marcus and that it was hanging in her closet. She did not reveal her secret until the day of the inaugural.

In conjunction with her humor, she possessed a no-nonsense, hands-on way of running the Governor's Mansion. On January 20, 1931, when her husband Ross Shaw Sterling was inaugurated governor of Texas, she moved to the mansion and continued with her quiet routine. She had always preferred to stay at her comfortable home called Miramar, which was twenty-five miles from Houston, in La Porte. There, she loved to fish from the pier, do needlework, and garden. Being first lady was a different matter, but it did not change Maud. Even with four servants at the mansion, she answered the door herself when she could. She dressed plainly, and her simple frocks were generally made of Texas cotton.

One afternoon, while she was in the downstairs hall, she noticed a man in blue coveralls wandering around the front yard. Immediately, she went out to meet him. The man, a carpenter, making an assumption based on her plain mode of dress, asked her if she was the housekeeper at the mansion. She replied that she was indeed. After chatting a while he proceeded to forcefully ask for a tour of the house, stating that he had heard it was in bad condition and he wanted to come see for himself. After an extensive look around, as he prepared to leave, he asked Maud her name. She sweetly smiled and said "I'm Mrs. Sterling." As she gently closed the front door, she left a very surprised carpenter on the front porch.

Maud brought her own silver to the mansion, including a handsome coffee service and serving pieces and flatware. When a teacher came into the State Dining Room with a class in tow, Maud overheard her explaining that everything in the mansion belonged to the state. The teacher boldly opened a drawer in the buffet and showed the class the fine workmanship of the flatware. She said that even these beautiful things were owned by the state of Texas. Maud told the teacher, as she gently as she could, that the majority of the silver and all of the flatware on display was the property of the Sterling family. Among the things Maud did not bring to Austin were numerous needlework tapestries and wall hangings that she had made. When asked why she preferred to leave them in her bayfront home, she joked that there might be moths in the Governor's Mansion.

When Maud first moved into the mansion she was alarmed at the expense of running the place. The first electric bills ran nearly fifty dollars a month, so she got the Austin Power Company to reread the meter and reduce the bills. She was a thrifty shopper as well, having fruit and vegetables trucked in from her country farm. Her eggs, butter, hams, and poultry arrived at the mansion on a regular basis. What she could not grow was purchased from grocery markets in Austin. She did her own grocery shopping and was frequently seen holding her shopping basket under her arm. Maud did everything on a strict budget, even though money was not a serious concern for her and her husband.

Maud grew native Texas wildflowers as a hobby and eventually made a small rock garden in what had once been Miriam Ferguson's chicken yard on the mansion grounds. She was familiar with the names of all the native species, having learned alongside her son when he was studying botany. Her success with flowers, particularly larkspur, was of interest to former first lady Mildred Moody, who had tried numerous times to grow it but with little success. Vibrant red tulips lined the front walk of the mansion, and the flower gardens changed with the seasons. Two large evergreen shrubs Maud set out at the front of the house thrived there for at least two decades.

While redecorating the downstairs rooms, Maude was horrified to learn that during previous administrations, several pieces of the mansion's original furnishings had been sold to a junk dealer. She was determined not to let this happen again and made a complete inventory of the furnishings. In the library, green carpeting and draperies, in rough green cloth with fringe trimmings, replaced tattered twenty-year-old hangings. A pair of small chairs covered in maroon tapestry flanked the fireplace. The family radio sat next to a sectional case filled with books and magazines.

Maud made the mansion a comfortable home, but after her time as first lady was over, she returned to her own home in La Porte, where she fished from the pier behind her house and tended her expansive gardens. Among the Sterlings' generous contributions to society was the gift of their La Porte residence to the Houston Optimist Club, which made it a boys' home.

Maud Abbie Gage Sterling

♦ BAY RIDGE STRAWBERRY PRESERVES

Bayridge Road is a long street running the length of the small town of Morgan's Point, Texas. Running parallel to the shore, it slopes downward to the water in a kind of ridge. The town used to be the site of the Morgan plantation (from which Emily Morgan, the fabled "yellow rose of Texas," had reportedly come).

The plantation acreage was eventually broken up and the land was sold in long, narrow plots to maximize the number of houses that could be constructed facing Galveston Bay. Houston residents prized houses along Bayridge Road as summer retreats where they could trade the heat and humidity of the city for the cooling breezes of the coast. The Sterling Mansion, home to Governor and Mrs. Sterling, occupied a large plot of land along the ridge and was designed to be a reduced-scale replica of the White House.

Strawberries grew in abundance on the Sterling property, and this recipe is a wonderful way to utilize them. Frances Sterling Thurlow, a niece of Maud and Ross Sterling, grew up eating her aunt's delicious preserves. She notes that figs can be used in place of the strawberries, with whole lemon slices added to the mixture. She says the lemons are delicious. They are.

Stem and wash strawberries. Cut away green or overripe portions. For each quart of strawberries use an equal amount of sugar. Place the strawberries on the bottom of a kettle and the sugar on the top. When this comes to a boil, keep at boiling point for 20 minutes (over slow fire). Let cool in the juice. Put in mason jars, cover top with paraffin, and seal. This recipe requires no water to be added unless the berries are very dry and the water in which they are washed does not stay on them sufficiently. ❧

♦ JOE BETSY MILLER ALLRED ♦
1935–1939

Joe Betsy Allred, who was born in Altus, Oklahoma, and her husband James Allred were fond of simple fare, and as first lady she served corn bread sticks at almost every meal in the mansion. There was always ice cream in the electric freezer for the governor and oatmeal cookies in the mansion pantry for their two young sons, Jimmie and David (one of whom is remembered for sliding down the banister during a party and landing in a bowl of sweet peas). The food the first family ate would have been very familiar to most cooks in Texas in the mid-1930s; the Allreds' eating habits mirrored those of many families in the state during the time immediately following the Great Depression.

The mansion's large vegetable garden, ably managed by gardener Robert Reed, provided for the family in abundance. Onions, radishes, beets, lettuce, green beans, and new potatoes were grown in the backyard for use on the governor's table. Joe Betsy purchased other types of vegetables from a peddler who would pull up to the back door of the mansion every morning. Seasonal fruits and vegetables were used whenever possible because they were less expensive.

Although she did not do a great deal of cooking herself, Joe Betsy would review daily menus with her cook (a convict from the Texas prison system who had formerly been a chef at a Dallas country club) and would often arrange the salads or assist with the garnishing of the desserts for large events. The cookbook that furnished almost all of the recipes used during the Allred administration was produced by the Wichita Falls Woman's Forum in 1932. A friend in Wichita Falls gave Joe Betsy this book, and it quickly supplanted all other cookbooks used at the mansion.

Company and special guests usually ate the same hearty fare as the Allreds. Occasionally, depending on who the company was, ham would be served instead of bacon for breakfast. Special dinners consisted of a grapefruit and orange salad or a salad made of shredded cabbage combined with almonds and cream cheese. Another interesting mealtime addition for the first family was prunes stuffed with cream cheese.

Hams and turkeys were often sent to the Allreds from well-wishers. These gifts were much appreciated and made their way onto the mansion table, served plain for family and garnished with parsley for festive occasions. White fluff salad, an Allred favorite, comprised an unlikely combination of cabbage, marshmallows, and pineapple.

The Allred family, circa 1936.
From the author's collection.

Spring salad was made with diced beets, hard-boiled eggs, and olives. Ordinary homemade mayonnaise was used as a dressing on or in almost all salads prepared by the mansion cook. Joe Betsy prepared the menu and floral arrangements for her sister-in-law's wedding at the mansion. On March 2, 1935, Hazel Allred married W. D. Stokes, Jr., of Gladewater in the mansion parlors.

In 1936 Texas celebrated the one-hundredth anniversary of its independence from Mexico. During that centennial year the governor was very busy traveling from one special event to another, and Joe Betsy would occasionally accompany him on the trips around the state. In June, they traveled to Dallas to open the official Centennial Exposition.

Just as the governor and first lady traveled around Texas in conjunction with the centennial, Texans were also on the go and thousands of tourists came to Austin from throughout the United States that year. (Often, the Allreds would come face to face with curious visitors peering through the windows.) The number of requests from people wanting to visit the mansion increased threefold during 1936, and Joe Betsy's secretary, Bobbie Wilson, coordinated such activities with the first lady. That year's visiting dignitaries (who always slept in the Sam Houston bed), included Jesse H. Jones, a Houston philanthropist, and the vice president of the United States, John Nance Garner.

In an effort to improve the appearance of the mansion, Joe Betsy selected several pieces of new furniture for the old home. Two chairs purchased during her time as first lady remain in use in the library. Later in 1936, Joe Betsy's schedule was interrupted as the time approached for another Allred to join the family at the mansion.

Sam Houston Allred was born at home in the Sam Houston bed. In March of 1937, the nation's first lady, Eleanor Roosevelt, stopped by the mansion during her Texas tour. Before leaving, she penned her best wishes to the littlest Allred in the mansion guestbook.

Joe Betsy loved living in the home and did much to preserve its heritage. Her bedroom was filled with furniture and mementos from the house's past. The beautiful carved walnut bed she slept in was used previously by Governor Hogg. Mrs. Moody had had it restored 1927. A grand piano and Joe Betsy's personal furnishings completed the room. Her husband James's bedroom was also filled with historic furnishings. His bedroom suite was from the home of Jesse Lincoln Driskill, cattleman and builder of the Driskill Hotel; former first lady Willie Hobby had acquired it for the mansion. Over the fireplace Joe Betsy hung an ornate round oak-framed mirror that she had discovered in the servants' quarters. Once it was resilvered and restored, it was placed back in the mansion.

The following recipes are from the *Woman's Forum of Wichita Falls Cook Book* published in 1932. This cookbook was Joe Betsy Allred's personal favorite, and in a 1935 interview she identified these dishes as having been served on a regular basis at the mansion. The book was reprinted in 1982, and the Woman's Forum was gracious enough to provide me with a copy.

Joe Betsy Miller Allred
♦ POTATO SALAD

This recipe was contributed to the Wichita Falls Woman's Forum cookbook by Mrs. Ola G. Hamlin and was a favorite at the mansion. The nuts are an interesting addition to the traditional mix. I tried pecans and walnuts and found them to provide the perfect amount of texture.

> 4 potatoes, boiled and cubed
> 3 hard-boiled eggs
> 1 cup nut meats, finely chopped
> 4 cubed apples
> 1 small minced onion

Dressing for potato salad:

> 2 eggs, separated
> ½ pint cream
> 1 teaspoon salt
> 2 tablespoons butter, melted
> ½ cup hot vinegar

Mix egg yolks with next four ingredients and cook in double boiler until thick. Take from fire and add the well-beaten whites of eggs. If desired, celery seed and mustard may be added to seasoning. Pour dressing over other ingredients and let stand an hour before serving. ❧

Joe Betsy Miller Allred
♦ WHITE FLUFF SALAD

This is really a nice, unusual salad.

> 1 small package marshmallows
> 1 cup shredded pineapple, drained

2 cups shredded cabbage
1 cup whipped cream
4 tablespoons mayonnaise
½ cup nuts

Add the marshmallows, cut in fourths, to the pineapple; crisp the finely shredded cabbage in ice water until serving time, drain thoroughly; add whipped cream to the mayonnaise and fold in nuts. Mix and serve. ⤚

Joe Betsy Miller Allred

◆ CHICKEN PIE

1 chicken
Salt/pepper
½ pound veal
¼ pound mushrooms (Mrs. Allred left these out)
2 tablespoons shortening
3 hard-boiled eggs
4 ounces bacon
Parsley, chopped
Chicken stock
English pastry
1 egg, beaten

Cut chicken into small points, season with salt and pepper. Slice veal thinly, line bottom of casserole with this, place on top layer of chicken. Chop mushrooms fine, sauté them in the shortening. Sprinkle half of this over the chicken, then a layer of hard-boiled eggs, then thin slices of bacon and chopped parsley. Continue in this way until all the ingredients are used. Fill dish ¾ full with chicken stock. Put a strip of pastry around the edge, then cut a piece to fit the top and press the edges of the pastry together. Bake. Brush top with beaten egg. Cook 1½ hours at 325 degrees. Serves 6. ⤚

Joe Betsy Miller Allred
✦ COCONUT PIE

1 cup sugar
10 tablespoons flour
¼ teaspoon salt
4½ cups sweet milk
4 eggs, separated
1 cup coconut
¾ cup nuts

Mix sugar, flour, and salt, and sift. Put part of milk on to scald.
Save enough to mix with dry ingredients. When milk scalds pour
in sugar mixture with the egg yolks. Cook until thick. Take off
stove and add coconut and nuts. Put in baked crusts. Put egg
whites on top, made into a meringue. ⌐

Joe Betsy Miller Allred
✦ STRAWBERRY ICE CREAM

1 quart single cream [whipping cream or heavy cream works
    fine]
1 quart berries
Sugar

Crush berries through a sieve, mix with cream, and sweeten to
taste. Freeze hard. ⌐

Joe Betsy Miller Allred
✦ ELECTRIC REFRIGERATOR ICE CREAM

The mansion cook would add blackberries and other fruits. This
recipe, though ancient, still works.

20 marshmallows, large
2 cups whole milk
Vanilla extract
1 cup double cream [heavy or whipping cream]

Place milk and marshmallows in the top of a double boiler and stir until marshmallows are dissolved. Cool; add vanilla and whipped cream and place in freezer compartment of an electric refrigerator until firm. Fruit may be added if desired.

Joe Betsy Miller Allred
♦ VEAL BIRDS

Have your butcher slice veal round very thin, remove bone, skin, etc. Cut in strips about 3 inches long by 2 inches wide, each strip making a bird. Make a well-seasoned dressing, using stock or milk to mix it. Place dressing on each bird, roll up, and fasten with a toothpick. Sprinkle birds with salt and pepper, dredge with flour, and sauté in hot fat or butter until brown. Place in baking pan and pour in milk to half cover the birds. Bake at 275 degrees until very tender. If gravy is not thick enough, remove birds and thicken gravy before serving. Serve hot.

Joe Betsy Miller Allred
♦ SWISS STEAK

$\frac{1}{2}$ cup flour
3 teaspoons salt
$\frac{1}{2}$ teaspoon pepper
2 pounds flank or round steak
3 tablespoons butter
1 medium can of tomatoes
1 medium onion, chopped

Mix flour, salt, and pepper together and pound into the steak. Brown floured steak in a hot frying pan to which the butter has been added. Boil tomatoes and chopped onion together for 5 minutes, pour over the steak, and bake about 2 hours in 325-degree oven. Serves 8.

Joe Betsy Miller Allred
◆ BAKED COCONUT CUSTARD

This is a wonderful simple custard and reflects the 1930s fascination with coconut as an ingredient in cooking.

    4 cups milk
    6 egg yolks, beaten
    6 egg whites, beaten
    1 cup sugar
    ¼ teaspoon salt
    2 cups grated coconut (fresh or dried)

Beat egg yolks and whites separately; add to milk. Add sugar, salt, and coconut. Pour into buttered custard cups. Bake in pan of hot water till set in a 325-degree oven for 20 to 25 minutes. ⤳

Joe Betsy Miller Allred
◆ CHOWCHOW

Joe Betsy Allred's daily menu choices are very typical of those foods served in the years immediately following the depression. This chowchow is a wonderful accompaniment to pinto beans.

    6 large onions
    1 medium cabbage
    12 green sweet peppers
    10 or 12 small hot peppers
    1 cup salt
    2 quarts vinegar
    2½ pounds of brown sugar
    Celery seed
    Pickling spices

Put all of the vegetables through a coarse food chopper. Add salt and vinegar, cook 30 minutes, then drain. Heat 2 quarts of vinegar and 2½ pounds of brown sugar, 1 package of celery seed, and 2 packages of pickling spices (the last wrapped in a little cheesecloth bag).

Mix drained vegetables in this, and after it has come to a boil, cook 20 minutes. Seal while hot. ⧏

Joe Betsy Miller Allred
◆ OLD-FASHIONED BLACKBERRY COBBLER

This is a remarkably simple dessert to prepare and was one of Governor Allred's personal favorites.

2 boxes of berries ($3\frac{1}{2}$ to 4 cups)
2 cups sugar
2 tablespoons flour, mixed with sugar
Butter

Clean and wash berries carefully and set aside. Line an $8\frac{1}{2}$-by-8-by-$1\frac{1}{2}$-inch pan or Pyrex® dish with a rather rich baking powder crust rolled a little thicker than a piecrust. Cover the bottom of the crust with mixture of sugar and flour, holding some of the sugar back. Crush the blackberries with a silver fork, pour into the crust, and dot with plenty of butter. Add the remainder of the sugar and cover with a top crust. Dampen the edges so the juice will not run out and make perforations to permit the steam to escape. Bake in a moderate oven until a nice brown color and until the juice looks thick. Cool and serve from dish, either plain or with cream. ⧏

Joe Betsy Miller Allred
◆ RATHER RICH BAKING POWDER PIECRUST

3 cups all-purpose flour
$1\frac{1}{2}$ teaspoons salt
2 teaspoons baking powder
1 tablespoon white sugar
6 tablespoons ice water
1 cup shortening

In a large bowl, combine flour, salt, baking powder, and sugar. Place $\frac{1}{2}$ cup of flour mixture in a small bowl and stir in water until smooth. Cut shortening into remaining flour mixture until it looks like coarse meal. Blend in the flour-water mixture. Wrap dough and chill in icebox until ready to use.

Joe Betsy Miller Allred
◆ BERRY ROLL

So many of the desserts served in the 1930s are very similar to those that have once again gained popularity in Texas. This roll is an elegant end to summertime meals.

> 1 small recipe biscuit dough, made extra rich
> 3 cups slightly crushed berries
> 2 cups sugar
> 2 tablespoons flour
> Butter
> 2 cups boiling water

Prepare a rich biscuit dough and roll out to a thickness of about $\frac{1}{4}$inch. Spread this with crushed berries that have been combined with 1 cup sugar and 2 tablespoons flour. Roll as a jelly roll and make slices about $1\frac{1}{2}$ inches wide. Dot this with butter. Place in an oiled baking pan. Melt remaining cup of sugar in iron skillet, add 2 cups boiling water. When sugar is completely dissolved, pour over roll and bake slowly until golden brown.

> Biscuit Dough:
> 2 cups flour
> 4 teaspoons baking powder
> $\frac{1}{2}$ teaspoon cream of tartar
> $\frac{1}{2}$ teaspoon salt
> 2 teaspoons sugar
> $\frac{1}{2}$ cup margarine or butter
> $\frac{2}{3}$ cup milk

Combine the flour, baking powder, cream of tartar, salt, and sugar through a sifter or strainer into a large mixing bowl. Cut the butter into small cubes. Work the butter into the dry ingredients. Mix well. Pour milk into the batter and stir it in with a fork. The consistency should be slightly lumpy.

Sift some flour on a countertop or other flat surface and spoon the dough onto it. Knead the dough for a few minutes until it is smooth. Too much kneading makes dough tough. Using a lightly floured rolling pin, flatten the ball into a circle. Work from center outward until the dough is about $\frac{1}{4}$ inch thick. ⇜

◆ WAR AND PEACE ◆
1938–1948

The mansion cuisine of the 1940s can be divided in two eras, those being the war years and the postwar years. Each time period featured a distinctly different set of food trends. In the war years, the availability of food products depended largely on wartime rationing. Even by the time the United States entered World War II in 1941, Texas consumers were already seeing the prices of their favorite imported food products skyrocket. Olive oil was priced at nine to eleven dollars a gallon. French chocolates, spices, bananas, and coconuts were expensive and hard to get.

The government system of rationing food products meant that the mansion cooks had to follow an elaborate point system that determined how much cheese, butter, sugar, coffee, and canned goods a household could buy. If households used up their allotment, they simply had to make do. Molasses, sorghum, and honey stood in for sugar; processed vegetable oils in the form of oleo took the place of butter. Ground beef, which required fewer rationing points than did steaks or roasts, was used by the mansion cooks in spaghetti, meatloaf, and hamburgers. For the most part, the governor's household had to follow the same rationing rules that everyone else did.

Even though there was some wiggle room in the rations for the chief executive, supplies in the mansion pantry remained tight, and nothing was wasted. The vegetable garden behind the mansion was expanded and called a victory garden. Tending wartime kitchen gardens was considered a patriotic duty, and millions of gardens were planted throughout the country. At the mansion, the produce was eaten fresh or canned by the cook, as it had been for years.

The war's end in 1945 brought big changes to Texas tables. Homegrown produce, at least in a town setting, was largely forgotten as Texans rushed to the market to buy canned vegetables and frozen fruits. Milk, cream, cheese, and eggs were consumed in enormous quantities. But mostly, Texans wanted their beef. No more meatless Mondays, no more eating "low on the hog"—it was time to eat meat. Women's roles also began to change. Made-from-scratch cooking was slowly sidelined as people began to utilize one-box mixes and convenience foods. Fast food also came into fashion with the opening of the first McDonald's and Dairy Queen later in the decade.

Years of not having new goods meant that postwar Texas cooks rushed to experience the latest kitchen time-savers. KitchenAid introduced the first automatic dishwasher, and across the state cast-iron stoves—a fixture through the depression and war years—were junked to make way for shiny new chrome and enamel cookstoves. Throughout the decade, the mansion kitchen never slowed.

✦ MERLE ESTELLE BUTCHER O'DANIEL ✦
1939–1941

All Merle O'Daniel wanted from the legislature in 1941 was a small appropriation for new linoleum in the mansion kitchen and a little more money to finish the rose garden. She had already managed to cut corners and find enough in the general budget to buy new venetian blinds in the dining room and to redo the dining room furniture. The high kitchen walls were repainted—pea green—and pantries added. The O'Daniels had brought many of their own furnishings with them to the mansion, including an old Edison phonograph, a large grandfather clock, a silver tea service, and an electric organ. Their twelve-year-old canary, Jerry, and a school of goldfish also made the trip from Fort Worth.

Merle's days as first lady were full. Arising between 6:00 and 6:30 A.M., she would make the necessary arrangements for breakfast.

*First Lady Merle O'Daniel, shown standing in the State Dining Room
with the dining table set for a reception. Note the Zuber "Scenic America"
wall coverings that were installed during the Moody administration.*
Courtesy Austin History Center, Austin Public Library, PICA 06596.

Meals for the O'Daniels were seldom private, with guests appearing even for breakfast. After the morning meal she would busy herself making out the week's grocery list, and once a week she would
do her own grocery shopping. After coordinating the day's correspondence with her secretary, Bobbie Wilson, and answering any
pressing letters, it would be time for lunch. On rare occasions the
family would be able to dine alone, but more often than not there
would be from one to fifteen guests at the mansion for a luncheon.
The rest of the afternoon was generally spent attending functions or
greeting any members of the public who would stop by for a peek
inside the governor's home. Merle set an ambitious schedule for
herself early in her husband's first term, hoping to have four "at-
home" functions each month. At the close of the day, she would
dress for dinner and try to find time to relax with her husband.

First Lady Merle O'Daniel, holding a bouquet of roses, watches her
husband Governor W. Lee O'Daniel on his Inauguration Day,
January 21, 1941. Radio newsman Pat Adelman stands next to him.
Courtesy Texas State Library and Archives Commission (1976/8-56).

Her hobby was gardening, and during her time as first lady she
had several old sheds at the back of the mansion property torn
down to make room for a large star-shaped rose bed. The majority
of the roses were the red Texas Centennial variety, which were sent
to the mansion from admirers in Tyler. The large bed was inter-
spersed with grassy walking paths. Other flower beds on the mansion grounds received her special touch; often she could be found
on her hands and knees setting out plants and weeding the beds
herself. The mansion lawns were grazed during the O'Daniel administration by a large mountain goat, a gift from an admirer.

Merle, tall and slender with piercing blue eyes, had met W. Lee
O'Daniel while they were both attending business college in
Hutchinson, Kansas. Soon after the couple met, he informed her
that they were going to wed and have three children, named Pat,

The Mansion grounds took a beating during the O'Daniel barbecue reception January 1, 1940. Thousands crowded into the yards.

Courtesy Texas State Archives and Library Commission (76/8-92).

This rare photograph shows the Mansion kitchen after a large event during the O'Daniel administration January 21, 1941. Note the box of Oxydol and the tin of Bon Ami next to the kitchen sink.

Courtesy Texas State Archives and Library Commission (76/8-60).

Mike, and Molly. They eventually married and his prediction came true. They settled in Fort Worth in 1925.

When daughter Molly married East Texas oilman John D. Wrather in 1941, the O'Daniels invited seemingly all of Texas to the wedding. An estimated twenty-five thousand spectators came to see the festivities and listen to the ceremony on loudspeakers as the young couple took their vows. Fruit juice and wedding cake were served in the front yard of the mansion to all the guests. Big events were a specialty of Merle's. When her husband invited, by radio, all of the citizens of Texas to his second inauguration in 1941, she oversaw the party, at which more than twenty thousand Texans lined up outside the mansion for a gigantic barbecue. The meal included thirteen hundred pickles, one thousand pounds of potato salad, and thirty-five hundred loaves of bread. Barbecue pits were dug on the mansion grounds to cook nineteen thousand pounds of beef for the inaugural dinner. Also on the menu were mutton, hot dogs, and a buffalo the governor had killed the week prior to the inaugural.

≈≈≈

Merle Estelle Butcher O'Daniel
♦ ORANGE BISCUITS

The marmalade caramelizes and gives these light biscuits an extra dimension of goodness.

    2 cups sifted flour
    4 teaspoons baking powder
    1 tablespoon sugar
    $\frac{1}{2}$ teaspoon salt
    $\frac{1}{4}$ cup shortening
    $\frac{1}{2}$ cup milk
    1 egg
    $\frac{1}{3}$ cup orange marmalade

Mix and sift dry ingredients together; cut in shortening thoroughly; combine lightly with milk and egg to make a soft, very slightly moist dough. Roll out on a lightly floured board to

Jovial First Lady Blanch Fay Stevenson.
From the author's collection.

$\frac{3}{4}$-inch thickness. Cut with a small biscuit cutter and place in muffin tins. Press into the top of each biscuit about 1 teaspoon orange marmalade. Bake in a very hot oven at 450 degrees for about 10 to 12 minutes. Yields 12 biscuits.

◆ BLANCH FAY WRIGHT STEVENSON ◆
1941–1942

One of the most engaging first ladies ever to grace the mansion did not get to enjoy the home for very long. Blanch Fay Stevenson was

Blanch Stevenson arrived in the Mansion in a wheelchair on
the day of her husband's Inaugural, August 4, 1941.
She passed away five months later.
Courtesy Texas State Library and Archives Commission (1976/8-804).

gravely ill when her husband Coke was elected governor. The old library, or the Green Room as it is sometimes known, had been used primarily as a reading room or office, but when Mrs. Stevenson came to the mansion it was converted into her bedroom to save her the effort of climbing the stairs to the second floor. The south entry of the mansion was closed in, and a small powder room was created. Despite all of the treatments she underwent, Blanch passed away just five months after her husband was inaugurated. Business and governmental offices in Austin and around the state were closed in her memory.

Coke, in honor of her wishes, had the standard mansion shrubs replaced with camellias and colorful azaleas. Smaller flower beds were filled with her favorite varieties of iris and tulips. The Stevensons' cocker spaniel Dusty roamed the old house for weeks looking for his mistress.

Blanch Fay Wright Stevenson
◆ DUCK GUMBO

The use of duck has once again come into fashion, and duck is almost as easy to find as chicken at your local specialty shop.

   ¼ cup cooking oil or shortening
   ¼ cup flour
   1 cup dry onion, chopped
   4 large ducks or 10 to 12 quail or 10 to 12 doves
   Black and red pepper
   1½ cups chopped bell peppers
   1½ cups chopped celery
   1 cup cooking parsley
   1 cup green onion, chopped

Make a roux (by heating the oil and adding the flour). Stir constantly until very brown. Add onion and cook till wilted. Then add meat, seasoning, peppers, and celery. Cover tightly and let simmer until cooked down (about an hour). Then add 1½ quarts of water, parsley, and green onion and cook till meat is tender (falls off the bone). May add more water as needed. Serve over rice. Serves 10. ~

Blanch Fay Wright Stevenson
◆ SPANISH MACARONI

A savory Stevenson family favorite, this dish is easily made and keeps well for a meal the next day. Mattie, the Stevensons' wonderful cook, always served this dish together with the Apricot Salad that follows.

4 tablespoons shortening
Minced large onion
2 tablespoons flour
1 chopped green pepper
1 can tomatoes
1 teaspoon sugar
1 pound ground meat
1 tablespoon salt
1 teaspoon chili powder
Macaroni
1½ pound grated cheese

Put shortening in a pan and heat. Add minced onion and sprinkle in flour. Fry until tender and add green pepper and tomatoes and sugar. After all this comes to a boil, add ground meat, salt, and chili powder. Let simmer until done. Add cooked macaroni. Don't cook over 20 minutes. Sprinkle grated cheese over mixture. ⤝

Blanch Fay Wright Stevenson
◆ APRICOT SALAD

Apricots are a very nutritious addition to your daily diet. This salad was once a staple at church potluck suppers.

1 egg
½ lemon
1 tablespoon sugar
Mustard
½ cup sweet milk (cream)
1 cup whipping cream
1 can apricots, drained
4 bananas

Whip the egg, add lemon juice, sugar, and mustard. Then add sweet milk. Cook in double boiler until thick. Cool. Whip cream, open apricots and drain, peel bananas. In salad mold place a layer of bananas then the apricots. Pour the sauce over the whole mixture. Chill in the icebox. ⤝

Blanch Fay Wright Stevenson
◆ COCONUT CAKE

This cake is light, airy, and delicious.

$\frac{1}{3}$ pound butter
$1\frac{1}{2}$ cups sugar
2 eggs, separated
1 teaspoon salt
3 teaspoons baking powder to $1\frac{1}{2}$ cups cake flour
$1\frac{1}{2}$ cups milk
1 teaspoon vanilla
$\frac{1}{2}$ cup coconut

Preheat oven to 350 degrees. Grease three 8-inch round cake pans. In a large mixing bowl with an electric mixer, cream butter and sugar until light and fluffy. Mixture will be lemon colored. Add egg yolks and blend well. Sift together, salt, flour, and baking powder. Add alternately with milk to above mixture. Blend well after each addition. Add vanilla, blend well. Set aside. Wash beaters in hot soapy water. Making sure bowl and beaters are absolutely grease-free, whip the egg whites until stiff. Fold egg whites and coconut into batter. Pour into cake pans. Bake about 30 minutes; toothpick inserted should come out clean. Cool completely. Frost with Coconut Filling.

Coconut Filling:
$1\frac{1}{4}$ cups sugar
$\frac{1}{2}$ cup milk
$\frac{1}{2}$ cup cream
2 cups coconut, fresh: tightly packed
3 tablespoons butter
$\frac{1}{2}$ teaspoon vanilla

Bring to a boil all ingredients. Then boil slowly for about 15 minutes. Don't beat too much. Pour filling over cake while it is still hot and of a jelly consistency. ⤚

Blanch Fay Wright Stevenson
✦ ITALIAN CHEESE PIE

For extra zip, add two cloves of fresh garlic, finely minced and lightly sautéed, to this easily made pie.

    6 eggs, small
    2 cups cream
    1 large onion, grated
    1 pound domestic Swiss cheese, grated
    Garlic salt, Worcestershire, pepper, salt

Beat eggs. Stir in other ingredients. This can be varied by using milk for cream, a sharper cheese, and shallots or chives for the onion. Pour the custard into two short raw pie shells. Bake at 450 degrees for 15 minutes. Dust tops generously with grated Parmesan cheese. Serve warm. Takes the full 45 minutes to cook. ↤

✦ MABEL BUCHANAN JESTER ✦
1947–1949

Mabel Jester was a tall, reserved woman who loved being first lady but cared little for joining clubs or other social organizations. Her chief concern was caring for family members who lived at the mansion: her husband Beauford and the two youngest children, Beauford, Jr., and Joan.

Jerry Wilke, the social secretary, helped Mabel schedule tours and special events. It was not uncommon for the first lady to prepare lunch for as many as forty people, many of them unexpected. Texas Ranger W. E. Harrell kept the crowds at the mansion under control and also served as chauffeur and family friend. For Mabel there seemed to be little quiet time.

She would usually rise at 7:30 and have a quick breakfast with the governor before he went to the office. Then she would go over the day's tasks with Miss Wilke, the secretary. Immediately thereafter she would discuss the day's meals with the cook. Once she finished in the kitchen, Mabel would give instructions for the day to the

Governor Jester's Inauguration day, January 21, 1947. Pictured left to right: In uniform Major Howard Burress, daughter Barbara Jester, Grandmother Jester, a beaming Governor Jester, First Lady Mabel Jester holding a huge bouquet of roses. Next to her is their other daughter, Joan.
Courtesy Texas State Library and Archives Commission (1976/8-745).

maid and laundress. Then, if there was time, she would begin a task that she dearly loved, that of arranging the flowers placed throughout the house. To further complicate her schedule, the mansion was also open to the public daily from 2:00 until 5:00.

The Jesters moved out of the mansion while peeling plaster was repaired, rooms were repainted, and the overloaded electrical system was replaced. The kitchen was modernized and a new deep-freeze locker was installed as well as the first electric dishwasher. New crystal chandeliers were also hung in the dining room and the main reception room. Upstairs, the Sam Houston bed received new hangings in red satin damask. The window treatments were of the same material, and the chairs were covered in red clipped velvet. The carpeting was gray, as was the patterned wallpaper. The bed also received new linens, all monogrammed with Sam Houston's initials. The towels in the green and white bathroom adjoining in the Houston bedroom were also monogrammed.

Mabel's time in the mansion came to a sudden and tragic end, when her husband died unexpectedly while on a train trip. Grief-stricken, she left the mansion with her family and returned to life as a private citizen.

≈

Mabel Buchanan Jester
♦ CHARLOTTE RUSSE

This elegant dessert is both simple to make and appropriate for a special dinner.

    1 tablespoon gelatin
    ¼ cup cold water
    3 egg yolks
    ½ cup sugar
    2 cups milk
    ½ cup sherry wine
    3 egg whites
    ¼ teaspoon salt
    2 tablespoons sugar
    2 cups heavy cream, whipped

Soften gelatin in cold water. Beat yolks slightly, add sugar and milk. Cook over hot water to form a custard. Add softened gelatin and heat until dissolved. Remove from fire. Add sherry, beat with rotary beater, cool. Beat whites until foamy, add salt and 1 tablespoon of the sugar. Beat until peaks just curl over. Fold into custard mixture. Whip cream with 1 tablespoon sugar and fold into custard. Pour into mold and chill until set. To serve, unmold and garnish with whipped cream. Yields 6 to 8 servings. ≈

Mabel Buchanan Jester
◆ WAFFLETTES OR ROSETTES

Mary Faulk Koock of Green Pastures restaurant fame used several of these recipes while catering for the mansion. Austin has produced few cooks as accomplished in traditional Southern cuisine.

1 egg, beaten
1 cup milk
1 cup flour
1 teaspoon sugar
$\frac{1}{8}$ teaspoon salt

Mix ingredients together to make batter. Dip a rosette iron in deep hot fat and then immerse half way (on the iron) into batter. Dip back in the hot fat until rosette floats off the iron when done. Brown to a light color, remove from fat with fork, and drain on absorbent paper. This is simple and takes only practice. They can be made several days in advance, kept in airtight containers, and run in a hot oven for only a minute when ready to serve. ～

Mabel Buchanan Jester
◆ CHOCOLATE SAUCE

This chocolate sauce is a treat that hardens over ice cream. Mabel Jester noted that this recipe is very much like the commercially made ice cream topping known as Elmer's Gold Brick Sauce®, a perennial Southern favorite made by Elmer's Candy Corp. of New Orleans.

4 squares chocolate
1 stick butter
$3\frac{1}{2}$ cups sifted powdered sugar
1 large can Pet [condensed] milk

Combine ingredients and cook 3 minutes. Add vanilla to taste. ～

Mabel Buchanan Jester
◆ SEVEN MINUTE FROSTING

1½ cups sugar
⅓ cup cold water
2 egg whites
2 teaspoons light corn syrup
¼ teaspoon cream of tartar
Pinch of salt
1 teaspoon vanilla

In the top of a double boiler, combine the sugar, water, egg whites, corn syrup, cream of tartar, and the salt. Beat with an electric mixer set at low speed for 30 seconds, then set the pan over boiling water (the pan bottom shouldn't touch the water). Beating at high speed, cook the frosting for about 7 minutes, or until it's stiff and glossy. Remove from the heat, add the vanilla, and beat 2 more minutes. ◆

Mabel Buchanan Jester
◆ CHOCOLATE BAVARIAN CREAM

2 squares unsweetened chocolate
⅓ cup sugar
1 cup milk
1 envelope gelatin
1 pint whipping cream
1½ teaspoons vanilla

Melt two squares chocolate in pan. Add ⅓ cup sugar. Heat milk and add gelatin softened in ¼ cup water. Add to chocolate mixture. Chill until slightly thickened. Add vanilla. Fold in whipped cream. ◆

Mabel Buchanan Jester
◆ CHICKEN AMANDINE (FOR 6 TO 8)

2 tablespoons butter, melted
2 tablespoons flour

1 teaspoon Beau Monde seasoned salt
1 teaspoon white pepper
1 tablespoon grated onion
Salt to taste
2½ cups hot chicken stock (1 tablespoon concentrated
chicken stock may be added to make richer stock if needed
3 tablespoons heavy cream
1½ cups cooked chicken, diced
½ cup mushroom slices, sautéed and drained
Small bowl of toasted, slivered almonds

Simmer butter and flour without browning for 5 minutes. Add Beau
Monde, white pepper, onion, salt, and chicken stock. Stir with wire
whip until smooth. Let simmer 15 to 20 minutes. Add heavy cream;
then strain and add diced chicken and mushroom slices. Place the
bowl of almonds near chafing dish to sprinkle on top of chicken. ❧

Mabel Buchanan Jester
◆ SHRIMP CREOLE

Mrs. Jester did not specify how much shrimp to use, but following
several delicious experiments I have found 1½ to 2 pounds of fresh
de-veined and peeled medium shrimp to be sufficient.

1 large onion chopped
1 green pepper chopped
2 stalks celery chopped
2 cloves garlic
1 tablespoon flour
2 tablespoons Lea & Perrins® Worcestershire sauce
1 can tomato soup
Liberal dashes of Tabasco® sauce
3 bay leaves
1 tablespoon chives
1 tablespoon dried parsley
1 tablespoon vinegar
1 teaspoon red pepper
½ teaspoon thyme

Cook onion, green pepper, and celery until glassy. Add garlic. Add flour, Lea & Perrins®, soup, and Tabasco®. Let simmer 30 minutes. Cook shrimp. Let water boil with bay leaves, red pepper, chives, parsley, thyme, and vinegar. Add shrimp to mixture. Serve over rice ring. (Cook 2 cups rice, but put in well-buttered ring.)

Mabel Buchanan Jester
◆ SPINACH SOUFFLE

1 package of chopped spinach
1 small onion
1 stick butter
4 or 5 tablespoons flour
$\frac{1}{2}$ teaspoon red pepper
2 cups milk
2 cups grated sharp aged cheese
4 or 5 eggs

Boil spinach with salt, strain, then grate onion in spinach. Set aside. Put stick of butter in double boiler and melt. Add flour, then let simmer for 20 minutes. Put in red pepper. Warm milk, then pour into mixture. Stir constantly until thick, then add cheese. Stir until cheese melts, beat together egg yolks, and pour yolks into mixture. Stir constantly, then pour spinach into mixture. Beat white of eggs and fold into mixture. Put in casserole. Set in pan of water, have oven hot, then turn down to 300 degrees. Cook 1 hour.

Mabel Buchanan Jester
◆ SOUR CREAM TWISTS

1 oz. yeast
4 cups sifted bread flour
$\frac{1}{2}$ teaspoon salt
1$\frac{1}{4}$ cups butter
3 egg yolks, beaten
1 teaspoon vanilla
1 cup commercial sour cream
Powdered sugar

Crumble yeast into flour and salt. Cut in butter with pastry blender until mixture resembles meal. Add beaten egg yolks, vanilla, and sour cream. Mix well. Divide into 7 balls. Roll each ball separately in powdered sugar and roll quite thin into a circle. Cut each circle into 8 pie-shaped wedges. Put 1 teaspoon filling (below) on each and roll tightly, starting at the broad end. Shape as a crescent and place on ungreased cookie sheet. Bake 15 to 20 minutes in 400-degree oven. Remove, sprinkle with powdered sugar. Makes 56.

Filling:
3 egg whites, stiffly beaten
1 cup sugar
1 cup ground pecans
1 teaspoon vanilla

Fold sugar, nuts, and vanilla into beaten egg whites.

Mabel Buchanan Jester
◆ HOT CHEESE STICKS

½ pound Old English cheese, grated
¼ pound bacon, cut in small pieces
2 eggs, beaten
1 medium onion, chopped
Dash Worcestershire sauce

Mix above ingredients and spread on rye bread cut into thirds or rounds, toasted on one side. Broil until cheese is melted and hot. ≈

A New Era

THE 1950S BROUGHT about many changes in entertaining at the Mansion, which reflected new socioeconomic realities. All varieties of grocery and convenience products could be purchased from neighborhood supermarkets. Innovations such as one-touch electric ranges, dishwashers, and refrigerators with built-in freezers changed the kitchen landscape.

The Texas economy was good. Beef production was at a postwar high, and although steak was still king, casseroles appeared with regularity on dining tables, even at the mansion. Cooks had discovered, thanks in part to television and the first cooking shows, that canned cream soups could be used as a time-saving base for one-dish meals.

In the 1950s the parties at the mansion would be characterized by a carefully orchestrated elegance and grace. The events set the example for thousands of Texans wanting the newest and best for their own parties. Being a trendsetter was not an easy task during the prosperous postwar years, but the first lady who occupied the mansion longer than any other was up for the challenge.

◆ MARIALICE SHARY SHIVERS ◆
1949–1957

Marialice Shary was born in Omaha, Nebraska. She lived there during her early childhood before moving to Mission, Texas, with her parents. Her father, John H. Shary, was a prominent citrus fruit grower, cattleman, banker, and realtor in the Rio Grande valley. Her mother was known throughout the region for her elaborate parties and seasonal open houses. The Shary home was large and seemed to always be filled with visitors and family from around the country, so Marialice grew up in an atmosphere of hospitality and entertaining. After graduating from high school she left the family home and moved to San Antonio, where she later graduated from Our Lady of the Lake University. While attending one of the many seasonal parties held by her parents, she met her future husband, Robert Allan Shivers. They married in 1937.

Allan had a desire to enter politics, and although she had envisioned a rather different path for their lives, Marialice supported her new husband. He was elected to the Texas senate when he was twenty-six. Eventually, Allan became lieutenant governor and then governor upon the unexpected death of Gov. Beauford Jester in July, 1949. For the next seven and a half years the Shivers family occupied the mansion. As first lady, Marialice's love of entertaining was boundless. She lived in the mansion at a time of prosperity in Texas and the United States. The postwar years saw a huge resurgence in entertaining and a much more elaborate social regime was established.

During her time in the mansion, she persuaded the typically stingy legislature to spend money on the one-hundred-year-old structure, which once again desperately needed work. The much-patched roof leaked. The heating was unreliable. The plumbing often rebelled at very inopportune times. Fortunately for the Shivers family, the mansion received extensive repairs and updates during their lengthy stay. Air-conditioning was installed, as was modern central heating. Television arrived in the mansion. And, for the first time, more than one person at a time could run a bath in one of the four bathrooms.

The Shivers family already had a household staff, and these individuals came to work at the mansion. Jerry Bell was headwaiter and a master of everything. Albert "Fats" Marshall was associate waiter and cook and also did odd jobs. Two sisters, Marie and Nina Alvarado, oversaw the cleaning and the laundry. The Shivers children were cared for as babies by Beatrice, the baby nurse. When they were older, Scottish-born Marion "Macky" MacBeth took over. Overseeing both the smaller family kitchen upstairs in the mansion's private quarters and, to a lesser degree, the large main entertaining kitchen downstairs was Tomas, or "Tommy" as the family knew him. Marialice supervised the staff's activities and focused her efforts on developing menus and overfeeding everyone. All of the Shivers staff worked for the family until age and infirmity precluded them from doing so.

The number of Shivers pets rivaled that of the Hogg family many years before. Living with them were Butch, a German shepherd; Dynamite, a boxer; Freddie, a Saint Bernard; Storky, a Welsh terrier; love birds; tropical fish; numerous canaries; and more than a few turtles.

Birthdays for the children were huge events. Marialice would have a school bus, bearing a birthday sign on the side, stop at Pease Elementary, where the children, their entire class, and their teachers would be loaded aboard and driven to the mansion. One of the most memorable of the birthday parties was one with a Davy Crockett theme. Seventy-five second- and third-grade students attended and were served cake and ice cream. Marialice designed the cake, which resembled a mountain with Davy Crockett's cabin on top. Mrs. Tula Knolle, mansion secretary, helped Marialice coordinate such events, which seemed to become more involved with each passing month.

Prior to the Shivers administration, every governor's family brought their personal dishes and silver for entertaining. During Marialice's time as first lady, the first official state china and silver were ordered. Bone-colored china in the Jefferson pattern by Pickard China and silver flatware in the Pointed Antique pattern were chosen. The new china bore the state seal in gold, and each piece of the new flatware was engraved with the seal and the years that Governor Shivers was in office. The flatware was ordered from Joe Koen & Sons Jewelers on Congress Avenue. Every successive governor has followed the tradition of adding to the state flatware.

When celebrating holidays at the mansion, Marialice Shivers did not hold back on decorating. For Christmas, she had two trees in the downstairs rooms, with decorations designed by Harold Eichenbaum of Austin. One tree was an enormous pink-flocked specimen with aqua-colored decorations and sequined butterflies, and the other was a large green-flocked tree decorated with golden orbs, strands of golden ornaments, and golden glitter spray. Hundreds toured the mansion at Christmastime to see the elaborate decorations, and each year's display tended to outdo the previous one.

Marialice Shivers was always active in social causes as well. She was founder of the Seton Development Board in Austin and was instrumental in supporting Seton Hospital's neonatal center, which was named for her. She was active with the University of Texas, the Shivers Cancer Center, the Allan Shivers Library and Museum in Woodville, Texas, the Allan Shivers Park at Texas Scottish Rite Hospital in Dallas, and the Sharyland Independent School District's scholarship program.

Marialice was first lady for almost all of the 1950s, a decade when entertaining became much more formal. Not since the elaborate multicourse dinners of the late nineteenth century had menus been so complicated. One of Marialice's traditional luncheon menus was

Shrimp in Avocado with Hot Sauce
Chicken Hash
Broiled Tomato
Texas Ruby Red Grapefruit Sections
with Poppyseed
Dressing
Cherry Angel Pie
Hot Homemade Rolls
Coffee

As a result of the expansive trends in entertaining, changing tastes, and the popularity of new foods, Marialice's collection of recipes is the largest in this book. She loved to try new things and was well known for making sure that everyone had their fill. Every recipe is included basically in its original form, as discovered. Together, they provide an interesting food-related testament to one of the most prosperous and optimistic times in Texas history.

⇌

Marialice Shary Shivers
◆ CHICKEN SALAD EXOTIC

2 cups diced chicken
1 cup thinly sliced celery
⅓ cup sliced canned water chestnuts
3 tablespoons chopped preserved ginger
¼ cup toasted coconut flakes
½ cup mayonnaise
1 tablespoon fresh lemon juice
Salt
Cayenne pepper
¼ cup toasted coconut
Cantaloupes and fresh cherries with stems (optional)

Boil, bone, and dice chicken. Combine chicken, celery, water chestnuts, ginger, and coconut flakes. Add mayonnaise and toss lightly to coat. Add lemon juice, salt, and cayenne pepper to season gently. Heap onto lettuce leaves on large plates. Arrange sliced cantaloupe around plate in fan shape and decorate with fresh cherries. Sprinkle toasted coconut flakes over all to serve. ⇌

Marialice Shary Shivers
◆ MUSHROOM SAUCE

This sauce is delicious over chicken or pork. It also works wonderfully well over pasta.

⅓ cup butter
¼ cup flour
1⅓ cup chicken stock
1 pound of sautéed mushrooms

Dash paprika
1 tablespoon lemon juice
2 egg yolks
¼ cup cream
Parsley

Place butter into top of double boiler, and stir in flour until smooth. Then add hot chicken stock and mushrooms and all seasoning. Cook until thick, and last add beaten egg yolks and cream. Parsley is used for the garnish. ❧

Marialice Shary Shivers
♦ ESCALLOPED EGGPLANT

Peel and cube 2 pounds of eggplant and cook until tender, drain, and mash. Eggplant can be tricky. Make certain you remove all of the bitter outer skin.

Add:
2 eggs
½ cup minced onions
1 cup cracker meal
½ cup milk
Salt and pepper to taste
4 tablespoons butter
Little garlic
1 cup grated American cheese

Pour into oiled baking dish, top with cheese (1 cup), and bake at 350 degrees for 30 minutes. ❧

Marialice Shary Shivers
♦ CLAM SUPREME

8 ounces cream cheese
1 tablespoon cream
1 tablespoon clam juice (reserved from clams)
2 6½ ounce cans minced clams, drained well

1 teaspoon onion, finely minced
1 teaspoon fresh garlic, minced
1 heaping teaspoon fresh parsley, chopped
Dash of hot pepper sauce
10 brown and serve clover leaf rolls
3 tablespoons butter
Chopped parsley
Parmesan cheese

Mix the cream cheese until light, adding the cream and clam juice slowly. Add minced clams, onion, garlic, parsley, and hot sauce. Mix until smooth.

Cut the rolls into three sections. Scoop out the center of each section leaving about $\frac{1}{8}$ inch crust on the sides and bottoms. Lightly butter and fill with the clam mixture. This can be made a day ahead up to this point and refrigerated. When ready to serve, sprinkle with chopped parsley and Parmesan cheese. Bake on a cookie sheet in 350-degree oven for 10 minutes. ❧

Marialice Shary Shivers
♦ CHEESE CORN BREAD

1 cup yellow cornmeal
1 cup all-purpose flour, sifted
$\frac{1}{4}$ cup sugar
$\frac{1}{2}$ teaspoon salt
4 teaspoons baking powder
$1\frac{1}{2}$ cups grated sharp cheddar cheese
1 egg
1 cup milk
$\frac{1}{2}$ cup shortening, softened

Sift together cornmeal, flour, sugar, salt, and baking powder. Stir in cheese. Mix in egg, milk, and shortening. Beat with a rotary beater about 1 minute or until smooth. Do not overbeat. Pour in a greased 8-inch square pan. Bake at 375 degrees for 30 minutes. Cut in squares. Serve hot. Serves 8. ❧

Marialice Shary Shivers
◆ CHICKEN BREASTS GOURMET

4 chicken breasts
Flour to dust chicken
2 tablespoons salt
½ teaspoon thyme
½ teaspoon marjoram
½ teaspoon paprika
Toast
Fat for frying
Sliced almonds

Roll chicken in flour that has been seasoned with salt, thyme, marjoram, and paprika. Fry in fat until golden brown. Arrange chicken in a roaster and cover with the following sauce. Roast at 350 degrees for about 1 hour or until tender. Baste 2 or 3 times to glaze. Arrange chicken on toast, pour sauce over, and sprinkle with almonds to serve. (Split whole breasts in half lengthwise.)

Sauce:
2 cups pineapple juice
¼ cup lemon juice
2 tablespoons cornstarch
2 tablespoons sugar
½ teaspoon curry powder

Mix pineapple juice, lemon juice, cornstarch, sugar, and curry powder in a saucepan. Cook and stir until mixture thickens slightly. ~

Marialice Shary Shivers
◆ OLD-FASHIONED GINGERBREAD
WITH LEMON SAUCE

½ cup butter
½ cup sugar
1 egg

1 cup dark cane syrup
2½ cups flour, sifted
1½ teaspoons soda
1 teaspoon cinnamon
1 teaspoon ginger
½ teaspoon nutmeg
¼ teaspoon cloves
½ teaspoon salt
1 cup boiling water
3 tablespoons preserved (crystallized) ginger, finely chopped
1 cup chopped pecans (optional)

Cream butter, sugar, and egg. Add syrup. Sift flour, soda, cinnamon, ginger, nutmeg, cloves, and salt and add to first mixture. Beat well. Add boiling water, ginger, and nuts. Grease and lightly flour a 14-by-10-inch baking pan. Pour in mixture and bake at 350 degrees for about 25 minutes. When done, cut in generous squares. Pour lemon sauce over squares to serve. ☙

Lemon Sauce:
2 eggs
¾ cup sugar
2 tablespoons flour
Juice of 2 lemons
⅛ teaspoon lemon rind
Pinch salt
2 tablespoons butter
1 cup very hot water

Mix all ingredients except hot water in a saucepan. (An electric blender does this trick in an instant.) When ingredients are well mixed, add hot water. Stir well and cook until thick, but do not boil. Note: For variation, omit the lemon juice and add a little nutmeg and cinnamon. ☙

Marialice Shary Shivers
◆ BROILED TOMATOES BROOKHOLLOW

4 ripe tomatoes, peeled and sliced in half
Italian salad dressing
1 6-oz. jar marinated artichoke hearts
Basil
Bread or cracker crumbs
Parmesan cheese
Butter

Early in the morning, peel and slice tomatoes in halves and lay in baking dish. Pour Italian salad dressing over the tomatoes and refrigerate. One hour before serving, slice artichoke hearts in halves and place one half on each tomato half. Sprinkle over each tomato: basil, crumbs, cheese, and a dab of butter. Bake at 350 degrees for 20 minutes. Serves 8. ⤳

Marialice Shary Shivers
◆ FROSTED GRAPES

These clusters of grapes are beautiful, but whether they are edible or not is questionable because the egg whites are uncooked. Eat them at your own risk, or better yet, use them in a centerpiece or other decorative display.

Several bunches of grapes, left in clusters
4 egg whites
1 cup sugar

Use any color grapes, but dark grapes look best. Wash, but do not separate or remove from stem. Beat egg whites until just foamy. Place sugar in a paper bag. Dip and roll grapes in egg whites; then drop into bag of sugar and shake gently to coat. Remove grapes gently and place on waxed paper to dry. Chill if desired. ⤳

Marialice Shary Shivers

◆ GOLLY'S CUCUMBER SALAD

No record exists as to who Golly was, but this is a delicious light salad.

> ¾ cup boiling water
> 1 package lime Jell-O®
> 1 cup mayonnaise
> 2 3-ounce packages soft cream cheese
> 1 teaspoon horseradish
> 2 tablespoons lemon juice
> ¾ cup grated unpeeled cucumber (drained and squeezed)
> ¼ cup finely chopped green onion.

Dissolve Jell-O® in boiling water, then add mayonnaise, cream cheese, horseradish, and lemon juice. Beat until smooth, then chill until thick. Remove from icebox and add cucumber and onion. Pour into mold and set.

Marialice Shary Shivers

◆ MINCE APPLE CRISP

> 3 pounds tart cooking apples
> ½ cup sugar
> ½ teaspoon ground cinnamon
> ¼ teaspoon ground nutmeg
> 2 teaspoons lemon juice
> ½ cup mincemeat
> ½ cup bourbon
> ⅓ cup honey
> 1 cup coarsely chopped walnuts
> ¼ cup butter, softened
> ½ cup light brown sugar
> ¾ cup sifted flour
> 1 cup heavy cream, whipped

Preheat oven to 375 degrees. Peel and core apples and slice ¼ inch thick. Use enough of the apples to get 8 cups of slices. Combine the sugar with cinnamon and nutmeg. Mix the apples with sugar-spice mixture and lemon juice in a large bowl. Set aside. A word of caution: Be sure the apples are tart, green ones, preferably. Also they should be crisp, not mealy. Taste one, and if it doesn't have a tang, increase the amount of lemon juice. Stir mincemeat, bourbon, and honey together. Add $\frac{1}{2}$ cup of the nuts. Set aside. To make the topping, cream the butter with the brown sugar and add the flour and the remaining $\frac{1}{2}$ cup of nuts. Mix well, using your fingers if necessary. The mixture should be crumbly. Butter an 8-by-8-by-2-inch baking dish or a $1\frac{1}{2}$ quart shallow casserole. Arrange a layer of apples in the bottom, add a layer of the mince-meat mixture. Repeat layers until the dish is full, ending with apples. Sprinkle the sugar-nut mixture over the top. Bake 40 to 45 minutes, or until the apples are tender when tested with a toothpick and the syrup begins to bubble. Serve with whipped cream.

Marialice Shary Shivers
 ◆ CHERRY ANGEL PIE

6 egg whites
2 tablespoons powdered sugar
$\frac{1}{4}$ teaspoon each salt and cream of tartar
$1\frac{1}{2}$ cups sugar
2 teaspoons vanilla
$1\frac{1}{4}$ cups whipping cream
$1\frac{1}{2}$ teaspoons vanilla
2 teaspoons lemon juice
1 can (1 pound, 5 oz.) prepared cherry pie filling

For the meringue shell, beat egg whites until foamy, add salt and cream of tartar, and beat until soft peaks form. Gradually beat in granulated sugar, 1 tablespoon at a time, until stiff peaks form when beater is withdrawn. Beat in the 2 teaspoons vanilla. Spread meringue on the bottom and sides of a buttered 10-inch cheese-cake pan or deep baking pan with removable bottom. Bake in a 300-degree oven for about 1 hour, or until pie is lightly browned and dry on the outside. Let cool (it settles as it cools). Several hours before serving, whip the cream until stiff and flavor with the 1½ teaspoons vanilla and the powdered sugar. Spread in the bottom of the meringue shell. Blend lemon juice into cherry pie filling and carefully spoon filling over the cream. Chill. Makes 8 to 10 servings. Ornament.

Marialice Shary Shivers
♦ JUBILEE SALAD MOLD

This is a wonderful light salad with cherries and raspberries afloat in a ruby ring. The addition of the wine and currant jelly makes for a wonderful flavor. Serve with celery fans.

1 10-oz. package frozen raspberries, thawed
½ cup currant jelly
2 cups water
½ cup sherry
¼ cup lemon juice
2 3-ounce packages red raspberry flavored gelatin
1 pound (2 cups) pitted dark cherries, drained

Drain raspberries, reserving syrup; combine jelly and ½ cup water, heat and stir until jelly melts. Add remaining 1½ cups water and the gelatin; heat and stir. Remove from heat, add sherry, lemon juice, and reserved raspberry syrup; chill until partially set. Fold remaining raspberries and cherries into gelatin and put into 6-cup mold.

Marialice Shary Shivers
♦ CUCUMBER JELLY RING

4 large cucumbers
4 tablespoons gelatin
½ cup water
2 cups boiling water
4 tablespoons vinegar
2 tablespoons lemon juice

¼ teaspoon salt
1 teaspoon grated onion
Dash cayenne

Peel, remove seeds, and grate cucumbers. Soak gelatin in small amount [½ cup] of water; when soft add boiling water, then vinegar and lemon juice. Mix with cucumbers and seasonings. Place in lightly greased ring mold and set in icebox to chill. Serves 8.

Marialice Shary Shivers
◆ CREAM SALAD DRESSING

2 egg yolks
1 tablespoon sugar
½ teaspoon mustard
Salt, pepper
3 tablespoons vinegar
1 teaspoon butter
½ cup cream, whipped

Beat egg yolks, add sugar and seasoning, then vinegar and butter. Cook in a double boiler until thick. Remove from fire, cool. Add whipped cream. Fill center of cucumber ring with purple cabbage slaw and serve with cream salad dressing.

Marialice Shary Shivers
◆ CHICKEN HASH

Poach a 2½-pound chicken in chicken broth for 45 minutes to 1 hour or until it is tender. Remove the chicken from the broth and let it cool. Cut the meat from the bones, dice it, and reserve it.

In a saucepan cook 1 cup wild rice in 4 cups boiling water, stirring frequently, for 20 minutes, or until it is tender, and drain it. In a skillet sauté the rice briefly in 1 or 2 tablespoons butter. Blend in ½ cup sherry and salt and pepper to taste, and cook the rice for 1 or 2 minutes more. Remove the pan from the heat and keep the rice warm.

In a skillet melt $\frac{1}{2}$ stick of butter, blend in 2 tablespoons flour, and slowly stir in 2 cups scalded milk. Cook the sauce, stirring until it is smooth and thickened, and simmer it gently for 10 to 15 minutes. Add $\frac{1}{2}$ cup light cream and salt and pepper to taste and stir in the reserved chicken. Keep the creamed chicken warm.

Prepare a Mornay sauce: In a skillet melt another $\frac{1}{2}$ stick or $\frac{1}{4}$ cup butter, blend in 2 tablespoons flour, and slowly stir in 2 cups scalded milk. Cook the sauce, stirring, until it is smooth and thickened. Add a little of the sauce to 3 egg yolks, beaten, blend the mixture thoroughly, and stir it into the rest of the sauce. Do not let it boil. Let the sauce cool and add 2 tablespoons whipped cream, $\frac{1}{2}$ cup grated Parmesan cheese, and salt and pepper to taste and cook the sauce, without letting it boil, until the cheese is melted and the sauce is blended and thickened.

In a shallow ovenproof serving dish arrange a border of the wild rice and heap the creamed chicken in the center. Pour the Mornay sauce over chicken and rice, sprinkle the top with grated Parmesan cheese, and place the dish under the broiler for a few minutes to brown the top. Serves 4 to 6. ❧

Marialice Shary Shivers
◆ ARTICHOKE DIP

1 (15-ounce) can artichoke hearts, drained
$\frac{1}{3}$ cup mayonnaise
1 tablespoon chopped onion
Juice of $\frac{1}{2}$ medium lemon
3 or 4 slices bacon, cooked crisp and chopped
$\frac{1}{8}$ teaspoon salt
$\frac{1}{8}$ teaspoon pepper
Tabasco®

Chop artichoke hearts. Add mayonnaise, chopped onion, lemon juice, and bacon: mix well. Add salt, pepper, and Tabasco® to taste: chill. Serve with crackers, corn chips, or raw vegetables for dipping. Yields 1 cup. ❧

Marialice Shary Shivers
◆ SHRIMP IN AVOCADO WITH HOT SAUCE

3 good sized ripe avocados
6 very thin slices bacon, fried crisp, drained and crumbled
1½ cups tiny Danish shrimp

Hot Sauce:
3 tablespoons butter
3 tablespoons tomato ketchup
3 tablespoons vinegar
3 tablespoons sugar
3 tablespoons Worcestershire sauce

Place the butter, ketchup, sugar, vinegar, and Worcestershire in the top of a double boiler and bring up to piping hot but do not cook. Cut the avocados in half lengthwise and remove the pits. Clean the centers. Place 1 slice of crumbled bacon in each avocado. Mix the shrimp in the hot sauce and spoon the mixture on top of the bacon in each avocado. Serve immediately. Serves 6. ⤳

Marialice Shary Shivers
◆ MRS. CARRUTH'S MERINGUE CAKE

Although seldom made these days, meringues are truly one of the most enjoyed desserts. This light and airy version was one of Mrs. Shivers's favorites. The maraschino cherries provide an interesting period touch to the finished cake.

5 egg whites
5 tablespoons sugar
½ teaspoon vinegar
Pinch salt
½ teaspoon vanilla

Topping:
½ box (12-ounce size) vanilla wafers
1 cup whipping cream

Maraschino cherries
Chopped nuts

Combine egg whites, sugar, vinegar, salt, and vanilla. Beat until stiff. Grease a square-cornered pan, then line with waxed paper so that paper extends on all sides. Grease sides and bottom of waxed paper. Spread meringue mixture into pan and bake 20 to 25 minutes at 275 degrees or until browned. Cool in pan. Repeat recipe again, pouring second meringue mixture into a second pan. Bake as directed.

While cakes cook, finely crush vanilla wafers for topping. Whip cream. Sprinkle a platter with some crumbs, remove first layer of meringue by grasping sides of waxed paper. Put meringue over crumbs, spread with whipped cream. Add more crumbs, stack second meringue layer, top with crumbs. Refrigerate until ready to serve. Garnish with maraschino cherries or nuts if desired.

Marialice Shary Shivers

◆ PINEAPPLE CUCUMBER MOLD

1 cup crushed pineapple, drained
1 small package lemon gelatin
½ teaspoon salt
½ cup finely grated carrots
1 envelope unflavored gelatin
¼ cup cold water
1 cup mayonnaise
½ cup half and half cream (sour cream may be used)
1 tablespoon grated onion
½ cup finely chopped celery
½ cup grated cucumber, drained
½ teaspoon salt

Drain pineapple. Add enough water to syrup to make 1½ cups liquid. Heat this to boiling and dissolve gelatin. Chill until slightly thickened. Add salt, carrots, and pineapple. Turn into ring or mold. Chill until firm. Soften unflavored gelatin in cold water, then dissolve over hot water. Combine remaining ingredients, adding gelatin, and blend. If desired, tint a pale green with food coloring. Pour over pineapple layer in mold. Chill until firm. Unmold onto serving plate, garnishing with salad greens. Serves 8 to 10. ⤳

✦ JEAN HOUSTON BALDWIN DANIEL ✦
1957–1963

In May, 1957, a twenty-four-pound chunk of plaster fell from the reception hall ceiling and narrowly missed the head of Gov. Price Daniel. The governor had just come down the mansion staircase to shake the hand of a guest. When he stepped forward to greet the visitor, the plaster fell and hit the step behind him. Without missing a beat, he turned to several of the startled guests and said, "You can't say our affairs aren't different." This reception coffee, held in honor of Governor Daniel's sister and aunts, certainly was different. Those attending talked about the events of that day for years.

Following the crashing impact, Jean Daniel rushed to the hall to check on her husband. Upon seeing he was not hurt, she quietly went back to greeting guests and directing them to the State Dining Room, where refreshments were being served. A huge chandelier hung only inches from the gaping hole where the plaster had fallen. The entire ceiling, much of it dating back to the time the mansion was built, was soon replaced. In addition to the ceiling being reworked, the hall foundation was reinforced and the rear wall of the hall was curved to conceal the six steel beams required for the job.

Jean was pleased when the structural work was completed, as the redecorating could then begin. Gold-and-ivory flocked wallpaper with a large design was chosen. Pale gold carpeting was placed in the upper and lower halls and on the staircase. In honor of Mrs. Daniel's work on behalf of the mansion, the State Official Ladies Club purchased a beautiful antique coffee urn for use at receptions. Outside, gardener Martin Westbrook, a fourteen-year veteran at the mansion, continued to cultivate the flowers used at dozens of receptions and events each year.

The Daniel family was thrilled when a 1958 General Electric console television was installed shortly after the repairs and redecorating were completed. It was the first television set at the mansion that was state property rather than a personal possession. The family and Shawn, a one-legged parakeet, enjoyed life at the home of the chief executive of Texas.

The pace of entertaining and the constant stream of visitors kept the daily routine interesting. One evening in 1960, well after midnight, two visitors arrived at the mansion. John F. Kennedy and Lyndon Baines Johnson, campaigning in the state, had stopped over in Austin for a speaking engagement. The kitchen staff had long since gone home, so Jean hurriedly set about getting refreshments together for the two men. The Daniel children were all on what they referred to as a "pimple diet," so the only beverage to be found in the refrigerator was skim milk. Jean sent her son Houston to find out what the men would prefer, water or the milk. They and the governor were served skim milk, and following several hours of conversation, all retired for the evening. John F. Kennedy was placed in the Houston room, but with his bad back he found the Sam Houston bed to be too soft. He was given the Daniels' "Pineapple" bed, which had that symbol of hospitality carved on each bedpost. Other distinguished guests at the mansion during Jean Daniel's time as first lady included Adolfo López Mateos, who was president of Mexico, and Konrad Adenauer, chancellor of West Germany.

The constant activity at the mansion only served to strengthen Jean's love of history. After the ceiling came crashing down, she knew she it was time to carry out an extensive study of the mansion's past. She collected mementos that formed the basis of the mansion collections. She collected information that had never been compiled previously, and it was eventually published as *The Texas Governor's Mansion* in 1984 by the Texas State Library and Archives Commission and the Sam Houston Regional Library and Research Center.

Jean Houston Baldwin Daniel
◆ TEXAS STAR SALAD

In the mansion, Jean used a mold in the shape of a Texas star and served this salad on a large tray garnished with small tomatoes, avocado slices, olives, celery, artichokes, carrot curls, and radishes.

 1 package cooked frozen shrimp or 1 pound fresh shrimp, diced
 1 can undiluted tomato soup
 3 packages cream cheese
 2 envelopes gelatin
 $\frac{1}{2}$ cup water
 $1\frac{1}{2}$ cups mayonnaise
 $\frac{1}{2}$ cup chopped celery
 $\frac{1}{2}$ cup chopped green bell pepper
 $\frac{1}{2}$ cup chopped onion

Clean, de-vein, and cook shrimp. Set aside. Heat soup, then add cheese and stir until well blended. Dissolve gelatin in tap water. Pour soup over gelatin in large bowl; stir until gelatin is dissolved. Add mayonnaise, celery, green pepper, onion, and shrimp. Blend, then pour into mold that has been rinsed with cold water. ⬳

Jean Houston Baldwin Daniel
◆ CHUTNEY

This chutney may be kept in the deep freeze for future use, as can the grated fresh coconut in the condiment and relish list that follows the next recipe, for Chicken Curry.

 1 cup juice from watermelon preserves or spiced peaches
 $\frac{1}{2}$ cup vinegar
 $\frac{1}{2}$ cup water
 1 cup sugar
 1 teaspoon salt
 1 tablespoon cinnamon
 1 tablespoon ground cloves

1 tablespoon curry powder
1 teaspoon white pepper

Boil together the above ingredients and then add:

1 cup watermelon preserves
1 cup pineapple chunks
1 cup seedless raisins
¾ cup green or red peppers
2 large apples, diced
½ cup candied orange peel

Boil until thick and seal in jars.

Jean Houston Baldwin Daniel
◆ CHICKEN CURRY

Families in southern Asia used to serve curry by having boys carry each condiment, and so they identified the dish as a two-, six-, ten-, or even fifteen-boy curry, depending upon the number of young men needed to serve each course. The condiments and relishes are served in individual dishes, and guests choose the ones they prefer to make the meal exotic and unusual.

1 large chicken
Salt
¼ teaspoon cayenne pepper (pepper pods may be used)

Boil the chicken until tender, adding cayenne pepper while chicken is boiling. Salt to taste. Let cool. Remove meat from bones and cut in large cubes. Add meat to following sauce according to instructions (turkey, lamb, beef, or seafood may be substituted).

Sauce:
4 cups stock
1½ onion, chopped
1½ cups celery

2 green apples, peeled and diced
3 squash, medium sized, chopped
1 green bell pepper, chopped
1 can mushroom pieces
Milk from one coconut
2 tablespoons curry powder
2 tablespoons Worcestershire sauce
4 tablespoons flour

Combine stock, onion, celery, apples, squash, green pepper, mushrooms with liquid, coconut milk, curry powder, and Worcestershire sauce. Boil all until vegetables are soft and well done. Add flour that has been browned in chicken fat or vegetable oil, to thicken. If sauce is too thick, add a can of bouillon or celery soup. At this point, "taste for balance," as a veteran cook once advised. This means the sauce might need a little more curry powder, a dash of cayenne, a pinch of salt, a pinch of thyme, a small portion of ginger, or a small clove of garlic chopped fine.

About 30 minutes before serving (or time enough to ensure the dish will be piping hot), add the cubed meat to sauce and heat in a casserole or double boiler. Serve over fluffy rice, with a selection of condiments and relishes. The success of curry lies in the condiments or relishes that are served with it.

Some condiments are considered "musts," and these have been marked with an asterisk in the following list. Others are optional with the hostess, who can prepare them ahead of time. Ten to fifteen side dishes arranged around the curry and rice make a colorful and delicious whole-meal party dish. This recipe serves from eight to ten people.

Suggested Condiments:
*Chutney
*Grated fresh coconut
*Crushed peanuts
*Crumbled crisp bacon
*Riced hard-boiled egg whites
*Riced hard-boiled egg yolks
*Chopped crystallized ginger

*Relish, either sweet or sour
*Boiled puffed raisins
*Minced green onions
Tomatoes cut up fine
Diced bananas sprinkled with lemon juice, to keep them
    from turning dark
Diced bell pepper
Broiled mushrooms
Thinly sliced radishes (very colorful and good)
Very small chunks of pineapple
Thin marinated avocado slices
Crumbled French-fried onions (may be canned ones)

Jean Houston Baldwin Daniel

◆ ROLL RECIPE OF MRS. ROBERT A. JOHN

Mrs. Robert A. John, granddaughter of Sam Houston and grandmother of Jean Daniel, used this recipe for decades. More than
likely it predates even Mrs. John. It is a delicious addition to most
any meal.

I cake Fleischmann's yeast in $\frac{1}{2}$ cup cold water
$\frac{1}{2}$ cup butter
3 tablespoons sugar
I teaspoon salt
$\frac{1}{2}$ cup hot water
I egg, beaten
3 cups unsifted flour

Soak cake of Fleischmann's yeast in $\frac{1}{2}$ cup of cold water. Cream 3
tablespoons of sugar and I teaspoon of salt in $\frac{1}{2}$ cup of butter.
Add $\frac{1}{2}$ cup hot water. Stir until dissolved. When cool, add I well-
beaten egg, the yeast, and 3 cups of unsifted flour. When well
mixed, grease slightly and put in a greased bowl. Set into refrigerator about 12 hours. Make into rolls about 2 hours before
baking and allow to rise. Bake at 325 degrees for 20 or 25 minutes
until golden. ➤

Jean Houston Baldwin Daniel
◆ MY FAVORITE COOKIE RECIPE

As the mother of four schoolchildren who loved cookies, Jean Daniel always tried to keep a supply available, both baked and unbaked. Doubling this recipe from her Great-Aunt Jennie always ensured that there would be plenty of cookies on hand when they were needed.

    2 sticks of butter
    1 cup granulated sugar
    1 cup brown sugar
    2 eggs, beaten
    1 teaspoon soda
    1 teaspoon salt
    1 teaspoon vanilla flavoring
    2 cups pecans, broken
    4 cups flour

Let butter soften in a large mixing bowl; mix well with sugar and brown sugar. Add eggs, soda, salt, and vanilla flavoring. Add 2 cups of pecan meats and mix well. Gradually stir in flour. Keep stirring or working until all is thoroughly mixed. Tear off six pieces of waxed paper about 18 inches long. Divide the dough into six parts. Shape each part on the sheet into a long roll, working the dough so that the roll will be round and compact. Store in the icebox until cold and firm. Slice in thin slices and cook on the waxed paper dough was rolled in on a cookie sheet. Bake in oven about 350 degrees until light brown. Remove the batch from the cookie sheet and let cookies cool on the waxed paper; then they are easily removed to cookie jar. Will keep in cookie jar indefinitely but are better fresh from the oven. Each roll should make about three to four dozen cookies. ≈

Jean Houston Baldwin Daniel
◆ TEXAS TEA CAKES

This recipe was one of Jean Daniel's favorites. It has been used by six generations of her family.

 1 cup butter
 1 cup sugar
 2 eggs, well beaten
 1 teaspoon baking powder
 1 teaspoon vanilla or lemon flavoring
 ½ teaspoon salt
 3½ cups flour
 Raisins, optional

Mix as written. When it is stiff enough to handle, take a little of the dough at a time and roll thin on floured board or waxed paper. Cut into cookie shape using a State of Texas–shaped cutter. Dredge with sugar and place a raisin where your city should be located. Bake in a 350-degree oven until edges are light brown. Remove cookies from sheet leaving them on waxed paper to cool. Pack in tins. This recipe should make five dozen cookies. ≈

Jean Houston Baldwin Daniel
◆ SHRIMP-CHEESE MOLDED SALAD

Although molded gelatin salads are not as popular as they once were, this one is truly exceptional. It is easily prepared the day before it is needed.

 1 can undiluted tomato soup
 3 packages Philadelphia cream cheese
 2 envelopes gelatin dissolved in ½ cup water
 1½ cups mayonnaise
 1½ cups chopped celery, green pepper, and onion (combined)
 1 package cooked frozen shrimp, cut up, or 1 pound fresh shrimp cooked and cut up

Heat soup, add cheese, and blend well. Pour over gelatin mixture in large bowl. Stir. Add mayonnaise, chopped celery, etc., and shrimp. Pour into mold that has been rinsed with cold water. Congeal in refrigerator. ⇘

✦ NEW TRENDS ✦
1962–1972

Entertaining at the mansion changed considerably during the first few years of the 1960s. Texas food trends followed those of the nation. Far from the Texas "White House," the Kennedys were turning the national White House into a glittering center for entertaining. Glamorous Jackie Kennedy captured the nation's attention as a gracious hostess. Her dinner parties, prepared by a French chef, raised formal entertaining to an art form. Beautiful, easily prepared food was something everyone wanted.

On television's *The French Chef,* Julia Child was also at the peak of her popularity. If the food served at the White House did not inspire Texas cooks, then Julia Child's first cookbook and nationally televised show did. Her detailed instructions for formerly daunting dishes such as coq au vin or chocolate mousse made cuisine, once considered exotic, achievable for the average cook. Cooking in general became a popular avocation far beyond merely providing workable meals for one's family and guests. Following this trend, a new era of elegant Texas-style entertaining at the mansion began.

✦ IDANELL BRILL CONNALLY ✦
1963–1969

Despite the fact that Gov. John Connally and his wife, known as Nellie, usually served elaborate and elegant food at parties, the governor's favorite supper was corn bread crumbled in sweet milk. When Nellie, a popular former "Sweetheart" at the University of Texas, would answer the door of the mansion to greet guests, she would smile and say, "Y'all come in this house!" Her style at the mansion never failed to put guests at ease.

The Connally family, Christmas in the Mansion, 1963.
Courtesy Friends of the Governor's Mansion.

When the Connallys arrived at the mansion, the family was short one member. Patch, the family's long-legged dachshund, was left in Fort Worth. Mark Connally, then ten years old, gloomily reported that "Mother gave him to the maid." It was one of the first times the mansion had been without an official "First Pet."

The family's first meal at the mansion was an interesting affair. They had just moved in, their clothing and other personal effects had not yet arrived, and they were exhausted after all the inauguration activities. There was, at first, no cook, no housekeeper, no maid, and no porter for the large house, so Annie Menzel, a staff member in charge of taking care of the family at that time, cooked supper. She filled the plates in the kitchen and brought them to the table. When Nellie asked her to bring the meat and potatoes to the table, for seconds, Miss Annie replied that she could not as there were no serving bowls. After supper, Nellie checked every cupboard downstairs, and sure enough, no bowls or serving pieces of any kind were to be found.

A full staff was eventually brought on board and was paid through a state allotment. Nellie went through a series of maids before finding just the right person. Often the First Lady, who loved to cook, would find herself in the kitchen with her sleeves rolled up just as the guests would begin to arrive. Her favorite cookbooks were *The Joy of Cooking* and *The New York Times Cookbook,* and her experiments in the kitchen were usually successful. Favorite foods included black-eyed peas and fresh corn on the cob cooked on an open fire. She admitted that while it sounded "hideous," it tasted grand.

Florence Morton, the mansion secretary, and then Evelyn Allen, both assisted Nellie. Together, they coordinated an increasing number of social events and receptions, including a coffee for the wives of the astronauts. The most important and famous reception Nellie ever planned never occurred. President and Mrs. Kennedy were scheduled to come to the Governor's Mansion after their luncheon stop at the Trade Mart in Dallas. She had been readying the mansion for weeks, and the governor wanted everyone there to meet the president. Nellie later wrote of her original plans for that tragic day, "I thought I had everything arranged—even down to what the children would wear. But what hostess doesn't have a qualm or two when she's going to entertain a President and his First Lady?" After the tragedy she stayed by her husband's side at Parkland Hospital while he recovered from his wounds.

During her less traumatic days as first lady, Nellie established the first formal landscaping plan for the mansion. It was still in use as the twenty-first century began. In 1966, original fencing from the Capitol was removed from storage and placed around the Governor's Mansion property. At the back of the house, the porte cochere was extended to accommodate the larger cars of the time. In 1968, the grounds of the mansion, covering two acres, were transformed into

*First Lady Nellie Connally's efforts to acquire more silver and
serving pieces for entertaining at the Mansion were successful, as this 1968
photograph from the* Austin American Statesman *shows.*
Courtesy *Austin American Statesman.*

an imaginative arrangement of flower beds with flowering shrubs and trees. The addition of patios, terraces, and walkways created formal garden areas bordered by an expansive lawn.

The first lady also began a campaign to outfit the mansion with silver, crystal, and other supplies needed for entertaining. It was not for the Connally family personally that she was collecting. In fact, she is often quoted as stating that her family could have gotten by drinking from jelly glasses if they had to. Before the new state silver and crystal arrived, she would borrow serving trays and dishes from wherever she could. Setting the table for twenty-four guests was a daunting task when the mansion's flatware supply included only twenty-two butter knives. During dinner parties it was not uncommon for the mansion steward to go around and gather used teaspoons and forks and whisk them away to the kitchen, where they could be quickly washed and used with the next course. Nellie hoped to enlarge the silver service to accommodate sixty people, with the number of teaspoons and salad forks being brought to at least one hundred.

Nellie's efforts were successful. One of the largest gifts came from the children of the late Herman Brown, the noted philanthropist. They gave the mansion ten serving pieces from their father's collection of antique silver. The State Official Ladies Club presented Nellie with a silver punch bowl, tray, and ladle. The Senate Ladies Club presented the mansion with two vegetable dishes.

Although Nellie left the Governor's Mansion much better equipped for gracious entertaining, she and her husband remained well known for their down-to-earth hospitality. When they attended their first Governors Conference, they adhered to the tradition of bringing presents to the other governors and first ladies. "I made Picosa Grape Jelly," Nellie noted, "and John picked the wild grapes at our Picosa ranch." She packed the jelly in small jars and labeled them "Picosa Grape Jelly / Picked by John / Jellied by Nellie / For your breakfast pleasure." Nellie had Neiman Marcus wrap the jars in grand style. The governors and first ladies laughed when the small jar of jelly appeared out of the beautiful package. "Every year," she reported, "they always asked for more—but in larger jars!"

Some of the recipes included in this section are from one of Nellie's own dinner menus:

Shrimp Newburgh served over Rice
Squash Pie
Mixed Greens Tossed Salad with Vinaigrette Dressing
Orange Biscuits
Iced Tea
Coffee
Picosa Peach Ice Cream or Pecan Pie

Idanell Brill Connally
◆ SHRIMP NEWBURGH

2 tablespoons butter
2 tablespoons flour
$\frac{3}{4}$ teaspoon salt
Dash cayenne pepper
2 cups of half and half
4 egg yolks, well beaten
1 pound peeled, de-veined shrimp
$\frac{1}{4}$ cup dry sherry

Melt butter, stir in flour, salt, cayenne pepper. When well blended, add half and half, cook over low heat until smooth and mixture boils. Stir a little sauce into the egg yolks and beat well; add to the rest of sauce. Makes about 2 cups. Sauté shrimp in butter and a little sherry. Serves 6 to 8 people. ❧

Idanell Brill Connally
◆ SQUASH PIE

This recipe was used by Annie Menzel when she cooked for Governor and Mrs. Connally.

Peel about 2 pounds medium size squash. Cut into medium slices. Add cup well-chopped onions. Cook in enough water to cover. Cook until well done. Stir constantly. When done, press through coarse sieve. Pour into mixing bowl.

Add:

$\frac{1}{2}$ teaspoon white pepper

3 well beaten eggs

$\frac{1}{4}$ cup melted butter

1 teaspoon salt

$\frac{3}{4}$ cup sugar

Mix well. Pour into 9-inch casserole bowl. Crush 30 saltine crackers fine. Sprinkle over top of squash until entire bowl is covered. Bake in oven at 350 degrees for 45 minutes. ～

Idanell Brill Connally

✦ CHRISTMAS BLACK CHERRY MOLD

2 cans (16 ounces each) pitted black Bing cherries

1 can (20 ounces) crushed pineapple

3 packages black cherry gelatin (3-ounce size)

4 cups liquid, comprised of 7-Up® and fruit juices

1 cup chopped nuts

3 ounces cream cheese, softened

Drain cherries and pineapple, reserving juices. Add 2 cups boiling water to gelatin and stir until dissolved. Add 7-Up® to reserved juices to make 4 cups liquid total. Add liquid to gelatin, stir, and set aside to gel until consistency of egg whites. Stir nuts into softened cream cheese. Stuff the cherries with cream cheese mixture. Add pineapple to gelatin. Rinse a $2\frac{1}{2}$-quart ring mold with cold water. Pour $\frac{1}{3}$ of the partially set gelatin into mold. Add a layer of stuffed cherries, a layer of gelatin, a layer of cherries, and top with remaining gelatin. Chill until firm. Unmold on a bed of Romaine or Bibb lettuce. Surround the mold with clusters of assorted grapes and place a bowl of Nellie's Salad Topping in center. Serves 16 to 18. ～

Idanell Brill Connally
◆ NELLIE'S SALAD TOPPING

This salad dressing is delicious and relatively simple to prepare.

½ cup sugar
2 tablespoons flour
1 cup pineapple juice
1 egg slightly beaten
2 tablespoons butter
1 cup cream, whipped
½ cup shredded American cheese
3 tablespoons Parmesan cheese

In saucepan, combine sugar and flour. Stir in pineapple juice and egg. Cook over low heat until mixture has thickened. Remove from heat. Add butter. Cool and chill. Fold in whipped cream and half the American and Parmesan cheeses. Spoon into a bowl and sprinkle with remaining cheese. Serve with Christmas Black Cherry Mold. ⤚

Idanell Brill Connally
◆ PICOSA FRESH PEACH ICE CREAM

Nellie Connally wrote on this recipe, "We all loved it. . . . [It] makes my mouth water today!"

6 eggs
1 (14-ounce) can sweetened condensed milk
1 cup sugar
2 cups mashed fresh peaches
2 teaspoons vanilla
Milk to fill freezer 2 inches from top

Mix all ingredients together except milk. Pour into freezer; add milk, stir, and freeze. Yields 1½ gallons. ⤚

Idanell Brill Connally
♦ ORANGE CUSTARD PUDDING

This recipe came from Mrs. Connally's paternal grandmother, Mrs. A. W. Brill. Nellie liked the orange flavor, but Governor Connally preferred it plain.

> 2 oranges
> 1 teaspoon sugar
> 1 quart milk
> 3 egg yolks
> 1 cup sugar
> 3 tablespoons flour
> 1 teaspoon vanilla
> 3 egg whites (4 makes it even better)
> 2 teaspoons sugar

Peel, skin, and cut oranges in pieces. Sprinkle the 1 teaspoon of sugar over oranges and set aside. Scald milk but do not boil. Mix egg yolks, 1 cup of sugar, and flour, then slowly add to scalded milk. Cook over medium heat until slightly thick. Remove from heat and add vanilla and blend. Pour into baking dish or individual custard baking dishes. Drop the pieces of sugared orange into the custard. Beat egg whites until stiff, gradually adding 2 teaspoons of sugar. Beat until smooth and shiny. Top custards with sugared egg whites and broil in oven until meringue turns golden brown. Cool and refrigerate. Serve ice cold. This can be a delicious basic custard recipe if the orange pieces are omitted. Coconut or bananas can be added for variety. ~

Idanell Brill Connally
♦ ORANGE BISCUITS

Annie Menzel made these biscuits all the time. She took good care of the Connallys and was loved by the whole family.

> 2 cups flour
> 4 tablespoons sugar

1 teaspoon salt
2½ teaspoons baking powder
4 tablespoons shortening
Rind of one orange, grated and chopped
1 cup liquid—half milk, half fresh orange juice

Sift dry ingredients together. Cut in shortening, mix in orange rind. Pour liquid all at one time, mix lightly enough to bind ingredients together. Roll on lightly floured board ¾ inch thick. Cut with biscuit cutter. Bake at 450 degrees for 20 minutes until golden brown. Yields about 8 servings.

Idanell Brill Connally
♦ SAUSAGE ROLLS

1 package dry yeast
½ cup warm water
1 cup milk
¼ cup sugar
½ cup margarine
1 teaspoon salt
2 eggs well beaten
4 cups flour
Sausage links

Dissolve yeast in warm water. Heat milk in saucepan; add sugar, margarine, and salt; stir. Pour milk mixture into mixing bowl and cool to lukewarm. Add well-beaten eggs and dissolved yeast. Add flour, a little at a time, beating well until dough resembles a soft sponge. Chill dough in icebox overnight. Allow dough to rise 30 to 45 minutes. Roll out dough to ⅛-inch thickness. Cut strips the size of sausage and wrap each sausage as in a blanket. Dip in melted butter, place on cookie sheet bake at 350 degrees until slightly browned. The sausage rolls may be frozen before the dough is baked. ⤳

Idanell Brill Connally
+ CRUSTY CORN BREAD

This recipe for corn bread is the one Nellie used in the mansion. It
is a family favorite.

  1 cup flour
  1 teaspoon salt
  3 teaspoons baking powder
  2 tablespoons sugar
  $\frac{3}{4}$ cup yellow cornmeal
  2 eggs
  1 cup milk
  $\frac{1}{4}$ cup melted shortening

Sift together flour, salt, baking powder, and sugar. Then mix with
cornmeal. Combine eggs and milk and add to the dry ingredients, beating well. Add melted shortening. Bake in 400-degree
oven for about 20 minutes. ~

Idanell Brill Connally
+ ARTICHOKE BOTTOMS WITH SHRIMP (SERVES 6)

  1 jar artichoke bottoms
  3 tablespoons olive oil
  1$\frac{1}{2}$ tablespoons wine vinegar
  Salt and pepper to taste
  1 cup cooked shrimp, cut into small pieces
  $\frac{1}{2}$ cup green pepper, finely diced
  $\frac{1}{3}$ cup mayonnaise
  2 teaspoons lemon juice
  Paprika to taste
  6 cooked whole shrimp

Marinate the artichoke bottoms in a mixture of olive oil, wine
vinegar, salt, and pepper for about 1 hour. Mix the cut-up shrimp,
green pepper, and mayonnaise seasoned with lemon juice and
paprika. Drain the artichoke bottoms and place on serving plates.

Pile the shrimp mixture on top of each artichoke bottom, cover with a thin layer of mayonnaise, and garnish each with a whole shrimp. Very pretty and delicious. ↞

Idanell Brill Connally
◆ BROILED STUFFED MUSHROOMS
(MAKES 12 HORS D'OEUVRES)

12 large mushrooms
3 tablespoons butter
1 small onion, chopped
1 cup bread crumbs
½ cup chopped cooked shrimp (or chicken, ham, or chopped nuts)
2 tablespoons cream or sherry
Salt and pepper to taste
Sweet marjoram, rosemary, or oregano to taste

Preheat broiler; remove and chop mushroom stems. Heat 1 tablespoon of the butter in a skillet and add onion and chopped mushroom stems; cook about 2 minutes. Add crumbs, shrimp, enough cream or sherry to moisten, and all the seasonings. Place mushroom caps on a baking sheet and brush with remaining butter, melted. Broil, cup side down, in preheated broiler about 2 minutes. Invert and fill with the stuffing. Brush with melted butter and broil about 3 minutes longer. ↞

Idanell Brill Connally
◆ GOVERNOR CONNALLY'S BEEF TACOS

These tacos make a wonderful Sunday night supper at home.

1 medium white onion
Enough bacon to make a good pan of dripping
1 pound ground beef
Head of lettuce
Favorite picante sauce
Salt, pepper, and cumin to taste

Corn tortillas
4 ripe tomatoes
Sharp cheddar cheese
Optional:
1 4-ounce can of green chilies
1 tablespoon chili powder
Minced garlic to taste

Sauté chopped onion in a little bacon drippings, then add ground meat. Cook until done. Add finely chopped lettuce and a sound dash of picante sauce. Salt and pepper to taste.

Fry tortillas in hot oil. Drain on paper towels, tortillas either flat or folded. Fill with meat mixture. Add chopped lettuce and tomato. Top with grated cheese and serve immediately. Have chopped onions and more picante available for those who desire them. ⤳

Idanell Brill Connally
◆ CORN PONE

If there is a common thread that runs throughout the food history of the Governor's Mansion, it is corn pone. This version was a favorite of the Connally family before, during, and after their time at the mansion. It is delicious when served very hot with butter. Mrs. Connally wrote that this corn pone was "very fattening but good."

1 cup cornmeal
1 teaspoon baking powder
$\frac{1}{2}$ teaspoon baking soda
2 tablespoons margarine, butter, or bacon fat
$\frac{1}{3}$ to $\frac{1}{2}$ cup water or milk

Mix cornmeal, baking powder, and soda. Rub in margarine or butter, until it is crumb-like. Mix in milk until it is at a dropping consistency. Mold in hands or drop by spoonfuls and fry in a hot frying pan in margarine, butter, or bacon fat. Drain. ⤳

✦ IMA MAE SMITH SMITH ✦
1969–1973

Ima Mae Smith was a popular first lady whose sense of history about the mansion and its furnishings led her to compile a booklet about the house. She was keenly aware of the importance of keeping and documenting the treasures in the home's collection. One of her most lasting contributions was the restoration of the Napoleon clock, which had been purchased for the mansion in the 1940s by Miss Ima Hogg. The ornate long-case clock, reputed to have belonged to the famous French ruler, had quit working and been relegated to the basement. Former first lady Marialice Shivers visited with Ima Mae about the old timepiece, and shortly thereafter it was brought out of storage. Ima Mae had it restored by inmates of the Texas prison system. It now occupies a place of honor on the second floor of the mansion. As one state trooper working at the mansion quipped many years before, the clock does everything—except keep time.

Ima Mae oversaw a fairly massive restoration campaign during her stay in the mansion. New paint, wallpaper, and carpet, in shades of spring green, were applied and installed. The carpeting on the lower floor of the mansion dated to the late 1950s and was beginning to show wear. During 1969 alone, thirty-eight thousand visitors walked on it.

The lower parlors were repainted in a soft blue tone. Furniture was refinished and reupholstered by inmates of the Ramsey Prison Unit at Huntsville. A small bench, formerly stored in the mansion basement, and a sofa, stored in the garage, were restored and place back in the mansion. The odd little powder room off the State Dining Room was reworked and updated. The powder room had been created years earlier for Blanch Stevenson. It featured red rose wallpaper and had a green tile floor with a drain in the middle, a small commode, and a basin that hung on the wall. For all those years it had been the only public restroom on the first floor. Remodeling included lowering the ceilings and adding new fixtures. The rose-patterned wallpaper was replaced and a small chandelier that had previously hung in this small powder room was reinstalled.

The State Dining Room retained its flocked red wall coverings, and the red carpeting was shampooed. The trim throughout the room was repainted. The chairs, previously covered in red leather, were reupholstered in antique white satin brocade. In the family dining room, the ancient rug, possibly dating to the Sayers administration, was replaced and the floors were refinished. All the furnishings were inventoried and stored, and the empty rooms got a thorough cleaning. When Ima Mae could not find a professional firm willing to clean the mansion chandeliers, she asked the mansion porter to do it. His patient efforts yielded professional results.

The mansion kitchen was freshened, and new sheet vinyl in a pattern named Algiers was put down throughout the service areas. New washer and dryer connections were installed, and a small back closet was created to house the coats and wraps of mansion guests.

Outdoors, the landscaping project initiated by Nellie Connally was maintained and improved. The Austin Rose Society created new rose beds. Azaleas were replanted, and the giant red cannas, donated by Texas Tech, were divided and reset. A new riding lawn mower was purchased, much to the relief of the groundskeeper. Although a sprinkler system was needed, the mansion grounds were still watered by one man in a daylong process.

Ima Mae left the mansion better than she found it. The Napoleon clock she so lovingly had restored still enjoys a prominent spot in the upstairs hall. It still does not keep time.

~

Ima Mae Smith Smith
♦ DATE PUDDING

1 cup sugar
2 teaspoons baking powder
1 cup flour
1 cup milk
1 teaspoons vanilla
$\frac{1}{2}$ teaspoon salt
1 cup dates, chopped
1 cup nuts, chopped
$1\frac{1}{2}$ cups brown sugar

2 cups hot water
2 tablespoons butter
Whipped cream to garnish
Maraschino cherries to garnish

Combine 1 cup sugar, baking powder, flour, milk, vanilla, salt, dates, and nuts. Simmer together for a few minutes the brown sugar, hot water, and butter. Pour brown sugar liquid in a baking dish and cover the top with the batter. Don't stir. Cook 20 minutes at 450 degrees. Serve with whipped cream topped with a maraschino cherry. Serves 12. Ornament. ✦

Ima Mae Smith Smith
✦ BAKED TROUT, RED SNAPPER, OR BASS

1 (14- to 16-inch) trout, red snapper, or bass
3 to 4 fresh onions, sliced
Butter
Garlic salt, to taste
Salt, to taste
Black pepper, to taste
1 to 1½ ounces or more red wine
1 lemon

Place fish on large piece of heavy foil. Put 2 or 3 fresh onions inside and 1 out. Add a pat of butter inside and out. Sprinkle well with garlic salt, salt, and black pepper. Add wine. Squeeze lemon over fish then drop the rind into package. Carefully wrap fish in foil (sprayed with vegetable spray.) Bake over hot coals or in a 450-degree oven for 30 minutes on one side, turn and bake 15 more minutes. Open and enjoy. ✦

Ima Mae Smith Smith
✦ CHESS PIE

Chess pie has appeared, at one time or another, on practically every first lady's table since the mansion was first occupied. This version is slightly more custard-like in texture, and very good.

4 eggs, slightly beaten
1½ cups sugar
1 teaspoon vanilla
1 tablespoon vinegar
¼ cup melted butter

Beat eggs then add remaining ingredients and blend well. Pour into unbaked, 9-inch pie shell. Bake 45 minutes at 375 degrees. If you like the flavor of nutmeg, sprinkle a little over the top. ❧

Ima Mae Smith Smith
◆ CUCUMBER SALAD

1 package lemon Jell-O®
1 cup hot water
½ cup mayonnaise
1 tablespoon vinegar
1 large grated cucumber
1 small grated onion
½ pint small curd cottage cheese
½ cup broken nutmeats (your choice)
Pinch of salt

Dissolve Jell-O® in hot water. Add mayonnaise and vinegar. Chill until thick. Drain grated cucumber and add along with onion and cottage cheese to thickened Jell-O®. Add nutmeats and salt. Chill until set. ❧

Ima Mae Smith Smith
◆ CHICKEN WALDORF SALAD

1½ cups chicken, cooked and diced
⅔ cup whole green grapes
½ cup chopped pecans
⅔ cup chopped celery
½ teaspoon salt
⅔ cup mayonnaise

Blend all ingredients together and chill before serving.
Serves 4. ⤚

Ima Mae Smith Smith
◆ TEXAS HASH

2 onions, medium size
1 cup chopped celery
3 tablespoons cooking oil
1 pound ground steak
2 cups of tomatoes or juice
16 ounces elbow noodles, cooked
1 teaspoon chili powder
2 teaspoons salt
½ teaspoon pepper

Cook onions, celery in oil until yellow. Add meat and cook until
redness leaves. Add tomatoes, noodles, and seasoning and mix.
Put into large oiled casserole. Cover and bake at 350 degrees for
45 minutes. Serves 8. ⤚

Ima Mae Smith Smith
◆ PECAN PIE

3 eggs, slightly beaten
¾ cup sugar
1 cup corn syrup (light)
1 teaspoon vanilla
¼ teaspoon salt
1 cup pecans

Mix first five ingredients together. Pour over pecans in an
unbaked shell. Bake at 350 degrees for 40 minutes. ⤚

◆ BETTY JANE SLAUGHTER BRISCOE ◆
1973–1979

The Briscoe family has Texas roots back to 1832, when ancestors settled in what is now Fort Bend County. Andrew Briscoe signed the Texas Declaration of Independence, led a company of volunteers in the Battle of San Jacinto, and was appointed the first judge of Harris County by Sam Houston. Gov. Dolph Briscoe's father, Dolph, Sr., moved his family to Uvalde in 1910 and established a cattle business. Upon his father's death, Dolph, Jr., became the operator of the ranch. By 1972, Dolph was the state's largest individual landowner.

When Dolph was elected governor, he and First Lady Janey moved much of their own furniture into the private quarters of the Governor's Mansion. The furniture that had been in the rooms was stored in the carriage house at the back of the mansion property. The one thing they did not bring was their own bedding and mattress. Following a very uncomfortable first night, they sent to the ranch for their own bed.

Janey Briscoe loved living in the mansion. During her time in the house, she oversaw extensive redecorating and influenced every detail of the mansion interiors with her own special touch. The most apparent reflection of her tastes was the use of red throughout the home. Red carpeting covered the floors downstairs, and she repainted the traditional blue rooms in white to achieve a more harmonious effect with the red carpeting. Huge draperies with a contrasting border of gold and red hung in the downstairs rooms. Upstairs in the private quarters, Janey and Dolph added a large wood-burning fireplace.

The Sam Houston bedroom was redone with funds and gifts from the Arts and Humanities Commission. The room was lightened and the original floors stripped, sanded, and refinished. Janey replaced the heavy draperies with less formal versions and ordered a new hand-crocheted white coverlet for the bed. On the floors she placed a beautiful Baktiari rug. In the transom over the door, she placed a specially designed glass panel with the initial "H" etched in the center.

Janey loved to cook and was well known for her home-cooked

meals. She often prepared the evening meal herself, which she and Dolph would eat late, usually well after the staff had gone home. She used fresh, locally grown produce and beef from their ranch. As her six years in the house drew to a close, she made arrangements to have their personal belongings shipped back to the ranch in Uvalde. She and Dolph left the mansion and took a long vacation in New York and Europe. Although the splendors she saw while traveling were magnificent, she often said that nothing compared to her time in the Texas Governor's Mansion.

Betty Jane Slaughter Briscoe
♦ SPINACH RING

The Briscoes served many business luncheons at the Governor's Mansion, and Janey found that men preferred medium-rare rolled roasts or sirloin strips. The roasts were prepared simply, merely seasoned with salt and pepper. Occasionally dried cayenne pepper was inserted into the meat as an additional seasoning and a surprise. The steaks were always charbroiled to medium rare. This spinach ring is a perfect accompaniment.

$2\frac{1}{2}$ cups chopped cooked spinach
1 cup milk
3 tablespoons butter
3 tablespoons flour
$\frac{1}{3}$ teaspoon nutmeg
1 teaspoon grated onion
2 tablespoons lemon juice
2 eggs, well beaten
1 teaspoon salt

Mix together and pour into a well-buttered quart ring mold. Place in pan of hot water and bake at 375 degrees until firm. Unmold on hot round tray or plate. Can be made and served in individual molds. ◜

Betty Jane Slaughter Briscoe
✦ RIO FRIO RANCH ROLLS

1 cup boiling water
1 cup shortening
1 cup sugar
1½ teaspoons salt
2 eggs, beaten
2 packages dry yeast
1 cup warm water
6 cups flour, unsifted

In mixing bowl pour boiling water over shortening and dissolve. Blend in sugar and salt. When cool, add eggs. Dissolve yeast in warm water; then add to mixture. Blend in flour a little at a time, mixing well. Place in icebox. Roll out rolls on lightly floured board; cut and place on lightly greased pan. Let rise 1 to 2 hours before baking. Bake at 350 degrees for 20 minutes. Yields 2 to 3 dozen.

The dough will keep in the icebox for approximately a week, and it can also be used to make marvelous cinnamon rolls. ✑

Betty Jane Slaughter Briscoe
✦ SUGAR COOKIES

3½ cups flour
1¾ cups sugar
1 teaspoon soda
2 eggs
2 sticks oleo [or butter]

Mix together flour, sugar, soda; add beaten eggs and melted butter. Divide into four parts, shape into rolls, wrap in wax paper, and refrigerate overnight. Slice, then bake on ungreased cookie sheet at 450 degrees about 5 minutes. Remove from cookie sheet while still hot; sprinkle with sugar. ✑

Betty Jane Slaughter Briscoe
♦ VANILLA ICE CREAM

6 eggs
2 quarts sweet milk
2 cups sugar

Beat eggs and add other ingredients. Cook over hot water until
the custard thickens and coats spoon; strain, cool, then add:

1 pint heavy cream
1 teaspoon vanilla
1 teaspoon lemon extract

Blend all ingredients and freeze in a 4-quart freezer or freeze in
the freezer compartment of your icebox with waxed paper over
the top, stirring often until frozen. ～

Betty Jane Slaughter Briscoe
♦ BRISCOE PICOSO

This is a wonderful salsa that was enjoyed at both the mansion and
the Briscoe ranch.

22 green chilies
4 pods of garlic
1 lemon
1 teaspoon salt
2 large cans tomatoes (whole stewed)

Boil chilies in plain water until they lose their bright green color.
Peel and place in blender 4 pods of garlic, the juice of the lemon,
salt, and cooked peppers. Blend until a smooth paste. Add
(drained) stewed tomatoes to paste in blender and barely turn on
and off, to keep from making into a smooth paste; bits of the
tomatoes should be recognizable. ～

Betty Jane Slaughter Briscoe
◆ SPOON BREAD

The wife of John Nance Garner, who served as vice president under Franklin Roosevelt, gave this spoon bread recipe to Janey
Briscoe. It was a cherished keepsake in her recipe collection and was
used often over many years, including those spent at the mansion.

> 3 cups of milk
> 1½ cups cornmeal
> 2 tablespoons butter
> 3 eggs (beat yolks and whites separately)
> 2 teaspoons baking powder
> 1 tablespoon sugar
> 1 teaspoon salt

Scald milk thoroughly. Stir in meal and butter and let stand to
cool. Add well beaten yolks, baking powder, sugar, and salt.
Gently fold in stiffly beaten egg whites. Turn into buttered
baking dish (which can be used for serving) and cook in 350-
degree oven for 45 minutes, or until the consistency of thick
custard. Serve with spoon. ↞

Betty Jane Slaughter Briscoe
◆ 7-UP ® CAKE
This is another Briscoe family favorite.

> 2 sticks oleo
> ½ cup shortening
> 3 cups sugar
> 5 eggs
> 3 cups flour
> 1 teaspoon vanilla
> 1 teaspoon lemon extract
> 1 can of 7-Up®

Cream oleo, shortening, and sugar. Add eggs one at a time,
beating until well blended and creamy. Add flour gradually. Add

vanilla and lemon extract slowly. Lastly, add a whole can of 7-Up®. Blend until thoroughly mixed. Pour into greased tube cake pan. Bake 1 hour and 10 minutes at 325 degrees. ❧

Betty Jane Slaughter Briscoe
◆ ANGEL GINGERBREAD

½ cup butter
½ cup sugar
1 egg
¼ cup molasses
½ cup boiling water
1 cup flour
1 teaspoon salt
1 teaspoon ginger
1 teaspoon soda

Combine all ingredients and blend well. Pour into generously buttered baking dish and bake at 350 degrees for 25 to 30 minutes. Serve hot with whipped cream. ❧

Betty Jane Slaughter Briscoe
◆ OLD-FASHIONED POUND CAKE

1 cup butter
1¾ cup sugar
1 teaspoon vanilla
1 teaspoon lemon extract
5 eggs
2 cups flour

Beat and mix butter and sugar until thick like cream. Add vanilla and lemon extract. Break in eggs, one at a time, beating furiously after each addition. Mix flour lightly into mixture. Pour at once into a prepared baking pan and bake slowly for 1 hour. ❧

Betty Jane Slaughter Briscoe
✦ A VARIATION OF TEXAS PICANTE SAUCE

This recipe appears to be an earlier version of the Briscoe Picoso. It packs a lesser punch but is still very good. The use of serrano peppers gives it is slightly smoky flavor. Picante sauce is now so popular in Texas that one seldom sees this salsa recipe in printed form.

Janey Briscoe kept a large container of home-fried tortilla quarters in the pantry. They are wonderful to use with this hot sauce. It is equally delicious on eggs and in some salads as a dressing. She claimed it could be used on a million things. Make some of this fresh, spicy salsa and see for yourself.

18 serrano peppers or green chili peppers
2 garlic cloves
1 teaspoon Mazola® oil
Dash salt
3 large cans whole tomatoes

Boil peppers in water until they have lost their bright color and are an olive drab green. When the peppers are ready, put them in a blender with the garlic, oil, and a sprinkling of salt. Grind until they are completely pureed. Turn blender off and add tomatoes. Blend them all together, pour into a large container. This makes about 1 quart and keeps well in the refrigerator. ❧

Betty Jane Slaughter Briscoe
✦ TOMATO JUICE FRAPPÉ

While not often heard in kitchens today, the word frappé merely refers to a frozen or semifrozen beverage served as either an appetizer or dessert. When Governor Briscoe was in office, Janey Briscoe found it was very helpful to serve guests assembling for lunch either cold soup or fruit juice or the following vegetable juice frappé.

1 large can tomato juice
1 bay leaf
1 teaspoon Lea & Perrins®

Juice of ½ lemon
Tabasco®

Simmer the above in a 1-quart saucepan. Do not allow mixture to boil, but merely simmer so the bay leaf flavor is extracted and other spices are well blended. Then place in a large container to freeze. Take out later in the day (or the next day) and allow to thaw only enough to whip or stir vigorously. Serve in wine glasses or sherbet glasses. Place in freezer to be kept firm, but not refrozen. ❧

Betty Jane Slaughter Briscoe
♦ HORSERADISH DRESSING

Salads for business luncheons at the Governor's Mansion were usually quarter heads of lettuce with this delicious dressing. It is particularly good with the addition of tomato wedges. Make sure all elements of the salad are thoroughly chilled.

> 1 cup sour cream
> 1 teaspoon lemon juice
> ¼ teaspoon onion juice
> 2 teaspoons chopped chives
> ½ cup mayonnaise
> ¼ teaspoon dry mustard
> 1 tablespoon prepared horseradish

Mix thoroughly. Chill. ❧

Betty Jane Slaughter Briscoe
♦ VENISON CHILI

This venison chili is especially popular in South Texas.

> 1½ pounds bacon
> 1½ pounds ground venison
> ½ gallon cooked kidney beans
> 1½ teaspoon pepper

1 tablespoon chili powder
1 tablespoon salt
1 quart onions
½ gallon tomatoes or 4 no. 303 cans
½ teaspoon comino seed

Cut bacon into small pieces, brown to a crisp. Add venison and brown. Combine rest of ingredients in large kettle. Add the browned meat and enough water to cover. Simmer for 2 hours. Serves 20. ❧

Betty Jane Slaughter Briscoe
◆ CARAMELIZED BREAD PUDDING

The Briscoes liked to serve this simple pudding with an entrée that has a sharp flavor, such as Mexican food. It was a staple in the mansion icebox as it is a light and subtle dessert for people to eat before bedtime or just as a snack.

Butter
8 white bread slices
2 cups of brown sugar
6 eggs, lightly beaten
4 cups milk
2 teaspoons vanilla
½ teaspoon salt

Butter the bread and cut into cubes. In the top of a double boiler, mix brown sugar with buttered bread cubes. Combine eggs, milk, vanilla, and salt and pour over the bread and sugar. Do not stir. Cook over boiling water for 1 hour or until custard is formed. The brown sugar in the bottom of the pan forms the sauce. You can put the ingredients in a soufflé dish and proceed as above. ❧

Restoration

THE MANSION'S CONDITION by the last quarter of the twentieth century was deplorable. Cosmetic changes and cover-ups disguised many of the flaws, but structurally the old house was in danger. Something drastic had to be done. A full-scale restoration was on the horizon.

◆ RITA CROCKER CLEMENTS ◆
1979–1983, 1987–1991

Rita Crocker, a native of Kansas, grew up on ranches there and in Texas. She graduated from the Hockaday School in Dallas and attended Wellesley College before completing her undergraduate degree at the University of Texas. Her education amply prepared her for being first lady, and she took the role in stride.

Rita had heard that the mansion was in poor condition, but upon moving into it she was still shocked at what she found. By 1979 the mansion had served Texas' governors for more than 120 years. It was tired and worn. Rita knew that something beyond simply repainting had to be done. The last full-scale work on the home had taken place nearly a decade before.

Just prior to the Clementses' arrival, a section of wall in one of the mansion's double parlors collapsed. The wall was literally glued back into place, but an enormous crack revealed that serious repairs were needed. The woodwork above the doorways throughout the house was rotted in spots. The one small, ill-conceived powder room still served the entire first floor. There was no silver closet, and the carpeting was well worn throughout. The mansion kitchen was so cramped and cobbled together that for large events, food had to be stored outside in the garage.

At the request of Governor and Mrs. Clements, the legislature appropriated one million dollars for a complete structural and cosmetic restoration. The Friends of the Governor's Mansion, a nonprofit organization that Rita helped found, raised the additional three million dollars needed to refurbish the interiors.

The Clementses were very involved in the decoration of the mansion. Governor Clements suggested the theme for the rug in the conservatory. It features the seals of the six nations that have ruled Texas as well as Texas wildflower designs. The wallpaper throughout the house was removed, and the walls were painted and restored to their nineteenth-century appearance. Historic mansion furnishings were retained and restored, and a fine sampling of nineteenth-century American antiques furnished the remainder of the house. By 1982 the work was completed, and Governor and Mrs. Clements opened the house to the people of Texas with a press conference. Never before had the mansion been so complete and so perfect. For the first time in its history, there was nothing left to be fixed or redone in the entire house.

For her commitment to historic preservation and particularly her work in restoring the Texas Governor's Mansion, Rita Clements received the Miss Ima Hogg Special Award from the Winedale Society and the Ruth B. Lester Award from the Texas Historical Commission.

Rita Crocker Clements

◆ BAILEY SQUARE CHOCOLATE CAKE

This cake is the one I was served by Sarah Bishop during one of my first interviews with her in the mansion kitchen. She cut me a huge slice of and set it before me. I casually asked how it tasted. She stared at me with her intense eyes and said flatly, "It's pretty damn good." Perhaps because I was in the mansion kitchen, or because I was with superchef Sarah, this cake tasted like the best cake anywhere. The recipe has been used there for many years; in fact, it predates Sarah's time working at the house. The cake had recently been served to five former governors who were there to reminisce about their time in the mansion; I had eaten a leftover piece of the governors' cake.

> 4 cups all-purpose flour, unsifted
> 4 cups granulated sugar
> 1 teaspoon salt
> 2 cups water
> $\frac{1}{2}$ pound butter
> 1 cup salad oil
> $\frac{1}{2}$ pound Moreau-Hubin baking chocolate
> 4 whole extra large eggs
> 3 teaspoons vanilla
> 1 cup buttermilk
> $2\frac{1}{2}$ teaspoons baking soda

In a large mixing bowl stir together the flour, sugar, and salt. In a deep saucepan place the water, butter, oil, and baking chocolate. Bring to a boil, stirring constantly. Add chocolate mixture to dry ingredients and mix well on medium speed of mixer until well blended. While still hot, add the eggs, then the vanilla. Mix at medium speed until well blended. Then add the buttermilk to which the soda has been added. Mix at medium speed only until blended. Grease and flour a $2\frac{1}{2}$-by-$10\frac{1}{2}$-by-16-inch pan. Pour batter in and bake in a 350-degree oven for 40 to 45 minutes. Do not overbake. ❧

Rita Crocker Clements
✦ CHOCOLATE PECAN FROSTING

½ pound butter
½ pound Moreau-Hubin baking chocolate
2 pounds powdered sugar, sifted
½ cup plus 3 tablespoons cream or milk
2 teaspoons vanilla
1 pound chopped toasted pecans

In deep saucepan, heat all ingredients, stirring constantly until well blended. Pour hot frosting on hot cake. Cake is good served hot. If desired, 8 tablespoons cocoa can be substituted for the pound chocolate in both cake and frosting. Also, the batter can be baked in two 9-by-13-inch baking pans. Reduce the baking time slightly. Garnish finished cakes with pecans. ⇜

Rita Crocker Clements
✦ BAKED CHEESE GRITS

Mansion chef Sarah Bishop grew up eating these grits as prepared by her mother, an East Coast transplant who readily embraced good Southern food. Sarah in turn fixed them for all of the governors for whom she has cooked. It is a dish well liked by them all.

1 cup grits
1 teaspoon salt
3 cups water (boiling)
1 stick butter
8 ounces medium sharp cheddar cheese (grated)
½ cup milk
2 eggs (well beaten)

Stir grits into boiling, salted water. Add butter and cheese. Stir until blended. Add milk and eggs. Bake at 325 degrees for 1 hour and 10 minutes. Let stand before serving. Note: Works well made without butter. ⇜

Rita Crocker Clements

◆ MORE

This delicious casserole is a perfect family meal. It is for all practical purposes a "one-dish dinner." Hearty and robust, it is easily prepared.

2 onions, diced
1 green pepper, diced
1 large jar mushrooms, diced
2 small garlic cloves, diced
Salad oil
1½ pounds ground round beef
1 tablespoon chili powder
Salt
Pepper
1 can tomatoes
1 can tomato sauce
1 package frozen English peas
1 can whole kernel corn
½ cup cooked shell macaroni
Sharp cheddar cheese, grated

Sauté onions, green pepper, mushrooms, and garlic in a small amount of olive or vegetable oil; add ground meat and chili powder. Salt and pepper to taste. Add tomatoes and tomato sauce and let simmer for a while. Then add peas, corn, and cooked macaroni. Pour into a large Pyrex® dish and sprinkle with sharp cheddar cheese. Bake at 350 degrees for 30 minutes. ⤝

Rita Crocker Clements

◆ GOVERNOR CLEMENTS ANCHO CHILI CON CARNE

1 cup yellow onion, peeled and finely chopped
1 tablespoon garlic cloves, finely minced
1 tablespoon oregano
1 tablespoon cumin
7 tablespoons Ancho chili powder

1 teaspoon brown sugar
2 teaspoons salt
1½ teaspoon red hot chili pepper
1½ pounds beef chuck roast, boned and trimmed
1½ pounds pork roast, boned and trimmed
3 tablespoons bacon drippings
2 tablespoons vegetable oil (oil and drippings for browning meat)
¼ cup bacon drippings
¼ cup vegetable oil
¾ cup all-purpose flour

Prepare onions and garlic and set aside in a bowl. Measure and combine spices in bowl, set aside. Hand cut meat to fine dice. In iron or cast aluminum Dutch oven heat 3 tablespoons bacon drippings and 2 tablespoons vegetable oil and brown meat. Drain oil and remove meat. Put Dutch oven on high heat to evaporate juices. Heat ¼ cup bacon drippings and ¼ cup vegetable oil to smoking and add flour, stirring constantly with whisk or wooden spoon. Cook to medium brown. Remove from heat and add onions and garlic; continue to stir. Add herb and chili mixture. Add water slowly and continue to stir. Add meat and bring to slow boil. Reduce heat to simmer, adding water as needed (a cup at a time). Cook slowly, uncovered, 4 to 5 hours. Cool and refrigerate overnight. Warm and serve. ⤚

Rita Crocker Clements
◆ 3 OF 6 ICE CREAM

The Clements family loved homemade ice cream. This recipe is both popular and kind of clever.

3 bananas, mashed
3 oranges, juiced
3 lemons, juiced
3 cups sugar
3 cups milk
3 cups heavy cream

Mash bananas. Add strained juiced. Add sugar. Stir until sugar dissolves. Freeze a little. Add milk and heavy cream. Finish freezing. This can be easily doubled if a higher quantity is desired.

Rita Crocker Clements
♦ PECAN TASSIES

6 ounces cream cheese
½ stick butter
1½ cups flour

Cut cream cheese and butter into small portions. Whip with mixer on medium speed until light and fluffy. Add flour in thirds and mix well after each third is added. Form 3 dozen balls about 1 inch in size. Press into small muffin tins, bottoms and sides, to form a tart shape.

Pecan Filling:
2 eggs
1½ cups brown sugar
4 tablespoons butter, melted
2 teaspoons vanilla
Dash salt
1½ cups coarsely chopped pecans

Beat eggs lightly, add sugar, butter, vanilla, and salt and beat well. Divide pecans in half; line pastry cups with half. Fill cups with egg mixture and top with remaining half of pecans. Bake at 325 degrees for 25 minutes. Cool. Remove from pans carefully. These may be frozen for a month in freezer.

Rita Crocker Clements
♦ CHICKEN ENCHILADAS

3 large chicken breasts
1 cup chopped onion
1 clove garlic, minced
2 tablespoons margarine

1 (16-ounce) can tomatoes, cut up
1 (8-ounce) can tomato sauce
$\frac{1}{4}$ cup chopped green chilies
1 teaspoon sugar
1 teaspoon ground cumin
$\frac{1}{2}$ teaspoon salt
$\frac{1}{2}$ teaspoon dried oregano, crushed
$\frac{1}{2}$ teaspoon dried basil, crushed
12 corn tortillas
$2\frac{1}{2}$ cups shredded Monterey Jack cheese
$\frac{3}{4}$ cup sour cream

In saucepan, simmer chicken breasts in water to cover until tender. Drain, and carefully remove skin and bones. Sprinkle chicken with a little salt. Cut into 12 strips; set aside. In another saucepan, cook onion and garlic in margarine until tender. Add tomatoes, tomato sauce, chilies, sugar, cumin, salt, oregano, and basil. Bring to boiling, reduce heat and simmer covered for 20 minutes. Remove from heat. Dip each tortilla in tomato mixture to soften. Place one piece of chicken and about 2 tablespoons of cheese on each tortilla; roll up and place seam down in long baking dish. Blend sour cream into remaining sauce mixture, pour over tortillas, and sprinkle with remaining cheese. Cover and bake at 350 degrees until heated thoroughly.

Rita Crocker Clements
◆ MANSION'S APPLE CAKE OR
GOVERNOR CLEMENTS'S FAVORITE APPLE CAKE

Longtime mansion executive chef Sarah Bishop adapted this recipe for the Clements family. She has continued to make it for him on subsequent visits.

1 cup cooking oil
2 cups sugar
2 eggs
2 cups flour
2 teaspoons baking powder

1 teaspoon baking soda
1 teaspoon salt
1 teaspoon cinnamon (ground)
1 teaspoon nutmeg (ground)
1 teaspoon vanilla
4 cups Granny Smith apples (peeled and cored)
1 cup pecans (chopped)

Preheat oven to 350 degrees. Combine oil and sugar. Beat each egg in one at a time. Sift together the dry ingredients and stir into egg mixture. Fold in vanilla, apples, and pecans. Pour into an 8-by-11-inch pan that has been sprayed with cooking oil. Bake for 55 to 60 minutes or until knife inserted in the center comes out clean. ≋

◆ LINDA GALE THOMPSON WHITE ◆
1983–1987

Linda Gale White was one of the only first ladies that did not have to worry about a leaky roof or some other portion of the mansion needing repairs. The house was in the best condition it had ever been in during its century-plus history.

Linda Gale grew up in Irving, Texas, and after graduating from high school she attended Baylor University and earned a degree in business administration in 1964. She married Mark White in 1966. Linda then began a teaching career at Johnson High School in Austin, where she worked from 1960 to 1970. During the mid-1970s, she left teaching to pursue a career in real estate. The pace of her life was hectic, but she always found time for her three children and to volunteer with numerous social organizations.

After Mark was elected governor and the family moved into the mansion, Linda loved the entertaining and would often assist in preparing the food and hors d'oeuvres. Her entertaining schedule was especially heavy during the Sesquicentennial in 1986 as Texas celebrated the 150th anniversary of its independence from Mexico. She was equally adept at entertaining royalty or serving up a family-style supper for her friends and relatives. Although she was a working mother, she was no stranger to the kitchen and truly enjoyed the pace of her life as first lady.

Working in the small kitchen in the private quarters, she made the majority of the family's evening meals. During legislative sessions, when Mark would be working very late in the Capitol, she would have food and snacks waiting for him when he finally made it back to the mansion. Members of the staff who worked during the White administration recall those years as "family time."

Linda had always been active in volunteer work, and as first lady she made prevention of child abuse and other family-related issues her priority. She served as honorary chair and board member of the PTA Child Abuse Prevention State Advisory Council and as honorary chair of the Pebble Project, a Travis County effort to combat child abuse and neglect. Through her efforts, these programs gained statewide exposure and much-needed support.

When Mark's term was over and it was time to leave, Linda did so with a degree of sadness. The four years she and her family had spent in the "Texas White House" were special.

❧

Linda Gale Thompson White
◆ VICTORIAN PINEAPPLE UPSIDE DOWN CAKE

Sarah Bishop used this recipe during the terms of Governors Clements, Richards, and Bush. It is an especially light cake that is really delicious.

$\frac{1}{3}$ cup brown sugar
$\frac{1}{2}$ cup butter
1 pineapple, peeled and sliced into rounds
3 cups sifted cake flour
1$\frac{1}{2}$ to 2 cups sugar
4 teaspoons baking powder
1$\frac{1}{2}$ teaspoons salt
1 cup butter, softened
$\frac{2}{3}$ cup simple syrup [equal parts water and sugar boiled until smooth]

$\frac{2}{3}$ cup milk

2 teaspoons grated lemon peel (approximate)

$1\frac{1}{2}$ to 2 teaspoons vanilla

$\frac{1}{2}$ to 1 teaspoon almond extract

2 eggs

Melt butter with sugar in cast-iron skillet. Arrange pineapple slices to cover bottom and sides of pan.

Resift cake flour with sugar, baking powder, and salt. Cream the butter in mixer. Add dry ingredients to mixer then add syrup, milk, and flavorings. Beat for 2 minutes on medium speed. (Scrape down bowl.) Fold in the eggs and beat 2 minutes more. Pour batter into prepared pan. Bake at 350 degrees about 50 minutes. Remove from oven and let stand in pan 5 to 10 minutes. Turn out cake and leave pan over top for a few minutes to let syrup run over top of cake. Yield: 1 10-inch cake.

Linda Gale Thompson White
◆ CHICKEN FLAUTAS

Marinade:

1 cup Italian dressing

$\frac{1}{2}$ teaspoon cumin

$\frac{1}{4}$ teaspoon granulated garlic

$\frac{1}{2}$ teaspoon onion powder

$\frac{1}{2}$ teaspoon chili powder

Flautas:

1 5- or 6-ounce chicken breast

3 tablespoons butter

1 teaspoon grated onion

$\frac{1}{4}$ teaspoon minced garlic

$\frac{1}{4}$ cup flour

$\frac{1}{4}$ teaspoon salt

1 cup chicken stock or broth

1 tablespoon fresh parsley

$\frac{1}{2}$ teaspoon cumin

$\frac{1}{2}$ teaspoon chili powder

White pepper to taste
4 cups oil for frying
8 corn tortillas

Early in the day combine all marinade ingredients. Add chicken breast and marinate for 6 hours.

Preheat grill. Remove from marinade and grill for 3 minutes on each side. Dice into small pieces.

In a medium skillet, melt butter; add onions and garlic and sauté until just softened. Blend in flour and salt. Add chicken stock and cook until thickened. Add spices and herbs. Stir in chicken and cook slightly. Heat oil to 350 degrees. Soften tortillas in hot oil, one at a time, and place approximately 2 tablespoons of chicken mixture in each tortilla. Roll into cylinders as thick as your thumb. These can be cut in half for hors d'oeuvre size flautas. Fry at 350 degrees until crisp and lightly browned. Drain on paper towels. Serve with toothpicks and your favorite avocado sauce or guacamole. Yields 8 large or 16 small flautas. ⥮

Linda Gale Thompson White
◆ QUAIL WITH GRAVY

Chicken breasts may be substituted for quail with equal success in this delightfully rich dish.

6 tablespoons butter, divided
1 medium onion, finely chopped
$\frac{1}{2}$ pound fresh mushrooms, sliced
1 tablespoon oil
8 to 12 quail breasts
$\frac{1}{2}$ cup dry white wine or vermouth
1 large can cream of mushroom soup ($10\frac{3}{4}$-ounce size)
1 cup light cream (half and half)

Melt 3 tablespoons butter and sauté onion and mushrooms until tender. Remove from pan. Melt 3 tablespoons butter and oil and sauté birds until brown. Remove from pan. Pour off remaining fat. Add white wine or vermouth; scrape up particles on bottom of skillet. Add mushroom soup, onions, mushrooms, and cream; stir until well blended. Return birds to pan, spooning sauce over them. Cover and simmer for 30 minutes.

Linda Gale Thompson White
♦ PERENNIAL TEA PARTY SANDWICHES

These party sandwiches are probably just like the ones your grand-mother made. The Whites served them to members of the British royal family when they visited the mansion. The fillings can be pre-pared up to two days in advance, but it is recommended that you make the actual sandwiches the day you wish to use them. To keep them from drying out after they are made, drape a clean damp cot-ton dishtowel over the top of the sandwich container.

Basic Seasoned Cream Cheese for Tea Sandwiches:
8 ounces cream cheese, softened
1 tablespoon chili sauce
1 small carrot, finely grated
¼ cup grated cheddar cheese
2 green peppers, chopped and squeezed dry
Dash of white pepper
Dash of Worcestershire
Pinch of salt
Dash of hot pepper sauce
Bread (1 regular loaf makes approximately 100 canapés)

Beat the cream cheese. Add remaining ingredients (except bread) and mix well. Chill. This can be made ahead. To vary this mix-ture, add watercress to the basic seasoned cream cheese. Cut the bread into triangles.

For a cucumber version, add:
1 nice cucumber
½ cup finely chopped nuts
Dill (optional)

Score the cucumber lengthwise with the tines of a fork so the soft green is revealed in contrast to the darker green of the skin. Cut in half length-wise, remove seeds, and cut into $\frac{1}{4}$-inch slices. Spread bread with basic cucumber mixture. Cut the spread slices of bread into circles using a cookie cutter. Place a half slice of cucumber on the cheese. Sprinkle the other half of the circle with chopped nuts. For variety, add dill to the cream cheese mixture. These can be made into little sandwiches by placing another piece of bread on the dressed half. ➤

Linda Gale Thompson White

◆ GREEN ENCHILADAS WITH SPICY SAUCE

1 dozen corn tortillas
$\frac{1}{2}$ cup oil
2 cups shredded Monterey Jack cheese
$\frac{3}{4}$ cup chopped onion
$\frac{1}{4}$ cup butter
$\frac{1}{4}$ cup flour
2 cups chicken broth
1 cup sour cream
1 can (4 ounces) jalapeno peppers, seeded and chopped

Spicy Sauce:
1 medium tomato, finely chopped
$\frac{1}{2}$ cup onion, finely chopped
2 jalapeno peppers with seeds, finely chopped
$\frac{1}{4}$ cup tomato juice
$\frac{1}{2}$ teaspoon salt

To make enchiladas, cook tortillas, one at a time, in hot oil in a skillet for 15 seconds on each side. Do not overcook them or tortillas will become stiff and not roll properly. Place 2 table-spoons of the cheese and 1 tablespoon of the onion on each tortilla: roll up. Place seam side down in a baking dish. Melt butter in another saucepan, blend in flour. Add chicken broth, and cook stirring constantly until mixture thickens and bubbles. Stir in sour cream and peppers. Cook until heated through, but do not boil. Pour over tortillas. Bake at 425 degrees for 20 minutes. Sprinkle remaining cheese on top and return to oven for 5 minutes or until cheese melts. Serve with Spicy Sauce, which is made by combining all sauce ingredients. Serves 6.

Linda Gale Thompson White
♦ MOCK CHEESE BLINTZES

3 loaves white sandwich bread
$\frac{1}{2}$ cup cinnamon
2 cups sugar
3 pounds cream cheese
2 egg yolks
1 cup sugar
$\frac{2}{3}$ teaspoon salt
$\frac{1}{2}$ teaspoon vanilla
$\frac{3}{4}$ teaspoon lemon peel
$\frac{1}{2}$ tablespoon cinnamon
$\frac{1}{2}$ teaspoon nutmeg
1 pound butter, unsalted, melted

Prepare bread by removing crusts. Flatten, using a rolling pin or a pasta machine. Combine $\frac{1}{2}$ cup cinnamon and 2 cups sugar and set aside. Beat cream cheese in a large mixing bowl. Add eggs and beat until creamy and smooth. Add 1 cup sugar and remaining ingredients (except melted butter). Spread on flattened bread; roll up (cigar style) and cut in half. Dip one side first in the melted butter, then in the cinnamon-sugar mixture. (The blintzes can be frozen at this point.) Bake in 350-degree oven for 12 to 15 minutes, on the upper rack of the oven. Serve with Blueberry Sour Cream for dipping. The blintzes are best when served warm. Makes approximately 108 pieces.

Blueberry Sour Cream:
1 pint fresh blueberries (when using frozen berries make sure you defrost them on paper towels to absorb the moisture)

1 pint sour cream
1 teaspoon sugar
Dash of nutmeg

Linda Gale Thompson White
◆ ASPARAGUS ROLLUPS

1 1-pound loaf thin white sandwich bread
1 pound cheddar cheese, shredded (4 cups)
4 ounces cream cheese, softened
Horseradish to taste
Cayenne pepper to taste
1 green pepper, chopped
2 drops hot pepper sauce
1 15-ounce can asparagus spears, drained

Topping:
1 cup Parmesan cheese
$\frac{1}{2}$ cup bread crumbs
Dash of cayenne (for color)
Dash of chili powder (for color)

Prepare bread by removing crusts and flattening using a rolling pin
or a pasta machine. Set aside, covered with plastic wrap or a damp
towel. Combine cheeses, seasonings, green pepper, and hot pepper
sauce; mix well. Spread cheese mixture evenly on slices of bread.
Place an asparagus spear on one end of each slice and roll up, jelly
roll style. Repeat until all bread and/or asparagus is used. Combine
ingredients for topping. Dip one side of each rollup first in some
melted butter, then in the topping (can be frozen at this point).
Preheat oven to 375 degrees. Bake for 10 to 12 minutes. ❧

Linda Gale Thompson White
◆ STRAWBERRY CREAM STARS

8 ounces cream cheese, softened
$\frac{1}{4}$ cup confectioner's sugar

$\frac{1}{8}$ teaspoon cinnamon
1 tablespoon lemon juice
1 quart fresh strawberries

Combine cream cheese, sugar, cinnamon, and lemon juice in a mixing bowl and beat until smooth. Cover and refrigerate. This can be made ahead. Clean and hull strawberries. Place on paper towels, hulled side down. With a sharp knife, cut an "X" through the pointed end of each berry, being careful not to cut all the way through. Gently open the berry slightly. Using a pastry bag and a large star tip, pipe filling into the center of the berries. Berries can be filled up to 2 hours in advance. Place filled berries in paper petit four cups for easy serving. Yields about 36 filled strawberries. ≈

Linda Gale Thompson White
◆ TACO SOMBREROS

Filling:
1 cup tortilla chips, coarsely crumbled
1 cup sour cream
1 egg beaten
2 ounces ripe olives, diced
2 tablespoons taco sauce

Combine ingredients and refrigerate.

Sombreros:
1 pound lean ground beef, cooked and drained
$1\frac{1}{2}$ teaspoon black pepper
2 teaspoons chili powder
2 teaspoons granulated garlic
1 teaspoon onion powder
1 tablespoon cumin
$\frac{1}{2}$ teaspoon salt
2 tablespoons ice water
4 ounces cheddar cheese, shredded

Preheat oven to 375 degrees. Combine beef, seasonings, and ice water, and mix. Using a heaping tablespoon of mixture, roll meat into balls. Press into small muffin tins—1½-inch cups—forming a "tartlette" shell, covering the bottom and sides of the cups. Into each sombrero shell place a spoonful of the filling, mounding it slightly. Sprinkle the tops with shredded cheddar cheese. Bake at 375 degrees for 10 to 12 minutes. Remove immediately and serve. These can be cooled, frozen, and served later. Yields about 30 sombreros. ~

Linda Gale Thompson White
◆ COUNTRY NOODLE CASSEROLE

1 pound sliced bacon
1 package (1 pound) very fine vermicelli noodles (DO NOT OVERCOOK)
3 cups cottage cheese
3 cups sour cream
2 cloves garlic, crushed
2 medium onions, minced
2 tablespoons Worcestershire sauce
⅛ teaspoon Tabasco® sauce
2 teaspoons salt
5 tablespoons horseradish
1 cup grated Parmesan

Fry bacon until crisp. Drain on paper towels and crumble. Cook noodles "al dente" according to package directions. Drain well. Mix all remaining ingredients, except Parmesan cheese. Add noodles and bacon and toss until well mixed. Put in deep buttered casserole. Cover and bake at 350 degrees 30 to 40 minutes. Sprinkle with Parmesan cheese before serving. ~

Linda Gale Thompson White
◆ CALICO GARDEN MOUSSE

In this recipe you can also use 6 ounces of olives available in bulk at your local specialty shop or even some grocery stores. Get the best, most delicious variety you can. Most bulk olives must be pitted prior to use. Canned olives, which have little flavor, are not recommended.

Mousse:
2 tablespoons unflavored gelatin
$\frac{1}{2}$ cup water
1 can ($10\frac{3}{4}$ ounces) tomato soup
1 package (8 ounces) cream cheese, softened
1 cup mayonnaise
1 cup chopped celery
1 bunch green onions, finely chopped
$\frac{1}{4}$ cup slivered or sliced almonds
1 small jar olives, drained and chopped
2 cups chicken, deboned and diced

Soften gelatin in water and combine with soup. Carefully mix into cream cheese until smooth and combine with remaining ingredients. Chill.

Avocado Dressing:
1 avocado, mashed
$\frac{1}{2}$ cup sour cream
1 teaspoon seasoned salt
Dash of cayenne pepper

Mix avocado, cream, and seasonings until smooth.

Linda Gale Thompson White
◆ PRALINE BARS

12 graham crackers
1 cup butter or margarine
$1\frac{1}{2}$ cups light brown sugar
$1\frac{1}{2}$ cups chopped pecans
1 teaspoon vanilla
1 teaspoon imitation rum flavoring

Line a 15-by-10-by-1-inch jelly roll pan with whole graham crackers. Bring butter and sugar to a rolling boil and cook for 3 minutes, stirring with a whisk. Remove from heat. When the bubbling stops, add the nuts, vanilla, and rum flavoring. Spread mixture evenly over crackers. Bake at 350 degrees for 10 minutes. Cut each cracker into pieces at the natural scored lines. Yields approximately 4 dozen cookies.

Linda Gale Thompson White
♦ CUCUMBER/SHRIMP BISQUE

1 quart buttermilk
1 tablespoon Dijon mustard
1½ pounds cooked shrimp, de-veined, peeled, and sliced
1½ pounds English cucumber, peeled and finely diced
1 tablespoon fresh dillweed, chopped
1 tablespoon chives, finely chopped

Mix the buttermilk and mustard. Fold in shrimp, cucumber, dillweed, and chives. Chill mixture at least 4 hours before serving. Yields 6 servings.

Linda Gale Thompson White
♦ GOVERNOR WHITE'S FAVORITE SHORTCAKE

This strawberry shortcake recipe was the one used by Gov. Mark White's aunt, Mary Ann McColpin. This dessert was a summertime favorite at the mansion.

4 cups all-purpose flour
2 teaspoons sugar
2 teaspoons salt
1⅓ cup chilled shortening
4 tablespoons chilled butter
8 tablespoons ice water

Sift flour, sugar, and salt together into mixing bowl. Combine shortening with butter and cut into flour mixture with a pastry blender. Work it until it has the grain of coarse cornmeal. Sprinkle the dough with water and toss lightly with a fork. If needed to hold dough together, add an additional teaspoon or so of water. Form dough into two balls; wrap with waxed paper and refrigerate for at least 2 hours. Then roll dough out on lightly floured board to $\frac{1}{2}$-inch thickness. Cut ten 3-inch rounds out of each ball. Place rounds on cookie sheet and prick entire surface of each round with a fork. Bake at 400 degrees for 12 minutes or until lightly browned. Cool on rack.

Glaze:
$\frac{1}{2}$ pint strawberries
$\frac{1}{2}$ cup sugar
1 cup water
1 tablespoon arrowroot
1 tablespoon cold water
1 tablespoon kirsch
1 teaspoon lemon zest

Hull berries. Combine with sugar and water in a saucepan. Bring mixture to a boil and simmer for 5 minutes. Strain mixture. Return to saucepan and bring to a boil. Stir in arrowroot that has been dissolved in cold water. Remove mixture from heat. Stir in kirsch and lemon zest. Cool before using.

Fruit:
Remove stems from 2 pints of strawberries, cut into halves.

Cream:
1 pint whipping cream
2 tablespoons powdered sugar

Combine whipping cream and sugar and beat until stiff. Line ten pastry rounds with a layer of berries. Drizzle with glaze. On the bottom side of second set of pastry rounds, spread $\frac{1}{8}$-inch layer of whipped cream. Place cream side down over strawberries. Add second layer of strawberries and glaze. Garnish top of each shortcake with remaining whipped cream and a sprig of fresh mint.

✦ THE HONORABLE ANN WILLIS RICHARDS ✦
1991–1995

Dorothy Ann Willis was born in Lakeview, Texas, in 1933 and graduated from Waco High School in 1950. She later attended Baylor University on a debate scholarship. After graduating, she went to the University of Texas at Austin, where she earned a teaching certificate. She taught social studies and history at Fulmore Junior High School in Austin during the 1955–56 academic year. She later said that teaching was the hardest work she had ever done.

It was while she was attending the University of Texas that Ann had gotten her first taste of politics. This drive remained with her, even after her four children were born. Despite the demands of her

Governor Ann W. Richards.
Courtesy Texas State Library and Archives Commission (1993/30-6).

family, Ann volunteered in local and statewide campaigns and worked for social causes in which she believed. The skills she received during this phase in her life served her well.

Her earliest political victory was in 1976. Against all odds, she had defeated a three-term incumbent for a seat on the Travis County Commissioners Court. Her family and friends were not really all that surprised, as they knew that Ann could do whatever she set her mind to. Six years later, Ann was urged to run for state treasurer. She received more votes in that election than any other statewide candidate on the ballot and became the first woman elected to statewide office in Texas in fifty years. In 1986 she was reelected without opposition. Her star rose to a national level in 1988 when she was chosen to speak at the National Democratic Convention. In 1990, Ann did something few women in Texas had ever done. She decided to run for governor.

Although it did not cause quite as much of a stir as it had in 1925 when Miriam Ferguson ran for governor, Ann's campaign caused its own political commotion. After a campaign that held the attention of the state, Ann was elected the forty-fifth governor of Texas. Her family and friends were again not terribly surprised.

Ann was governor and first lady rolled into one. She loved to entertain in a casual, breezy way. Texas food was always served, and her guests were usually reluctant to leave her parties. Her family always came first, though, no matter what she was doing. When the queen of England came to call at the mansion, Ann's proudest moment was introducing her family to Elizabeth.

Ann cooked many of her own meals in the small upstairs kitchen in the private quarters. The private rooms were decorated in a relaxing, eclectic, minimalist style with white and off-whites being the dominant colors. Her pet bird, Amazing Gracie, kept her company. She loved the mansion and all that it represented. Although there was no "First Spouse" to run interference at the special dinners and receptions, Ann played the dual role with consummate ease.

Ann Willis Richards
◆ MRS. LOVETT'S GINGERSNAPS

Recipes at the Governor's Mansion come from a surprising variety of sources. Singer Lyle Lovett's mom, Birnell Lovett, gave this delicious recipe to Sarah Bishop when she was visiting at the Lovett home in Spring, Texas.

$\frac{3}{4}$ cup of shortening
1 cup sugar
$\frac{1}{4}$ cup molasses
1 egg
2 cups sifted flour
2 teaspoons soda
2 teaspoons salt
1 teaspoon cloves
1 teaspoon cinnamon
1 teaspoon ginger
$\frac{1}{2}$ cup flour, to touch

Cream together the shortening and sugar. Add molasses and egg. Mix in flour soda, salt, and spices. Add $\frac{1}{2}$ cup flour to touch. Hand roll into balls. Dip in sugar. Place 2 inches apart on cookie sheet. Bake at 375 degrees for 15 minutes. ꒱

Ann Willis Richards
◆ MEXICAN SPOON BREAD

This recipe is from the mother of Sarah Bishop, the mansion chef. Her family used it after they settled in Houston during the late 1960s. Sarah prepared this delicious treat during Ann Richards's term and later during the years when the Bushes lived in the mansion.

1 16-ounce can of cream-style corn
$\frac{3}{4}$ cup milk
$\frac{1}{3}$ cup butter (melted)
2 eggs (beaten)

2 bunches green onions (sliced)
1 cup yellow cornmeal
$\frac{1}{2}$ teaspoon baking soda
1 teaspoon salt
1$\frac{1}{2}$ cups cheddar cheese (grated)
2 4-ounce cans green chilies (diced and drained)

Stir together corn, milk, butter, eggs, and onions. Stir together cornmeal, baking soda, and salt. Add dry ingredients to liquids. Heat iron skillet in oven with oil until almost smoking. Dust with cornmeal. Add $\frac{1}{2}$ mixture, then cheddar cheese and chilies, then other $\frac{1}{2}$ of mixture. Bake at 350 degrees approximately 1 hour. Let stand 10 to 15 minutes before serving. ≈

Ann Willis Richards
♦ JALAPENO CHEESE CORN BREAD

Governor Richards notes, "This is a wonderful recipe. It is particularly good with chicken, pork, and any vegetable." Governor Richards used lots of bacon, pimento, and garlic; you can add any of these items to suit your taste.

1$\frac{1}{2}$ cup corn bread mix
$\frac{3}{4}$ cup milk
1 egg
$\frac{1}{2}$ green onion, chopped
$\frac{1}{2}$ cup creamed corn
$\frac{1}{4}$ cup chopped jalapeno
$\frac{3}{4}$ cup grated cheese
Bacon, pimento, garlic
1 tablespoon sugar
2 tablespoons oil

Mix well. Pour into buttered baking dish and bake at 325 degrees for about 25 minutes or till done. ≈

Ann Willis Richards

◆ THE MANSION'S WONTON RAVIOLI
WITH LEMON CREAM SAUCE

1 pound ground chicken
2 green onions (minced)
1 tablespoon minced ginger root
1 tablespoon minced garlic
1 tablespoon sesame oil
1 tablespoon soy sauce
1 tablespoon cornstarch
40 wonton wrappers
Sauce:
1 tablespoon minced shallots
2 tablespoons clarified butter
3 tablespoons flour
1 cup chicken stock
1 cup heavy cream
1 tablespoon lemon juice
Salt and pepper to taste
Vegetable medley:
3 carrots (cut into matchsticks)
3 zucchini squash (cut into matchsticks)
3 celery stalks (cut into matchsticks)
2 cups green sweet peas
2 tablespoons cooking oil

To make the ravioli, combine chicken, green onions, minced ginger, minced garlic, sesame oil, soy sauce, and cornstarch. Place 1 tablespoon of mixture in center of each wonton wrapper. Dip finger in water and moisten sides of wonton. Fold into a triangle and seal outer edges. Moisten the two opposite corners and twist to seal. Allow wontons to dry for a few minutes on a sheet pan dusted with cornstarch. Cover with a slightly damp cloth. To make sauce, sauté shallots in clarified butter over low heat for one minute. Blend in flour and cook slowly for 2 minutes. Remove from heat and whisk in chicken stock. Return to heat and bring to boil, whisking constantly. Remove from heat and add heavy cream, lemon juice, salt, and pepper. Keep warm until ready to serve. To cook ravioli, bring a pot of water to a simmer. Drop ravioli gently into water, adding no more than 12 or so at a time. Cook about 6 minutes. Remove gently with a slotted spoon. Keep warm. While ravioli are cooking, sauté vegetables in oil until crisp-tender, adding peas at the very end. To serve, place sautéed vegetables on each plate, arrange 5 or 6 ravioli on top. Ladle cream sauce over both. ≈

Ann Willis Richards
♦ LEMON YOGURT CAKE

1 cup yogurt
2½ cups sugar
1 cup butter or margarine
6 eggs, separated
2 teaspoons grated lemon peel
1 teaspoon lemon extract
3 cups cake flour
1 teaspoon soda
1 teaspoon salt

Beat yogurt and 1½ cups of sugar with electric mixer until creamy. Add egg yolks, lemon peel, and lemon extract and beat until thick and pale yellow. Sift the flour, measure, and sift again with the soda and salt. Into the creamed butter mixture alternately mix the flour and the yogurt. Beat the egg whites until soft peaks form; then gradually add the remaining 1 cup sugar, beating until glossy. Fold batter into beaten egg whites and pour into a greased 10-inch tube pan. Bake at 350 degrees for 45 minutes or until done. Cool 15 minutes in pan, then turn out on a rack. Serves 12 to 15. ≈

Ann Willis Richards
♦ CHOCOLATE MINT BROWNIES

Brownies:
½ cup butter
2 squares unsweetened chocolate
2 eggs

½ teaspoon salt
1 cup sugar
1 cup flour
1 teaspoon vanilla
½ cup nuts, chopped

Melt butter and chocolate. Let cool. Beat eggs, salt, and sugar. Add chocolate mixture. Mix in flour and add remaining ingredients. Bake at 325 degrees in an 8-by-8-inch pan, coated with cooking spray, for 25 to 30 minutes. Cool.

Filling:
2 teaspoons butter
1 cup powdered sugar
1 teaspoon peppermint flavoring
1 drop green food coloring

Mix all ingredients and spread on top of cooled brownies. Refrigerate until cold.

Glaze:
1 1-ounce square unsweetened chocolate
1 tablespoon butter

Melt chocolate with butter and spread over cold brownies. Refrigerate. Cut into squares and serve. Yields 16 brownies. ⤛

Ann Willis Richards
♦ DELICIOUS FRUIT SMOOTHIE

The smoothie is an Austin tradition made famous at the old Martin Bros. take-out in the Whole Foods store at Tenth and Lamar (the second location of the original store before it became a large chain). This smoothie also became a favorite of Governor Bush. In your blender put two or three frozen strawberries, three or four slices of peaches, and half of a banana. Add about one-fourth to one-half cup of protein powder or muscle-building powder (MET-Rx, Spirutein, or others available at health food stores), one small carton of yogurt (flavored or plain) and one cup of apple juice. Add crushed ice if you want. Blend together into a smooth drink. Add more apple juice if it is too thick. Other kinds of health powders may be added as desired, as well as other fruits. This is a great breakfast or lunch, a high-energy strength builder. ~

Ann Willis Richards
◆ TARTAR SAUCE

Governor Richards proclaims this to be one of the best tartar sauces she has ever tasted. It is wonderful with fish, shrimp, or crab.

    1 cup mayonnaise
    2 tablespoons chopped "dill" pickles
    2 tablespoons chopped stuffed olives
    1 tablespoon grated onion
    1 tablespoon capers
    1 tablespoon lime juice or lemon juice
    $\frac{1}{4}$ teaspoon garlic salt

Mix preceding ingredients together. ~

Ann Willis Richards
◆ BURNT SUGAR ICE CREAM PIE

Sarah Bishop, chef at the mansion for Governor Richards, developed this recipe. It is a little work, but so good!

    $\frac{3}{4}$ cup sugar
    $1\frac{1}{2}$ cups milk
    3 egg yolks
    Pinch of salt
    3 tablespoons cornstarch
    $1\frac{1}{2}$ teaspoon vanilla
    $1\frac{1}{2}$ cups heavy cream
    Whipped cream for garnish (optional)
    Candied orange peel for garnish (optional)
    8-inch gingersnap pie crust

In large heavy skillet cook sugar over medium high heat, stirring constantly with a fork, until melted completely and a deep golden caramel. Remove from heat; stir caramel to prevent further darkening. Into skillet add milk carefully. The caramel will harden when milk is added. Cook caramel mixture over moderate heat, stirring, until the caramel is dissolved. Remove skillet from heat. In a bowl, whisk together egg yolks, salt, and cornstarch. Add caramel mixture in a slow stream, stirring. In a heavy saucepan, cook caramel mixture over moderate heat, stirring constantly with a wooden spoon until the mixture comes to a boil. Boil, stirring constantly, for 2 minutes. Strain the custard through a fine sieve into a metal bowl set in a larger bowl filled with ice and cold water. (This will cool the mixture down quickly.) Allow custard to cool, stirring; chill it, covered, until it is cold. Stir in vanilla and cream until mixture is combined well. Freeze mixture in ice-cream freezer, according to manufacturer's instructions.

Gingersnap Pie Crust:
1½ cups gingersnap cookies (approximately ½ box)
1 cup sugar
1 ounce unsalted butter, softened
¾ cup semisweet chocolate, melted

Preheat oven to 350 degrees. Break gingersnap cookies, and place in food processor: pulse until they are finely pulverized. Add sugar. Work in butter. Press into an 8-inch pie plate and bake for 8 to 10 minutes. Place in freezer to set up. When well chilled, remove from freezer and brush inside of piecrust with melted chocolate.

Assembly:
Spoon ice cream into pie shell; smooth with spatula. Store in freezer for 3 hours or until ready to serve. Garnish with sweetened whipped cream and candied orange peels. Yields 6 to 8 servings. ⤳

Ann Willis Richards
♦ JEFFREY'S FLAN

For ten years Sarah Bishop worked with Raymond Tatum at
Jeffrey's in Austin. She usually made a batch of flan every day. This
version of the creamy, traditional Mexican delight is wonderful.

2 quarts of half and half
1 cup sugar
1½ cups of sugar
12 eggs
8 egg yolks
Vanilla

Combine in a saucepan half and half and 1 cup of sugar. Bring to
a boil. Let cool in ice water. Caramelize 1½ cups of sugar and ladle
into bottom of flan cups. Whisk 12 eggs together. Add the 8 egg
yolks, whisk. Add vanilla. Add to cooled half and half mixture.
Strain the mixture through a fine cloth. Bake at 400 degrees in
pan filled with water to top of flan. Place a loose-fitting lid over
the top of pan. Check in 1 hour; turn pan and bake another 20 to
30 minutes. Yield: about 14 cups. ❧

Ann Willis Richards
♦ GRANDMA CLARK'S SODA BREAD

4 tablespoons unsalted butter
3 cups unbleached flour
1½ teaspoons salt
1 tablespoon baking powder
1 teaspoon baking soda
¾ cup sugar
1¾ cups buttermilk
2 eggs, well beaten
2 tablespoons unsalted butter, melted and cooled

Spread 2 tablespoons butter evenly over the bottom and sides of a 10-inch cast-iron skillet. Heat 5 minutes. Preheat oven to 350 degrees. Sift dry ingredients together in a large bowl. In another bowl, whisk together the buttermilk, eggs, and melted butter. Add this to the dry ingredients and mix just until blended. Do not overmix.

Spoon the batter into the prepared skillet, and smooth the top gently with a spatula. Dot the top with the remaining 2 tablespoons butter. Place the skillet in the oven and bake until the bread is puffed and golden brown, about 1 hour. Cool in the skillet for 10 minutes and serve warm, or transfer the bread to a wire rack to continue cooling. Cut into wedges to serve. ～

✦ LAURA WELCH BUSH ✦
1995–2000

Laura Welch was born and raised in Midland. She received a bachelor of science degree in education from Southern Methodist University in 1968 and a master's in library science from the University of Texas at Austin in 1973. She was an elementary school teacher and school librarian in Dallas, Houston, and Austin from 1968 to 1977. She met George W. Bush at a backyard barbecue at the home of friends Joe and Jan O'Neill in 1977. Three months later, in November of 1977, the couple married. In 1981 they welcomed Barbara and Jenna, who were named for their grandmothers.

Laura and George W. Bush moved into the Governor's Mansion with their thirteen-year-old twin daughters in January, 1995. Completing the Bush family at the mansion were the "First Dog," Spot, and two cats, Cowboy and India.

Laura's love of education and reading inspired her to utilize her public role as first lady to herald the work of Texas authors and artists and to promote breast cancer awareness. She also created and endorsed numerous programs stressing the importance of reading and education. Laura traveled thousands of miles across the state giving speeches for causes in which she believed. Everyone from those involved in the Texas Main Street Program of the

First Lady Laura Welch Bush.
Courtesy Texas A&M University Press.

Texas Historical Commission to representatives of the National Trust for Historic Preservation benefited from her candid, personal speaking style.

Laura treasured the mansion and was keenly interested in its preservation and its place in Texas history. She carefully chose historic Texas pieces from the mansion collections for the private quarters. Light fixtures were changed and carpets replaced, and slowly the mansion became a home. From the flowers she selected for the mansion gardens to the elaborate Christmas celebrations and holi-

{ 258 }

day decor that she chose, the Texas Governor's Mansion evolved to reflect her style during the time Laura was first lady. Visitation increased steadily as her husband became more politically visible on the national level. The media scrutiny only served to emphasize Laura's commitment to her family and to the sanctity of their time together.

Laura carried out her duties as first lady of Texas with a notable air of calm and poise, and she will always be remembered as a kind and sensitive steward of the Texas Governor's Mansion. After her husband George was elected to the presidency of the United States and the family moved to the much larger and better known mansion in Washington, Laura perhaps missed the relative peace and quiet of the house at 1010 Colorado Street in Austin.

Sarah Bishop began working as executive chef at the Texas Governor's Mansion in the early 1990s and has, as of this writing, cooked for four different governors. Charming and creative, Sarah has infused her own distinctive style into the cuisine of the mansion. While working on this book, I sat with Sarah in the sunny, gleaming mansion kitchen, and she graciously shared her thoughts on Texas cooking, cooking for the governors, and her creative process in selecting and perfecting new recipes. In an unexpected gesture of honor, she made her files available to me. While they are not exactly top secret, the recipes she contributed certainly are treasures, and they have seldom been seen by the general public.

When asked about the food preferences of the forty-third president of the United States, Sarah smiled and pulled out the recipe files she and family chef Kathleen Delacy-Bourke created for the Bush family. She should know what they liked; she cooked for them for six years. The recipes she shared reveal that even though Texas food has changed a great deal since the mansion was built in the mid-nineteenth century, the essence of the state's cuisine remains the same. Sarah's creative preparation of hearty, healthy fare, with the freshest ingredients, beautifully presented, defines cooking at the mansion. ⤛

Laura Welch Bush
◆ SARAH'S CHEX MIX

This recipe is a Bush family favorite. When the president and first lady moved to Washington, they wanted "Chex mix" made for them there. Shortly after the inauguration, the chef at the White House called Sarah Bishop at the mansion. He said that he had made three different batches, but the president said the mix tasted different than Sarah's. Sarah wrote down her recipe and sent it to Washington; the White House kitchen finally got it right.

3 tablespoons butter
1 tablespoon Yucatan Sunshine Habanero Sauce®
1 tablespoon Tabasco®
2 + tablespoons Worcestershire sauce
$\frac{1}{4}$ teaspoon comino
$\frac{1}{4}$ teaspoon oregano
$\frac{1}{4}$ teaspoon garlic granules
1 bag of La Choy Oriental Noodles®
3 cups Corn Chex®
3 cups Rice Chex®
3 cups Wheat Chex®
1 cup pepitas (raw pumpkin seeds)
1 cup pistachio nuts
2 to 3 cups pretzels (either sticks or Pepperidge Farm® goldfish)

Coat bottom of large bowl with sauce and toss cereals with the rest of ingredients to coat. Bake at 300 degrees for three 15-minute intervals, stirring in between. ~

Laura Welch Bush
◆ CLASSIC MEXICAN HOT SAUCE

Serve this sauce with chips or over cooked fish. Garnish with jicama and avocado. The sauce can also be mixed with sour cream to create a dip with a smoother texture and milder taste.

1 15-ounce can stewed tomatoes
$\frac{1}{2}$ 4-ounce can mild jalapenos
2 fresh green chiles or serrano peppers
$\frac{1}{4}$ white onion
$\frac{1}{2}$ teaspoon salt
$\frac{1}{2}$ teaspoon ground cumin
1 tablespoon fresh lime juice
$\frac{1}{2}$ teaspoon sugar
2 tablespoons fresh cilantro

Combine all ingredients in a blender or food processor and process until puréed. ~

Laura Welch Bush
◆ FROZEN MARGARITAS

1 6-ounce can frozen limeade
9 ounces tequila
2 ounces triple sec
$\frac{1}{8}$ lime, diced
Coarse salt

Put first three ingredients in blender. Fill with ice and blend until smooth. Rub edges of glasses with lime and dip in coarse salt. Pour margaritas into glasses and serve. ~

Laura Welch Bush
◆ MANSION BBQ SAUCE

To barbecue means to slow-cook meat at a low temperature for a long time over wood or charcoal. In Texas, barbecue (or BBQ) originated in the late 1800s during the great cattle drives. Reserving the better cuts of meat for the lead drivers or the owners, cowboys were fed lesser cuts of meat such as the brisket. Generally tough and stringy, brisket usually requires five to seven hours of cooking to make it tender.

Kathleen "Katy" Delacy-Bourke developed this recipe for a delicious

BBQ sauce for the Bushes. She worked in the mansion kitchen for the six years the Bushes lived there.

> $\frac{3}{4}$ cup chili sauce or ketchup
> $\frac{1}{3}$ cup molasses
> 3 tablespoons soy sauce
> 1 tablespoon dark brown sugar
> 1 tablespoon Dijon mustard
> 1 clove garlic, crushed
> 3 tablespoons lemon juice
> $\frac{1}{2}$ cup water
> 1 teaspoon kosher salt
> 2 tablespoons Worcestershire sauce
> 1 tablespoon pureed chipotle in adobo sauce

Simmer for 15 minutes or so.

Laura Welch Bush

♦ CHOCOLATE PECAN PIE BARS

Some recipes at the mansion are favored by more than one administration. These chewy little delights were a favorite of Governor Richards and the Bush family. This wonderful treat is perfect for box meals.

> 3 cups unsifted flour
> $\frac{1}{2}$ cup sugar
> 1 cup butter, softened
> $\frac{1}{2}$ teaspoon salt

> Filling:
> $1\frac{1}{2}$ cups Karo® corn syrup light or dark
> 6 squares Baker's® semisweet chocolate or $1\frac{1}{2}$ packages of
>   Baker's German Sweet Chocolate®
> $1\frac{1}{2}$ cups sugar
> 4 eggs, slightly beaten
> $1\frac{1}{2}$ teaspoons vanilla
> $2\frac{1}{2}$ cups pecans, chopped

Grease bottom and sides of 15-by-10-by-1-inch baking pan. Be certain sides of pan are 1 inch high. In large bowl with mixer at medium speed, beat flour, sugar, butter, and salt until mixture resembles coarse crumbs. Press firmly and evenly into pan. Bake in 350-degree oven 20 minutes.

Meanwhile for the filling, in a 3-quart saucepan stir corn syrup and chocolate over low heat just until chocolate melts. Remove from heat. Stir in remaining sugar, then eggs and vanilla until blended. Stir in pecans. Pour filling over hot crust. Spread evenly. Bake in 350-degree oven 30 minutes or until filling is firm around edges and slightly soft in the center. Cool in pan on wire rack. Yields 48 bars. ～

Laura Welch Bush
✦ BUSH FAMILY ZUNI STEW

This vegetarian stew is very flavorful and hearty, too.

1½ cup pinto beans (soaked overnight and drained)
1 bay leaf
1 teaspoon dried oregano
1 teaspoon salt
2 tablespoons corn or vegetable oil
2 yellow onions (chopped into ¼-inch pieces)
2 garlic cloves (finely chopped)
2 tablespoons red chile powder (or more if you'd like)
1 teaspoon ground cumin
½ teaspoon ground coriander
1 pound fresh tomatoes (peeled, seeded, and chopped)
2 dried ancho chile peppers (de-veined, seeded, and cut into narrow strips)
1 pound yellow or zucchini squash (cut into 1-inch pieces)
4 ears corn (cut the kernels off)
8 ounces fresh green beans (cut into about 1-inch pieces)
4 ounces jack or Muenster cheese (grated)
½ bunch cilantro (roughly chopped—reserve a few whole leaves for garnish)

Place beans, bay leaf, and oregano in a saucepan; cover with plenty of water and cook over medium heat for 1½ to 2 hours. Remove from heat when beans are soft, but not mushy. Add salt. Drain beans, but save the broth. Heat oil in a large skillet; sauté onions over high heat for 1 to 2 minutes. Lower the heat, then add garlic, spices, and stir. Add a little bean broth so the chile powder doesn't scorch. Cook until onions begin to soften, about 4 minutes. Add tomatoes and cook for another 5 minutes. Stir in chiles and remaining vegetables, along with the cooked beans and enough of the broth to make a moist, thick stew. Cook at a high simmer until vegetables are done, about 20 minutes. Stir in cheese and chopped cilantro, and garnish with whole leaves of cilantro. Serve with corn bread or tortillas.

Laura Welch Bush
♦ PUMPKIN BREAD

This wonderful recipe comes from Sarah Bishop's mother, Julia Evans Bishop. Many of the tours and teas at the mansion since Sarah's employment there have benefited from this wonderful bread.

    3 cups flour
    1 teaspoon soda
    ½ teaspoon baking powder
    ½ teaspoon salt
    ½ teaspoon ground cloves
    1 teaspoon cinnamon
    1 teaspoon nutmeg
    3 cups sugar
    1 cup corn oil
    2 cups pumpkin, cooked and mashed
    3 eggs, slightly beaten

Sift together flour, soda, baking powder, salt, ground cloves, cinnamon, and nutmeg. Once sifted, then add sugar. Stir in oil, pumpkin, and eggs. Mix until smooth. Bake in loaf pans lined with wax paper for 1 hour and 25 minutes at 350 degrees.

Laura Welch Bush
♦ SWEET POTATO PECAN PIE

They love sweet potatoes at the mansion, so the staff are always on the lookout for a good "sweet potato anything" recipe. This one is wonderful.

Dough:
3 tablespoons butter (softened)
2 tablespoons sugar
$\frac{1}{4}$ teaspoon salt
$\frac{1}{2}$ whole egg (vigorously beaten until frothy)
2 tablespoons cold milk
1 cup all-purpose flour

Place softened butter, sugar, and salt in an electric mixer bowl; beat on high speed until it's a creamy mixture. Add the $\frac{1}{2}$ egg and beat 30 seconds. Add the milk and beat on high speed for 2 minutes. Add the flour and beat on medium speed 5 seconds, then on high speed just until blended, about 5 seconds more. Remove the dough and shape into a 5-inch patty about $\frac{1}{2}$ inch thick. Lightly dust with flour and wrap in plastic; refrigerate at least 1 hour, preferably overnight. On a lightly floured surface, roll out dough to thickness of $\frac{1}{8}$ to $\frac{1}{4}$ inch. Very lightly flour the top of the dough and fold into quarters. Carefully place dough in a greased and floured 8-inch round cake pan. Unfold the dough and arrange to fit the sides and bottom of the pan; press firmly into place. Trim edges and refrigerate 15 minutes.

Filling:
1 cup sweet potato pulp (cooked/baked)
$\frac{1}{4}$ cup brown sugar
2 tablespoons sugar
$\frac{1}{2}$ whole egg (vigorously beaten until frothy)
1 tablespoon heavy cream
1 tablespoon butter (softened)
1 tablespoon vanilla extract
$\frac{1}{4}$ teaspoon salt

¼ teaspoon ground cinnamon
¼ teaspoon ground allspice
¼ teaspoon ground nutmeg

Combine all ingredients in a mixing bowl. Beat on medium speed until batter is smooth, about 2 to 3 minutes. Set aside.

Syrup:
¾ cup sugar
¾ cup dark corn syrup
2 eggs
1½ tablespoon butter (melted)
2 teaspoons vanilla extract
Pinch salt
Pinch ground cinnamon
¾ cup pecan pieces

Combine all ingredients except pecans in a mixing bowl. Mix thoroughly on slow speed until syrup is opaque, about 1 minute. Stir in pecans and set aside.

Assembly:
Spoon filling evenly into the dough-lined cake pan. Pour the pecan syrup on top. Bake in a 325-degree oven until a knife inserted in the center comes out clean, about 1¼ hours. (NOTE: The pecans will rise to the top during baking.) Let cool and serve with whipped cream. ～

Laura Welch Bush

◆ SQUASH CASSEROLE

Sarah Bishop and Katy Delacy-Bourke developed this recipe for the Bushes. It is a wonderful addition to any meal.

¼ cup butter
1 cup onions
¼ cup flour
2 cups whole milk

1 cup poblanos
1 cup green onions, sliced
Salt and pepper
4 yellow squash, sliced $\frac{3}{8}$-inch thick, steamed until tender
1 cup bread crumbs

Preheat oven to 350 degrees. Melt butter and sauté onions on medium heat until softened. Stir in flour and continue to cook for 3 minutes more. Whisk in milk, stirring constantly until thickened. Remove from heat and add poblanos and green onions. Season to taste with salt and pepper. Fold in cooked squash. Pour into a casserole and top with bread crumbs. Bake for 30 minutes. Makes 10 big servings. ≤

Laura Welch Bush
♦ MONA'S COFFEE CAKE

Who is Mona? I don't know, but I love her cake. Sarah Bishop has eaten this coffee cake at Christmas breakfast her whole life. The Bush family made it a tradition as well. Serve it with bacon and orange juice. It makes a special day even more so.

1 cup butter
2 cups sugar
2 cups sour cream
4 eggs
2 teaspoons vanilla
4 cups flour
2 teaspoons baking powder
2 teaspoons soda
$\frac{1}{2}$ teaspoon salt

Topping:
2 cups pecans (chopped)
2 teaspoons cinnamon
$\frac{2}{3}$ cup sugar
$\frac{1}{2}$ cup brown sugar

Cream together butter, sugar, and sour cream. Add eggs and vanilla. Sift together remaining ingredients and add to liquid mixture in fourths. Mix well. Grease and flour two or three cake pans (8- or 9-inch). Fill halfway and add a layer of topping. Cover with remaining batter. Place remaining topping on each. Bake about 40 minutes at 325 degrees.

Laura Welch Bush
◆ BUSH SOUTHWESTERN POTATO SALAD

Mansion chef Sarah Bishop suggests that you can increase the amount of the mustard, cilantro, and oregano used in this recipe. If you go a little heavier on the seasonings in this delicious summertime favorite, you can't go wrong. A Bush family friend gave this recipe to Laura Bush. It became a family favorite at the mansion and was served at many casual functions.

> 12 medium red potatoes, with or without the skins
> 2 pickled jalapenos, chopped
> $\frac{1}{4}$ cup Kalamata olives, chopped
> 2 teaspoons grainy mustard mixed with $\frac{1}{2}$ cup mayonnaise (or more)
> 1 teaspoon cilantro, chopped
> 1 teaspoon oregano, chopped
> 2 large hard-boiled eggs, diced
> Salt and pepper, to taste

Boil potatoes until cooked; rinse in cool water. Slice or dice and mix with the rest of the ingredients.

Laura Welch Bush
◆ BUSH FAMILY GRANOLA

Sarah Bishop and Katy Delacy-Bourke, the chefs at the mansion, developed this granola for the Bush family. The possibilities for variation are endless; this version is just one. It is also low in fat— a very good thing.

5 cups oats
1 cup wheat flakes
1 cup Krestmer Wheat Germ®
1 cup bran
1 cup sliced almonds or other nuts
1 cup dry milk (nonfat)
1 cup brown sugar
$\frac{3}{4}$ cup hot water
$\frac{1}{4}$ cup vegetable oil
$\frac{1}{2}$ cup honey or maple syrup

Mix ingredients together and bake at 350 degrees. Stir every 15
minutes for 45 minutes to 1 hour. ～

Laura Welch Bush

◆ TEXAS GOVERNOR'S MANSION COWBOY COOKIES

This wondrous recipe was brought to Sarah Bishop's attention by
her longtime friend Marilyn Bellows, a fifth-generation Texan. It
quickly became a mansion favorite and a signature dish of the Bush
tenure in the mansion.

3 cups all-purpose flour
1 tablespoon each: baking powder, baking soda, and ground
    cinnamon
1 teaspoon salt
$1\frac{1}{2}$ cups (3 sticks) butter, at room temperature
$1\frac{1}{2}$ cups each: granulated sugar and packed light brown sugar
3 eggs
1 tablespoon vanilla extract
3 cups each: semisweet chocolate morsels and old-fashioned
    rolled oats
2 cups each: sweetened flake coconut and chopped pecans

Heat oven to 350 degrees. Mix flour, baking powder, baking
soda, cinnamon, and salt in bowl. In a second very large bowl,
beat butter with an electric mixer at medium speed until smooth
and creamy. Gradually beat in sugars; combine thoroughly.

{ 269 }

Add eggs one at a time, beating after each. Beat in vanilla. Stir in flour mixture until just combined. Stir in chocolate morsels, oats, coconut, and pecans.

For each cookie, drop $\frac{1}{4}$ cup (4 tablespoons) dough onto ungreased baking sheets, spacing 3 inches apart. Bake 12 to 15 minutes or until edges are lightly browned; rotate sheets halfway through. Remove cookies to rack to cool. Makes 3 to $3\frac{1}{2}$ dozen cookies. ✎

Laura Welch Bush
♦ JOHN MARSHALL PIE

This Bush family standard is wonderful any time of the year. Prepare a graham cracker piecrust in a 9-inch pie plate. Combine the following ingredients in a double boiler and cook until thickened:

> 3 egg yolks
> $\frac{1}{2}$ cup granulated sugar
> $\frac{1}{2}$ cup milk
> 1 envelope unflavored gelatin (softened in water)

Then beat 3 egg whites until stiff, and beat in $\frac{3}{4}$ cup granulated sugar and 1 teaspoon cream of tartar to make a meringue. Fold meringue into egg yolk mixture in double boiler. When thoroughly mixed, add 1 quart whipped cream and a dash of Grand Marnier. Pour mixture in piecrust, grate semisweet chocolate over top, and keep chilled until served. NOTE: Cool Whip may be substituted for whipped cream. ✎

◆ ANITA THIGPEN PERRY ◆
2001–

Anita Perry had been to the Governor's Mansion many times during the political career of her husband Rick. During his time as a member of the House of Representatives in the Texas legislature, then as Texas commissioner of agriculture, and finally as lieutenant governor, the Perrys attended numerous functions held in the gracious first-floor rooms of the mansion. When Gov. George W. Bush, under whom Rick Perry served as lieutenant governor, sought and won the presidency of the United States, Anita's and Rick's lives changed forever. Instead of merely attending the functions at the mansion, Anita was to be in charge of them.

First Lady Anita Thigpen Perry
Courtesy Governor's Press Office.

{ 271 }

The state's most historic house was a long way from the comfortable West Texas home of her parents, Dr. Joe and Beunis Thigpen, where she was raised. Her father practiced medicine as a family physician for almost fifty years in Haskell, Texas, and her mother was involved in local civic causes. Inspired by her father, Anita began a career in health care herself. In 1974, she received a bachelor of science degree in nursing from West Texas State University and later, a master of science degree in nursing from the University of Texas Health Science Center in San Antonio.

Her career included various roles in medical, surgical, and pediatric nursing, including teaching and administrative positions. After assuming the role of first lady, Anita used her professional nursing experience to focus on issues close to her heart, particularly efforts to improve health care for women and children. Anita also used her visibility to raise awareness of women's issues. She hosted with her husband the first Texas Conference for Women in October of 2000, and it became an annual event.

Anita and Rick first met at a piano recital when they were children. They became sweethearts during their teen years and kept in touch with each other even when Anita's nursing career and the governor's air force assignments kept them in different parts of the world. After five years in the air force, Rick returned home to work on the family's farm and ranch, and the couple married in 1982. Their first child, Griffin, arrived in 1983, and their daughter Sydney was born in 1986. Life in Haskell was good. Rick was elected to the state legislature and served for six years in the House of Representatives.

In 1991 Rick was elected Texas commissioner of agriculture, and the Perry family moved to Austin. Austin was a big change from the small town of Haskell, but the Perrys enjoyed the large capital city. Anita worked as a health care consultant on issues such as osteoporosis, and the family quickly made friends and settled into their new home city.

When Anita became first lady, she found herself facing a tremendous task. Although the mansion was only a few miles from their home, the family faced the move with the legislative session in full swing and their teenage children in the middle of the school year. The family, including their beloved pet dachshund Lady, eventually settled into their new surroundings and resumed its normal activities.

Anita's calendar of events was always full, and the mansion was likewise usually filled with the sounds of visitors. Logically, given the first lady's focus on health care, one of the first formal events she hosted was a benefit for the Austin Alzheimer's Association. Held on a spring evening, the "Gallery in the Garden" event enabled guests to wander the mansion lawns and view local artists' work before purchasing them in an auction, which was a great success. Anita also hosted events to promote awareness of family violence, an issue she was keenly aware of because of her experience working in hospital emergency rooms and intensive care units.

One of Anita's favorite events during her first year at the mansion was a special Halloween party for residents of the Austin Children's Shelter. Since those children, many of whom had been abused or neglected in their lives, could not participate in trick-or-treating because of safety concerns, the first lady invited them to the mansion to play in the expansive yard, decorate cookies, and break open a piñata full of treats.

The Perrys continued the tradition of the popular Governor's Picnic, held each year to commemorate the first party or levee held at the mansion. Tom Perrini, nationally known chuck-wagon chef, catered the event as he had done for many years. Guests lined up around the chuck wagon in the front yard of the mansion and were served Texas ranch food on metal-enameled speckle-ware plates. Jane Karotkin, administrator of the Friends of the Govenor's mansion, had arranged the table decor complete with napkins fashioned from calico bandannas. Under the shelter of an enormous white tent, illuminated by twinkling white lights, guests dined and visited as they have done since the mid-1800s, as guests of the governor and first lady.

Also in the spirit of tradition the Perrys hosted a special dinner for five of the state's former governors. Each erstwhile governor commented on the many changes and improvements in the mansion since their own terms in office.

The mood of the old house changed following the terrorist attacks of September 11, 2001. That morning as the governor was about to leave the mansion—the scene of so many historic events in Texas—Anita called him to come see the breaking story on the news. The Perry family grieved along with the nation, and large American flags were suspended from the front balcony and back portico of the mansion.

Despite or perhaps because of the somber mood in the nation, Anita was determined that the holidays at the mansion would be a warm and special time. She made certain that the mansion decorations conveyed a feeling of tradition and home. Visitors could see yards of flowing garlands and snowflake ornaments—which was daughter Sydney's way of creating a winter wonderland inside even as outside temperatures were typical for a balmy Texas December.

Anita also revived the tradition of decorating the mansion's Christmas tree with elegant holiday ornaments depicting Texas landmarks from various counties. She hoped that these ornaments would remind visitors that this house was indeed the symbolic home of Texans from all over the state.

❧

Anita Thigpen Perry
♦ TEXAS SALSA

The Perry family first used this salsa recipe while Rick was the state's commissioner of agriculture. It is a fine way to feature the fresh produce of Texas.

> 1 can ($4\frac{1}{2}$ ounces) chopped onions
> 1 can (10 ounces) tomatoes and green chilies
> 2 tablespoons cider vinegar
> 1 tablespoon olive oil
> 2 ripe tomatoes, diced
> 1 small onion, chopped
> $\frac{1}{8}$ teaspoon garlic powder
> 1 teaspoon salt
> $\frac{1}{4}$ teaspoon black pepper

Mix all ingredients; cover and store in icebox. Serve with tortilla chips. Serves 15 to 20 persons. ❧

Anita Thigpen Perry
◆ CRÈME BRULÉE

Sarah Bishop, mansion chef, prepared this recipe for the special dinner honoring the former governors and first ladies. Ann Richards raved about it. You will too.

8 egg yolks
½ quart heavy cream
¼ cup sugar
¼ teaspoon vanilla
Pinch of salt

Beat egg yolks in a large bowl. Set aside. Scald remaining ingredients in a heavy saucepan (nonaluminum). DO NOT BOIL. Slowly add hot cream mixture to yolks while mixing, being careful not to beat air into it. Set up cheesecloth to strain mix. Pour into ovenproof custard cups (about 4 ounces). To bake: Place in pan filled with water ⅔ up the side of the custard cup. Bake at 350 degrees for 25 to 40 minutes. Chill the Crème Brulée. Before serving, spread 1 to 2 teaspoons of light brown sugar on top. Place under broiler until bubbly and toasted. Variation: Use crystallized ginger mixed with granulated sugar for topping. ⌇

Anita Thigpen Perry
◆ TEXAS GOVERNOR'S MANSION SUMMER PEACH TEA PUNCH

The remarkable Sarah Bishop has made hundreds of gallons of this delicious summer tea for receptions and events at the mansion. It is incredibly popular, and the recipe, though somewhat complicated, is well worth the effort. The torch has been pased to Dean Peterson, who now makes the punch for various Mansion events.

3 family size tea bags
4 cups fresh mint
4 cups water
12-ounce can lemonade concentrate

2 bottles Knudsen's Peach Nectar® (Do not substitute.
    Purchase at Whole Foods Market or other health food store.)
2 liters ginger ale
2 liters soda
½ to 1 cup simple syrup (Simple syrup: 2 parts sugar to 1 part
    water. Bring to a slow boil until clear—about 4 minutes.)

Boil water to steep tea and mint. Steep about 15 minutes. Remove
tea bags. Leave mint in solution until cool. Strain into 2-gallon
containers. Add lemonade, peach nectar, and syrup concentrate.
Add 2 liters ginger ale and 2 liters soda. Taste before adding
simple syrup. Yields 2 gallons. ✦

Anita Thigpen Perry
♦ APPLE PIE

This wonderful recipe is the result of mansion associate chef Margit
Johnson's years of training.

Crust:
3 cups flour
¼ teaspoon salt
1 teaspoon sugar
12 ounces cold butter
4½ tablespoons Crisco®
6 to 9 tablespoons ice water

Pulse flour, salt, and sugar in food processor. Cut up butter and
Crisco® slightly. Add to flour mixture and pulse till crumbly.
Add ice water slowly, till ball forms.
    Pat dough out to make an 8-inch circle. Wrap in plastic film
and chill 1 hour. Roll out entire piece to ⅛-inch thickness. Trim
outer edge by 1 inch. Place in 10-inch glass pie pan.

Filling:
10 Granny Smith apples
¾ cup sugar
3 tablespoons cinnamon

Dash nutmeg
½ teaspoon salt
2 tablespoons lemon juice
2 cups fresh or frozen blueberries

Peel, quarter, and slice apples. Heat them in large saucepan with remaining ingredients except berries. When hot, stir in berries.

Assembly:
   Pour fruit mixture into piecrust, piling apples high. Fold dough up, ruffling the excess. Pat with water and sprinkle sugar over crust and apple mixture. Bake at 350 degrees for 1 hour and 15 minutes (bake pie on sheet pan to protect oven from spills). ↙

Anita Thigpen Perry
  ✦ CHICKEN SALAD SUPREME

Continuing the tradition of more "good Southern cooking" in the mansion, this recipe adapted from Helen Corbitt's cookbook is a favorite in the Perry family.

For chicken:
3 bone-in/skin-on chicken breasts
1 medium sliced onion
2 sliced carrots
2 sliced celery ribs
2 cloves garlic

Place chicken and vegetables in a pot of cold water seasoned with bay leaf, thyme, celery seed, whole black peppercorns, and fresh parsley. Put pot on high heat and bring to a simmer. Do not boil. Reduce heat and allow to simmer for about 30 minutes. Cool chicken, pull from bone, and cube.

For salad:
1 cup finely chopped celery
2 tablespoons minced parsley
1 cup mayonnaise

1 tablespoon lemon juice
½ cup heavy cream
1 cup sliced white grapes
½ cup toasted shredded almonds

Combine cubed chicken with celery, minced parsley, mayonnaise, lemon juice, and cream until thoroughly mixed. Fold in grapes and almonds, and add salt and pepper to taste. ❧

Anita Thigpen Perry
✦ BISHOP'S CAKE

½ pound unsalted butter
2 cups granulated sugar
2 cups unbleached flour
1 tablespoon fresh lemon juice
1 teaspoon vanilla extract
5 eggs

Preheat oven to 350 degrees. Grease and flour a 10-inch bundt pan. Cream butter and sugar gradually; beat until fluffy. Sift flour and add to butter mixture. Stir just enough to blend. Add lemon juice and vanilla; stir well. Add eggs, one at a time, mixing well after each addition. Pour batter into the prepared bundt pan. Bake for 1 hour and 15 minutes or until a cake tester inserted into the center of the cake comes out clean. (After 30 minutes, cover cake loosely with aluminum foil.) When cake is done, cool in pan on a cake rack for 10 minutes. Remove from pan and cool completely. ❧

Old-Fashioned Measurements and Their Modern Equivalents

1 pinch or dash = what can be picked up between thumb and first
   two fingers; less than $\frac{1}{8}$ teaspoon

$\frac{1}{2}$ pinch = what can be picked up between thumb and one finger

1 spoonful = 1 tablespoon, more or less

Butter the size of an egg = $\frac{1}{4}$ cup or 2 ounces

Butter the size of a walnut = 1 tablespoon

Butter the size of a hazelnut = 1 teaspoon

BAKING TEMPERATURES

Very slow oven	=	below 300 degrees (Fahrenheit)
Slow oven	=	300 degrees
Moderately slow oven	=	325 degrees
Moderate oven	=	350 degrees
Moderately hot oven	=	375 degrees
Quick oven	=	375 to 400 degrees
Hot oven	=	400 to 425 degrees
Very hot oven	=	450 to 475 degrees
Extremely hot oven	=	500 degrees or more

CAN MEASUREMENTS

Can Size	Liquid Measure	Cups
6 ounces	6 ounces	$\frac{3}{4}$
8 ounces	$7\frac{3}{4}$ ounces	1
Number 1	$10\frac{1}{2}$ ounces	$1\frac{1}{4}$
Number 300	$13\frac{1}{2}$ ounces	$1\frac{3}{4}$
Number 303	15 fluid ounces	2
Number 2	1 pint, 2 fluid ounces	$2\frac{1}{2}$
Number $2\frac{1}{2}$	1 pint, 10 fluid ounces	$3\frac{1}{2}$
Number 3	1 quart, 14 fluid ounces	$5\frac{3}{4}$

Timeline of Governors, First Ladies, Food, and History

1845–46   The Republic of Texas joins the United States.

1846–47   James Pinckney Henderson; Frances Cox
             Henderson
         Elias Howe patents the sewing machine.
         War breaks out between the United States
             and Mexico.

1847–49   George T. Wood; Martha Evans Gindrat Wood
         Wuthering Heights by Emily Brontë and *Jane Eyre*
             by Charlotte Brontë are published.
         Marx and Engels issue the *Communist Manifesto*.

1849–53   Peter Hansborough Bell
         Zachary Taylor becomes the twelfth U.S. presi-
             dent in 1849.
         Marshmallows as we know them are introduced.
         Millard Fillmore becomes the thirteenth U.S.
             president in 1850.
         The Compromise of 1850 resolves some slavery
             issues and Texas border disputes.
         Potato chips gain popularity.

1853   James Wilson Henderson; Laura A. Hooker
             Henderson

James Wilson Henderson serves as governor of
Texas for less than a month.

1853–57   Elisha Marshall Pease; Lucadia Christiana Niles
Pease
Franklin Pierce becomes the fourteenth U.S.
president.
Vincent van Gogh and Sigmund Freud are born.
Gail Borden receives first patent on condensed
milk.
Construction begins on the Texas Governor's
Mansion.
Jelly beans are introduced.
The Governor's Mansion is completed in June,
1856.

1857–59   Hardin R. Runnels; Martha Caroline Adams
Runnels
James Buchanan becomes the fifteenth U.S.
president.
Laying of the transatlantic cable begins.

1859–61   Sam Houston; Martha Moffatt Lea Houston
Abraham Lincoln becomes the sixteenth U.S.
president.
The U.S. population is approximately 32 million.
Louis Pasteur develops the germ theory of
fermentation.

1861   Edward Clark; Martha Melissa Evans Clark
Clark succeeds Houston as governor when the
latter refuses to swear loyalty to the Confederacy.

1861–63   Francis R. Lubbock; Adele Baron Lubbock
Texas secedes from the United States.
Civil War begins when Confederates attack Fort
Sumter on April 12, 1861.
Breakfast cereal is introduced.

1863–65   Pendleton Murrah; Sue Ellen Taylor Murrah
           Abraham Lincoln issues Emancipation
               Proclamation and gives Gettysburg Address,
               1863.
           General Lee surrenders at Appomattox on April 9,
               1865.
           President Lincoln is shot on April 14, 1865, and
               succeeded by Andrew Johnson.

1865–66   Andrew J. Hamilton; Mary Jane Bowen
               Hamilton
           The chuck wagon is invented by Charles
               Goodnight.

1866–67   James Webb Throckmorton; Ann Rattan
               Throckmorton
           Deviled ham is introduced.

1867–69   Elisha Marshall Pease; Lucadia Christiana Niles
               Pease
           Tabasco® sauce is invented.
           The Governor's Mansion is occupied by Gen. J. J.
               Reynolds, a federal army officer.
           General Sheridan restores military rule in Texas.
           Ulysses S. Grant becomes the eighteenth
               president of the United States.
           Richard Cadbury introduces the first Valentine's
               Day box of chocolates.
           Fleischmann's® yeast is introduced.
           Ice cream sodas are invented in San Antonio,
               Texas.
           Campbell's® soup is sold for first time.

1870–74   Edmund J. Davis; Anne Elizabeth Britton Davis
           Margarine is invented.
           Idaho potatoes are cultivated.
           California navel oranges are introduced.
           Ice cream sodas become popular.

1874–76   Richard Coke; Mary Evans Horne Coke
               Reconstruction ends.
               First modern toilet facility is installed in the
                   Governor's Mansion.
               First gas lights are installed in the mansion.
               Texas' first artificially produced ice is made in
                   Jefferson.
               Heinz Ketchup® is introduced.

1876–79   Richard B. Hubbard; Janie Roberts Hubbard
               Texas drafts a new state constitution.
               First performance of the opera *Carmen,*
                   composed by Bizet.
               Alexander Graham Bell invents the telephone.
               Saccharin is invented.
               Hire's® root beer is introduced.
               Rutherford B. Hayes becomes the nineteenth
                   U.S. president.
               Albert Einstein is born.

1879–83   Oran M. Roberts; Frances Wickliffe Edwards
                   Roberts
               The Governor's Mansion is plumbed for running
                   water.
               James A. Garfield becomes the twentieth
                   president.
               Malted milk is introduced.
               Candy corn is introduced.
               Chester A. Arthur is sworn in as president after
                   the assassination of Garfield.
               Pillsbury® flour enters the food market.

1883–87   John Ireland; Anne Maria Penn Ireland
               The Texas Capitol building burns down.
               Saltwater taffy is invented.
               Mark Twain's landmark novel *Huckleberry Finn*
                   is published.
               Dr Pepper® is invented.

Ball-Mason® jars are produced.
Evaporated milk is invented.
Coca-Cola® is invented.
The Statue of Liberty is dedicated.

1887–91   Lawrence Sullivan Ross; Elizabeth Dorothy
                Tinsley Ross
            Pizza is introduced.
            The newly completed Texas Capitol is dedicated.
            Queen Victoria of England celebrates her fiftieth
                year on the throne.
            George Eastman designs the Kodak® box
                camera.
            Aunt Jemima® pancake mix hits market shelves.
            Lipton® tea is sold for the first time.
            Benjamin Harrison is inaugurated as the twenty-
                third president.
            Calumet® baking powder is introduced.

1891–95   James Stephen Hogg; Sarah Ann Stinson Hogg
            Hogg is the first native Texan elected governor.
            First Lady Sallie Hogg requests the first wallpaper
                for the mansion.
            The internal combustion engine is patented.
            Henry Ford completes his first car.
            Cracker Jack® is invented.
            Eggs Benedict is invented.
            Lobster thermidor is invented.
            Cream of Wheat® is introduced.
            Wrigley's Juicy Fruit® and Spearmint® gum are
                introduced.
            Iceberg lettuce is introduced.
            Corn flakes are invented.
            Triscuit® crackers are introduced.

1895–99   Charles A. Culberson; Sallie Harrison Culberson
            William McKinley becomes the twenty-fifth
                president of the United States.

The *Maine* is sunk in Havana harbor, igniting the
　　Spanish-American War.
Tootsie Rolls® are invented.
Grape-Nuts® is introduced.
Mail-order fruitcakes are introduced in Corsicana.
Jell-O® invented.
1000 Island dressing is invented.
Texas sweet onions are introduced.

1899–1903　　Joseph D. Sayers; Orline Walton Sayers
Hershey introduces a milk chocolate bar.
The first major redecoration of the Governor's
　　Mansion is directed by First Lady Lena Sayers.
Electric lights are installed in the mansion for the
　　first time.
Valentine's heart candies with messages on them
　　are introduced.
The Galveston hurricane of 1900 kills an esti-
　　mated six thousand and devastates most of
　　the city.
Oil is discovered at Spindletop, Texas, in 1901.

1903–1907　　Samuel W. T. Lanham; Sarah Beona Meng
　　Lanham
The Wright Brothers make the first airplane flight
　　at Kitty Hawk, North Carolina.
Canned tuna is introduced.
Iced tea is sold for the first time.
Peanut butter, hamburgers, and ice cream cones
　　are introduced to the public.
The Daughters of the Republic of Texas gain
　　control of the Alamo.
Theodore Roosevelt becomes president of the
　　United States in 1905.
The hot fudge sundae is introduced.
The federal Pure Food and Drug Act is passed.
O'Henry's stories are published as a book entitled
　　Cabbages and Kings.

Kellogg's Corn Flakes® hit store shelves.

Picasso completes his Cubist painting, *Les Demoiselles d'Avignon*.

1907–11   Thomas Mitchell Campbell; Fannie Irene Bruner Campbell

Oklahoma becomes the forty-sixth state.

Ford produces the first Model T, and General Motors is formed.

Architect Frank Lloyd Wright completes the Robie House in Chicago.

Crisco® is invented.

French dip sandwiches are made for the first time.

Post Toasties® cereal is introduced.

1911–15   Oscar Branch Colquitt; Alice Fuller Murrell Colquitt

Colquitt becomes the first governor of Texas to have an automobile.

Ocean Spray® cranberry sauce is sold in cans for first time.

The Morton Salt girl trademark appears on the product label.

The Governor's Mansion receives a major structural addition in 1914.

The Houston Ship Channel opens.

Oreo® cookies are introduced.

Life Savers® premier.

The Gould Amendment requires packaged food contents to be "plainly marked on the package."

More than fifteen hundred persons die when the *Titanic* sinks in 1912.

Woodrow Wilson becomes the twenty-eighth U.S. president.

Fruit cocktail enters the market.

World War I begins in Europe in 1914.

1915–17   James E. Ferguson; Miriam Amanda Wallace
Ferguson

Corning introduces Pyrex® baking dishes.

Frigidaire unveils an electric refrigerator.

Alexander Graham Bell has the first American
transcontinental telephone conversation.

Mr. Peanut® is introduced.

Moon Pies® are introduced.

Mexican revolutionary general Pancho Villa raids
across the border into New Mexico.

The United States enters World War I in 1917.

Czar Nicholas II's abdication is followed by the
October Revolution in Russia.

Gov. Jim Ferguson is impeached on Sept. 24,
1917.

1917–21   William Pettus Hobby; Willie Chapman Cooper
Hobby

Lt. Gov. Hobby is sworn in as governor on
Sept. 26, 1917, replacing Ferguson.

The armistice ending World War I is signed on
November 11, 1918.

The 18th Amendment to the Constitution bans
alcoholic beverages.

Jack Dempsey becomes the world heavyweight
boxing champion.

President Woodrow Wilson wins the Nobel Peace
Prize in 1919.

KitchenAid introduces a standard electric mixer.

Fortune cookies are invented.

Warren G. Harding is inaugurated the twenty-
ninth president of the United States.

1921–25   Pat M. Neff; Myrtle Mainer Neff

King Tutankhamen's tomb is discovered in Egypt.

Wheaties® cereal is introduced.

Wonder Bread® goes on the market.

The first Girl Scout cookies are sold.

Sigmund Freud's *The Ego and the Id* is published.
Calvin Coolidge becomes president after the
death of Warren G. Harding.
Caesar salad is served for the first time in Tijuana,
Mexico.
Sixteen nations participate in the first Winter
Olympics.
Americans are using an estimated 2.5 million
radios.
Frozen foods are invented.

1925–27   Miriam A. Ferguson
"Ma" Ferguson becomes the first woman
governor of Texas, the second in the United
States.
A. A. Milne's *Winnie the Pooh* is published.
The opera *Turandot,* by Puccini, debuts at
La Scala in Milan.
Kool-Aid® is invented.
Bit-O-Honey® candy is introduced.

1927–31   Dan Moody; Mildred Paxton Moody
Charles Lindbergh flies nonstop in *Spirit of St.
Louis* from New York to Paris.
Walt Disney presents the first Mickey Mouse
films.
Composer Maurice Ravel completes his orchestral
piece "Bolero."
Alexander Fleming discovers penicillin.
Velveeta® is introduced.
American aviator Amelia Earhart becomes the
first woman to fly across the Atlantic.
The U.S. stock market crashes on October 24,1929.
Gerber baby food is introduced.
7-Up® premiers.
General Mills and General Foods are organized.
The electric range is available for the first time.
Chocolate chip cookies are created and named

after the Toll House Inn near Whitman,
Massachusetts.
The Good Humor® bar is invented.
Birds Eye introduced a line of "frosted" foods.
The city of Constantinople is renamed Istanbul.
Bisquick® is introduced.
Milk Duds® candy is introduced.

1931–33 Ross S. Sterling; Maud Abbie Gage Sterling
Population of the United States reaches
approximately 122 million.
Unemployment hits 13.7 million in the nation
and over 350,000 in Texas.
Franklin D. Roosevelt becomes the thirty-second
U.S. president.
Adolf Hitler becomes chancellor of Germany.
Campbell's cream of mushroom soup appears.
The first plastic-coated paper milk cartons are
introduced commercially.
The Chicago World's Fair opens.
Fritos® corn chips are introduced.
Red Hots® candies are introduced.

1933–35 Miriam A. Ferguson
Ritz® crackers are introduced.
Historic American Buildings Survey photographs
the Mansion and grounds.
The United States drops the gold standard for its
currency.
Prohibition is repealed in the United States.

1935–39 James V. Allred; Joe Betsy Miller Allred
Sam Houston Allred becomes the second child
born in the Governor's Mansion.
Texas celebrates the hundredth anniversary of its
independence from Mexico.
First Lady Eleanor Roosevelt visits the Texas
Governor's Mansion.

President Franklin Roosevelt signs the Social
Security Act.

Neville Chamberlain takes office as prime minister
of Great Britain.

American Airlines serves in-flight meals.

The first food standards are issued for canned
tomatoes, tomato purée, and tomato paste.

First drive-in opens in Glendale, California.

The Waring blender is invented.

Spam® arrives on the scene.

Krispy Kreme® donuts are introduced.

Kraft Macaroni & Cheese Dinner® is introduced.

Disney releases the animated film, *Snow White
and the Seven Dwarfs*.

Teflon® is developed.

1939–41   W. Lee O'Daniel; Merle Estelle Butcher O'Daniel

Germany invades Poland on Sept. 1, 1939.

Gov. "Pappy" O'Daniel invites all Texans to a
barbecue at the mansion after his inauguration.

Britain and France declare war on Germany.

"Deep in the Heart of Texas" becomes a popular
song in the United States.

The Borden company introduces Elsie the cow as
its trademark.

Nestlé creates first chocolate chips.

1941–47   Coke R. Stevenson; Blanch Fay Wright Stevenson

Gourmet magazine premiers.

M&Ms® candies are introduced.

General Electric unveils the first garbage disposal.

Japan attacks Pearl Harbor on Dec. 7, 1941.

Texas' First Lady Fay Stevenson dies in the
mansion on Jan. 3, 1942.

The Manhattan Project team begins work to
develop an atomic bomb.

The Allies begin their counteroffensive in France
on D-Day, June 6, 1944.

Harry Truman becomes president upon the death
of Franklin D. Roosevelt.

Reynolds Wrap® rolls out aluminum foil.

The war in Europe ends on May 8, 1945, and
Japan surrenders on August 14, 1945.

Tupperware® is invented.

Instant coffee is introduced.

Minute Maid® frozen orange juice concentrate is
introduced.

Betty Crocker® cake mixes are introduced.

1947–49   Beauford H. Jester; Mabel Buchanan Jester
Governor Jester dies of a heart attack while
traveling.

Sara Lee® cheesecake makes its debut.

The first Pillsbury Baking Contest takes place.

Pillsbury and General Mills launch cake mixes.

KitchenAid introduces the electric dishwasher.

Jolly Ranchers® candies are introduced.

Bubble gum cigars are introduced.

Junior Mints® are introduced.

Minute Rice® is distributed nationally.

1949–57   Robert Allan Shivers; Marialice Shary Shivers
Betty Crocker's Picture Cookbook is a best-seller.

Duncan Hines introduces a cake mix.

Central heating and air-conditioning are installed
in the mansion for the first time.

Oleomargarine Act requires prominent labeling of
colored oleomargarine, to distinguish it from
butter.

Saran Wrap® is introduced.

Lipton introduces onion soup mix.

Eggo® frozen waffles appear.

Cheez Whiz® is placed in test markets.

Queen Elizabeth II is crowned in Great Britain.

The mansion gets its first television in 1954.

Swanson unveils the first frozen TV dinner.

The first Burger King opens.
The first McDonald's opens.
Tappan introduces a microwave oven for home use.
The U.S. population is 150,697,999.
The first electric can opener is introduced.
Margarine outsells butter for the first time.
Sweet'N Low® is introduced.

1957–63   Price Daniel; Jean Houston Baldwin Daniel
Häagen-Dazs® ice cream becomes available to
    consumers.
Green Eggs and Ham becomes a popular
    children's book.
Edward A. Asselbergs invents instant mashed
    potatoes.
The Governor's Mansion receives Austin's first
    Texas Historical Landmark medallion.
Texan Van Cliburn wins the Tchaikovsky piano
    competition in Moscow.
John F. Kennedy becomes the thirty-fifth
    president of the United States.
The first Pizza Hut opens.
French cuisine becomes popular in the United
    States.
German chocolate cake is introduced to
    consumers.
Rice-A-Roni® is introduced.
Van Cliburn eats seventeen biscuits at Austin's
    Green Pastures.
The first aluminum beverage cans are introduced.
Trix cereal® is introduced.
The Berlin Wall is erected.

1963–69   John B. Connally; Idanell Brill Connally
President John F. Kennedy is assassinated in
    Dallas on November 22, 1963.
Governor Connally is wounded during the
    assassination of Kennedy.

Sweetarts® candies are introduced.

Julia Child makes her television debut.

Chicken wings are hatched in Buffalo.

Martin Luther King, Jr., wins the Nobel Peace
Prize.

Cool Whip® and Gatorade® are introduced.

Lyndon Baines Johnson wins the 1964
presidential election.

Tang® is launched.

Soviet spacecraft lands on the moon.

Pringles® potato chips are introduced.

Martin Luther King, Jr., and Robert F. Kennedy
are assassinated.

The Keebler Elf debuts.

1969–73   Preston Smith; Ima Mae Smith Smith

Neil Armstrong is the first man to walk on the
moon.

Richard Nixon is inaugurated as the thirty-
seventh president.

Jelly Belly® brand jelly beans appear on the
market.

The Dallas Cowboys win the 1972 Super Bowl.

Snapple® is invented.

Vice President Spiro Agnew resigns and is
replaced by Gerald R. Ford.

Secretariat wins the Triple Crown of horse racing.

Stove Top® stuffing is released.

1973–79   Dolph Briscoe, Jr.; Betty Jane Slaughter Briscoe

Richard Nixon resigns and is succeeded by Vice-
President Gerald R. Ford.

The United States celebrates its bicentennial in
1976.

Jimmy Carter becomes the thirty-ninth U.S.
president.

Elvis Presley dies.

1979–83	William P. Clements, Jr.; Rita Crocker Clements
	The Governor's Mansion undergoes structural restoration and interior redecoration.
	Ronald Reagan becomes the fortieth president.
	Skittles® appear on American candy counters.
	Searchers find the *Titanic* shipwreck in the Atlantic.
	Astronaut Bill Lenoir becomes first man to eat a jalapeno in outer space.
	The refurbished Governor's Mansion is reopened to the public on April 1, 1982.
1983–87	Mark Wells White; Linda Gale Thompson White
	Britain's Prince Charles visits the Governor's Mansion during the Texas Sesquicentennial.
1987–91	William P. Clements, Jr.; Rita Crocker Clements
	George Bush is inaugurated as the forty-first president.
1991–95	Ann Willis Richards
	Queen Elizabeth II and Prince Philip are honored at a reception in the mansion.
	Governor Richards hosts a meeting with the president of Mexico.
	U.S. President-elect Bill Clinton visits the Governor's Mansion.
	William Jefferson Clinton becomes the forty-second president.
1995–2000	George W. Bush; Laura Welch Bush
	The Texas Capitol Preservation and Extension Project is completed.
	Salsa outsells ketchup in the United States for the first time.
2001–	Rick Perry; Anita Thigpen Perry
	George W. Bush is inaugurated forty-third president.
	Starbucks opens its five-thousandth location.
	Terrorists use commercial airliners to attack U.S. targets on September 11, 2001.

Bibliography

◆ MANUSCRIPTS AND ARCHIVAL ◆ COLLECTIONS

Austin History Center, Austin, Tex. George and Laura Bush Files. Governors' Biographical Files. Pease-Graham Files and Carrie Pease Graham Registration File. Texas Governor's Mansion Files.

Bowen, Nancy Head. A Political Labyrinth: Texas in the Civil War—Questions in Continuity. Ph.D. dissertation, Rice University, 1974.

Calbert, Jack Lynn. James Edward Ferguson and Miriam Amanda Ferguson: The Ma and Pa of Texas Politics. Ph.D. dissertation, Indiana University, 1968. University Microfilms.

Center for American History, University of Texas at Austin. Thomas Mitchell Campbell Papers. Edward C. Clark Papers. Oscar Branch Colquitt Papers. James Stephen Hogg Papers. Taulman Collection.

Earle, Violet. The Administration of the Public Health Program in Texas. Ph.D. dissertation, University of Texas, 1950.

Friends of the Governor's Mansion Collection, Austin. First Ladies Files. Governors' Bibliographical Files. Governor's Mansion History Files.

Gray, Ronald N. Edmund J. Davis: Radical Republican and Reconstruction Governor of Texas. Ph.D. dissertation, Texas Tech University, 1976.

Griffin, Roger Allen. Connecticut Yankee in Texas: A Biography of Elisha Marshall Pease. Ph.D. dissertation, University of Texas at Austin, 1973.

Haynes, Leo C. Manufacturing in Texas: A Statistical Story. MBA thesis, University of Texas, 1929.

History Collection, Hardin-Simmons University, Abilene, Tex. Texas Governors' Vertical Files.

Miller, B. H. Elisha Marshall Pease: A Biography. Master's thesis, University of Texas, 1927.

Sam Houston Regional Library and Research Center, Liberty, Tex. Price Daniel Papers.

Southwest Collection, Texas Tech University, Lubbock. Pendleton Murrah File.

Texas Collection, Baylor University, Waco. First Ladies' Vertical Files. Governor's Mansion Vertical Files. Neff Collection.

Texas State Library and Archives, Austin. Thomas Mitchell Campbell Letters and Papers. Colquitt Mansion Invoices and Receipts. James Edward Ferguson Collection. Francis Richard Lubbock Papers. Hardin Richard Runnels Records. Coke Stevenson Papers.

Wagner, Robert Lancaster. The Gubernatorial Career of Charles Allen Culberson. Master's thesis, University of Texas, 1954.

◆ BOOKS AND ARTICLES ◆

Anderson, G. D., Mrs. *The Woman's Forum of Wichita Falls Cook Book.* 1932. Reprint, Wichita Falls, Tex.: The Woman's Forum of Wichita Falls, 1982.

Associated Press. "Many Orphans to Be Adopted for Christmas." *Dallas News,* December 22, 1940.

Atterberry, Ann. "Writers Will View Mansion." *Dallas Morning News,* March 1, 1970.

Austin Heritage Society. *The Old Bakery Bake Book.* Austin: Von Boeckmann-Jones, 1971.

Banks, Jimmy. *Money, Marbles and Chalk: The Wondrous World of Texas Politics.* Austin: Texas Publishing, 1971.

Barnes, Lorraine. "Herman Brown Silver Given State Mansion." *American Statesman (Austin),* November 30, 1964.

———. "Mansion Problem—Silver, Crystal Services Incomplete." *American Statesman (Austin),* September 19, 1963.

Barry, R. W. "Mrs. Sterling Has Endeared Self to Austin Residents." *American Statesman (Austin),* n.d., 1933.

Bengston, Carolyn Seay. "First Lady Returns to the Mansion." *Austin Statesman,* April 25, 1961.

Benner, Judith Ann. *Sul Ross: Soldier, Statesman, Educator.* College Station: Texas A&M University Press, 1983.

Bernhard, Virginia. *Ima Hogg: The Governor's Daughter.* Austin: Texas Monthly Press, 1984. Reprint, Saint James, N.Y.: Brandywine Press, 1996.

Biggers, Don H. *Our Sacred Monkeys (or), Twenty Years of Jim and Other Jams (Mostly Jim), the Outstanding Goat Gland Specialist of Texas Politics.* Brownwood, Tex.: Jones Printing, 1933.

Bolton, Paul. *Governors of Texas.* Corpus Christi: Caller-Times Publishing, 1947.

Brewer, Anita. "Attractive First Lady Wanted to Tame the Young, Wild Texas." *Austin American-Statesman,* August 4, 1956.

———. "Sarah Hogg Gave Dignified Elegance to Life of Political Hero in Mansion." *Austin American-Statesman,* August 25, 1954.

Brooks, Elizabeth. *Prominent Women of Texas.* Akron, Ohio: Werner Company, 1896.

Brooks, Raymond. "Mrs. Coke Stevenson Dies After Long Illness; Funeral Planned Today at Junction." *American Statesman,* January 4, 1942.

Brown, Norman D. *Hood, Bonnet, and Little Brown Jug: Texas Politics, 1921–1928.* College Station: Texas A&M University Press, 1984.

Buenger, Walter L. *Secession and the Union in Texas.* Austin: University of Texas Press, 1984.

Calmes, Jackie. "Governor's Mansion: Pride or Leaky Museum?" *Abilene Reporter-News,* April 24, 1979.

Caro, Robert A. *Means of Ascent.* New York: Knopf, 1990.

Cason, L. N., and Cora M. Oneal. "The Governor's Wife Answers Her Own Doorbell." *Dallas Morning News,* August 16, 1931.

Clark, James Anthony, and Weldon Hart. *The Tactful Texan: A Biography of Governor Will Hobby.* New York: Random House, 1958.

Clark, Morton G. *The Wide, Wide World of Texas Cooking.* New York: Bonanza Books, 1970.

Coleman, Arthur, and Bobbie Coleman. *The Texas Cookbook.* New York: A. A. Wyn, Inc., 1949.

Cook, Alison. "The Texas Food Manifesto." *Texas Monthly,* December, 1983, 138.

Cook, Molly Connor. "Mrs. O'Daniel Tells Plans for Mansion." *American Statesman (Austin),* January 22, 1939.

Cotner, Robert C. *James Stephen Hogg: A Biography.* Austin: University of Texas Press, 1959.

Creighton, Sue, comp. and ed. *Capitol Cook Book: Favorite Family Recipes of Texas Governors, Senators, and Other State Officials.* Waco: Texian Press, 1973.

Dallek, Robert. *Lone Star Rising: Lyndon Johnson and His Times, 1908–1960.* New York: Oxford University Press, 1991.

Daniel, Jean, Price Daniel, and Dorothy Blodgett. *The Texas Governor's*

Mansion. Austin: Texas State Library and Archives Commission and the Sam Houston Library and Research Center, 1984.

"Daughters of Only 3 Governors Were Married in Mansion." *Austin American-Statesman,* ca. 1942.

Davis, Clare Ogden. *The Woman of It: A Novel.* New York: J. H. Sears and Company, 1929.

"Davy Crockett Party Celebrated in Mansion." *Austin American-Statesman,* May 21, 1955.

Decherd, Kate J. "The Home That Belongs to All Texans." *Texas Outlook,* May, 1927.

DeShields, James T. *Stormy Petrels in Texas Politics.* Dallas: C. C. Cockrell, 1932.

———. *They Sat in High Places: The Presidents and Governors of Texas.* San Antonio: Naylor, 1940.

Deuson, Benny R. "Pendleton Murrah." In *Ten Texans in Gray,* edited by W. C. Nunn. Hillsboro, Tex.: Hill Junior College Press, 1968.

Dixon, Ford. "Oran Milo Roberts." In *Ten More Texans in Gray,* edited by W. C. Nunn. Hillsboro, Tex.: Hill Junior College Press, 1980.

Duncan, Merle Mears. "The Death of Senator Coke." *Southwestern Historical Quarterly* 63 (January, 1960).

Egerton, John. *Southern Food: At Home, on the Road, in History.* 1987. Reprint, Chapel Hill, N.C.: University of North Carolina Press, 1993.

"8 Marriages—Simple to Spectacular—Held in Historic Governor's Mansion." *Austin American-Statesman,* August 12, 1956.

Elliott, Claude. *Leathercoat: The Life History of a Texas Patriot.* San Antonio: Standard Printing, 1938.

Ex-Students' Association. *Cook 'em Horns.* Austin: Hart Graphics, 1981.

Farmer, Fannie Merritt. *The Boston Cooking-School Cook Book.* Boston: Little, Brown, 1918.

Farrell, Mary D., and Elizabeth Silverthorne. *First Ladies of Texas: The First One Hundred Years, 1836–1936.* Belton, Tex.: Stillhouse Hollow Publishers, 1976.

Federation of the Blind. *Where Good Cooks Get Together.* Austin, n.d.

Ferguson, Sheila. *Soul Food.* New York: Grove Press, 1989.

Fergusonism Down to Date: A Story in Sixty Chapters Compiled from the Records. N.p., 1932.

The First Texas Cook Book: A Thorough Treatise on the Art of Cookery. 1883. Reprint, Austin: Pemberton Press, 1963.

Fox, Saxon, ed. *Texas Capitol Collection: Cookery, Commentary, Portraiture.* Austin: Fox Press, 1991.

Friends of the Governor's Mansion. *The Governor's Mansion of Texas.* 2nd ed. Austin: Friends of the Governor's Mansion, 1997.

"Fund for Furnishing of Mansion Started." *Austin American- Statesman,* February 28, 1937.

Galvin, Lois Hale. "Shiverses to Spend Holidays in Gaily Bedecked Mansion." *Austin American-Statesman,* December 19, 1956.

Gantt, Fred, Jr. *The Chief Executive in Texas: A Study in Gubernatorial Leadership.* Austin: University of Texas Press, 1964.

"General Hancock's Reception." *Weekly Austin Republican,* January 29, 1868.

Gideon, Samuel E. "Landmarks and Places of Interest." *Daily Texan (Austin),* May 7, 1931.

Good Meals and How to Prepare and Serve Them. New York: Good Housekeeping, 1927.

"Gov. Clark's Wife Overshadowed by Mother-in-Law." *Austin American-Statesman,* August 12, 1956.

"Governor's Mansion Point of Interest." *Austin Statesman,* February 15, 1935.

"Governor's 20 Room Mansion Open to Students from 3 to 5." *Daily Texan (Austin),* October 20, 1946.

Haley, James L. *Sam Houston.* Norman: University of Oklahoma Press, 2002.

Hamilton, Jeff. *My Master: The Inside Story of Sam Houston and His Times.* Edited by Lenoir Hunt. Dallas: Manfred, Van Nort, 1940. Reprint, Austin: State House Press, 1992.

Harrison County Conservation Society, comp. *Heritage Sketch and Cook Book.* Harrison County, Tex., 1971.

Hendrickson, Kenneth E., Jr. *The Chief Executives of Texas: From Stephen F. Austin to John B. Connally, Jr.* College Station: Texas A&M University Press, 1995.

Hogan, William R. *The Texas Republic: A Social and Economic History.* Norman: University of Oklahoma Press, 1946. Reprint, Austin: University of Texas Press, 1969.

Holley, Mary Austin. *Texas.* 1836. Reprint, Austin: Texas State Historical Association, 1985.

Home Demonstration Club of Hurst. *Tested Recipes.* Hurst, Tex., n.d.

"Hundreds Greet Sterlings during New Year's Fete." *Austin American-Statesman,* January 1, 1932.

Jackson, Pearl Cashell. *Texas Governors' Wives.* Austin: Steck, 1915.

Johnson, Elizabeth Ann, ed. *The Helen Corbitt Collection.* Boston: Houghton Mifflin, 1981.

Jones, Billy M. "Miriam Amanda Ferguson." In *Women of Texas*. Waco: Texian Press, 1972.

Junior Group of the Dallas Symphony Orchestra League. *Noted Cookery*. Dallas: Dallas Symphony Orchestra League, 1973.

Keever, Jack. "History Stalks Corridors." *Dallas Morning News*, February 16, 1964.

Kerby, Robert L. *Kirby Smith's Confederacy: The Trans-Mississippi South, 1863–1865*. New York: Columbia University Press, 1972.

Koock, Mary Faulk. *The Texas Cookbook*. Boston: Little, Brown, 1965. Reprint, Denton: University of North Texas Press, 2001.

League Cook Book. *Famous Recipes by Famous People*. Austin: Cook Printing, 1933.

League of Women Voters of the Austin Area. *Capitol Cooking*. Olathe, Kans.: Cookbook Publishers, Inc., 1985.

"The Levee." *Texas State Gazette*, August 30, 1856.

Lewellyn, Hattie. "A Visit to Texas' Governor's Mansion." *San Antonio Express and News*, March 24, 1963.

Lubbock, Frances Richard. *Six Decades in Texas*. Austin: Ben C. Jones, 1900. Reprint, Austin: Pemberton Press, 1968.

"Mansion's Antiques Bring Memories of Early Texans." *Daily Texan (Austin)*, January 25, 1932.

Mercie Boone Guild, comp. *The Mansion Cookbook: A Treasury of Recipes, Household Hints and Assorted Information*. Seattle, Wash.: Ballard Printing and Publishing, 1976.

MacCorkle, Stuart A., and Dick Smith. *Texas Government*. 3rd ed. New York: McGraw-Hill, 1956. 5th ed. New York: McGraw-Hill.

MacNabb, Betty. "A Texas Bargain." *American Statesman (Austin)*, October 31, 1961.

"Mansion Exhibit Is Offered Today." *Austin American-Statesman*, January 4, 1963.

"Mansion's Menus Familiar to Average Texas Housewife." *Austin American-Statesman*, September 22, 1935.

McBee, Sue. "Mansion Takes on Christmas Air for Festivities." *Houston Chronicle*, December 12, 1956.

McKay, Seth. *W. Lee O'Daniel and Texas Politics, 1938–1942*. Lubbock: Texas Technological College Research Funds, 1944.

Moneyhon, Carl H. *Republicanism in Reconstruction Texas*. Austin: University of Texas Press, 1980.

Moody, Martha. "Mildred Paxton Moody: Former First Lady of Texas." *Texas Historian*, March, 1980.

Moody, Mildred Paxton. "Housekeeping in the Governor's Mansion." *Dallas News,* March 5, 1931.

"Mrs. O'Daniel Adds Homelike Atmosphere to Mansion." *San Antonio Express,* January 29, 1939.

"Mrs. O'Daniel Has Made Governor's Mansion Look Like Family Home." *Fort Worth Star-Telegram,* January 29, 1939.

Mullins, Mary Margaret. "First Lady of Texas." *San Antonio Express Magazine,* October, 1947.

Nalle, Ouida Ferguson. *The Fergusons of Texas; or, "Two Governors for the Price of One."* San Antonio: Naylor, 1946.

"New Garden at the Governor's Mansion," *Gossip,* April, 1931.

"New Silver for Mansion." *American Statesman (Austin),* January 6, 1957.

"New Wall Panels for Mansion." *Austin American-Statesman,* December 16, 1928.

"19,000 Pounds of Meat Ready for Barbecue." *Austin Daily Tribune,* January 18, 1941.

Nixon, Pat Ireland. *The Medical Story of Early Texas, 1528–1853.* Lancaster, Pa.: Lupe Memorial Fund, 1946.

Nozick, Betsy, Tricia Henry, and Rebecca W. Chastenet de Gery, comp. *Texas Tuxedos to Tacos: The Mystique of Entertaining.* Austin: Eakin Press, 1997.

Nunn, William C. *Texas under the Carpetbaggers.* Austin: University of Texas Press, 1962.

"Official Ladies Fete Guests, Honor Mrs. Jester at Mansion Tea." *Austin American-Statesman,* March 30, 1947.

"Pappy Passes the Biscuits as O'Daniels Move into Texas' Governor's Mansion." *Life,* January, 1939, 9-13.

Patrick, Carolyn. "Three Recall Mansion Life." *Dallas Morning News,* March 25, 1966.

Patterson, Caleb Perry, et al. *State and Local Government in Texas.* New York: Macmillan, 1940.

Paulissen, Maisie. "Pardon Me, Governor Ferguson." In *Legendary Ladies of Texas,* edited by Francis Edward Abernethy. Dallas: E-Heart Press, 1981.

Perry, George Sessions. *Texas: A World in Itself.* New York: Whittlesey House, 1940.

Phares, Ross. *The Governors of Texas.* Gretna, La.: Pelican, 1976.

Phelan, Charlotte. "New Governor's Mansion Needed—Mrs. Connally." *Houston Post,* June 23, 1963.

Pi Beta Phi: Cook Book. Los Angeles, 1936.

Pickrell, Annie Doom. *Pioneer Women in Texas.* Austin: Steck, 1929.

"Reception at Mansion Last Night." *Austin Daily Statesman,* January 2, 1913.

The Reliable Cook Book. Belton, Tex.: Woman's Home Mission Society, 1908.

Reston, James, Jr. *The Lone Star: The Life of John Connally.* New York: Harper and Row, 1989.

Rider, Lecta. "Mrs Allred Is Glad That Texas Will Not Build New Executive Mansion While She's First Lady." *Houston Chronicle,* December 3, 1936.

Roberts, Madge Thornall. *Star of Destiny: The Private Life of Sam and Margaret Lea Houston.* Denton: University of North Texas Press, 1993.

Roe, Ethel J. "Back-Door Gossip with First Lady of Texas—Mrs. Moody Tells of Some Mansion Housekeeping Problems, and Gives Recipe for Dan's Favorite Dessert." *Farm and Ranch,* October, 1928.

Rutherford, Bruce. *The Impeachment of Jim Ferguson.* Austin: Eakin Press, 1983.

Sager, Lois. "News of Women." *Dallas News,* January 16, 1949.

Scott, Mrs. Fred. "Love, Tragedy, Sorrow, Romance, War, Splendor, Pomp and Ceremony Are Interwoven in Story of the Mansion." *American Statesman (Austin),* April 25, 1915.

———. "Women Worth While." *American Statesman (Austin),* n.d., 1918.

Seale, William. *Sam Houston's Wife: A Biography of Margaret Lea Houston.* Norman: University of Oklahoma Press, 1970.

Shank, Dorothy E. *Magic Chef Cooking.* Saint Louis: American Stove Company, 1936.

Smith, Annette. "Mansion Has Varied through Years from Dull to Gay, Staid to Informal." *American-Statesman (Austin),* August 12, 1956.

Smith, Rick. "Life in the Mansion." *American Statesman (Austin),* n.d., 1979.

Spaight, Ashley Wood. *The Resources, Soil, and Climate of Texas.* Galveston: Belo, 1882.

Steen, Ralph W. *Twentieth Century Texas: An Economic and Social History.* Austin: Steck, 1942.

"Stork Avoids Governor's Mansion." *Austin American,* May 1, 1927.

Sutherland, Carol. "First Family Adapts to Mansion." *Austin American-Statesman,* March 17, 1957.

Texas Celebrity Cookbook. Fort Worth: Gardner-Farkas Press, 1984.

"Texas' First Lady Has an Aim: She Wants Legislature's Signal for New Kitchen Linoleum." *Dallas News,* January 21, 1941.

Trahey, Jane, ed., and Marihelen McDuff, comp. *A Taste of Texas: A Book of Recipes*. New York: Random House, 1949.

Treasure Pots. Austin: Austin's Woman's Club, 1940.

Turner, Martha Anne. *Richard Bennett Hubbard: An American Life*. Austin: Shoal Creek Publishers, 1979.

Twichell, Alice. "Governor's Mansion Houses Administration Souvenirs." *Daily Texan (Austin)*, January 25, 1932.

Tyler, Ron, et al., eds. *The New Handbook of Texas*. 6 vols. Austin: Texas State Historical Association, 1996.

Ulrich, Jane. "Mansion Changes Hands—Janey's Presence Everywhere." *Waco Tribune Herald*, January 14, 1979.

Victoria Junior Service League. *Entertaining in Texas*. Victoria, Tex.: Hart Graphics, 1982.

Vorwerk, Ed. "Remodeling." *Austin American-Statesman*, May 11, 1958.

Wagner, John. "Plates of Barbecue Served to 20,000 in Front of Mansion." *Dallas News*, January 22, 1941.

Wakefield, Eleanor. *Housekeeping in the State Executive Mansion*. Houston: Houston Post Press, 1932.

——. "Woman's Work Never Done in Texas Mansion—Styles Change So Often." *San Antonio Express*, July 3, 1932.

Waller, John L. *Colossal Hamilton of Texas: A Biography of Andrew Jackson Hamilton, Militant Unionist and Reconstruction Governor*. El Paso: Texas Western Press, 1968.

Welch, June Rayfield. *The Texas Governor*. Dallas: GLA Press, 1977.

"The Whist Club Holds Its First Meeting at the Governor's Mansion Thursday Night." *Austin Daily Statesman*, August 30, 1890.

"Wife of Governor Dies; Rites Today at Junction." *Dallas News*, January 4, 1942.

Winchester, Robert G. *James Pinckney Henderson, Texas' First Governor*. San Antonio: Naylor, 1971.

Women's Symphony League of Austin. *Enjoy!* Dallas: Taylor Publishing, 1980.

Ziemann, Hugo, and Mrs. F. L. Gillette. *The White House Cook Book*. New York: Saalfield Publishing, 1915.

Index

ISBN 1-58544-254-2

90000